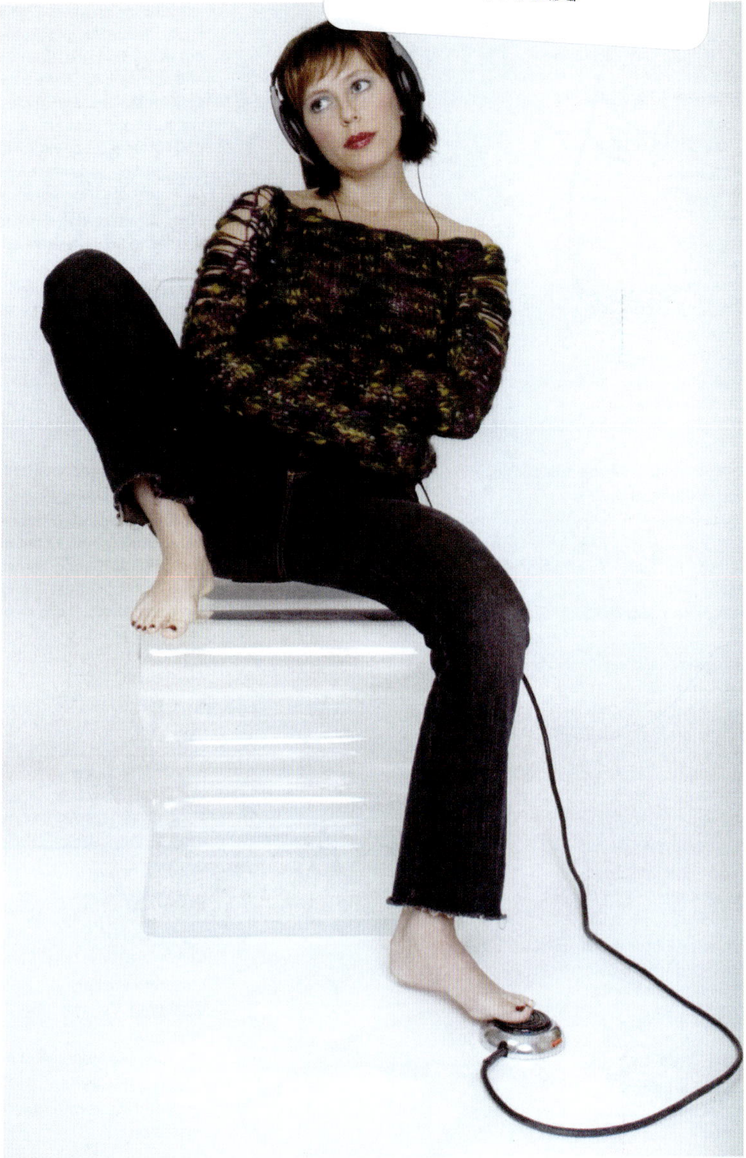

Textile

EDITED BY
CATHERINE HARPER
AND DORAN ROSS

THE JOURNAL OF
CLOTH AND CULTURE

VOLUME 7
ISSUE 2
JULY 2009

ORDERING INFORMATION

Three Issues per volume. One volume per annum.
2009: Volume 7

ONLINE
www.bergpublishers.com

BY MAIL
Berg Publishers
C/O Turpin Distribution Services
Pegasus Drive
Stratton Business Park
Biggleswade
Bedfordshire SG18 8TQ
UK

BY FAX
+ 44 (0)1767 601640

BY TELEPHONE
+ 44 (0)1767 604951
For Subscription Enquiries
email custserv@turpin-distribution.com

ENQUIRIES
Editorial: Julia Hall
email jhall@bergpublishers.com
Production: Ken Bruce
email kbruce@bergpbublishers.com
Advertising: Corina Kapinos
email ckapinos@bergpublishers.com

SUBSCRIPTION RATES
Institutional
Print and online: 1 year: £158/US$307; 2 year: £252/US$491
Online only: 1 year: £134/US$261; 2 year: £214/US$481
Individual
Print: 1 year: £46/US$79; 2 year: £74/US$126
Full color images available online
Access your electronic subscription through
www.ingentaconnect.com
Berg Publishers is the imprint of
Oxford International Publishers Ltd.

AIMS AND SCOPE

Cloth accesses an astonishingly broad range of human experiences. The raw material from which things are made, it has various associations: sensual, somatic, decorative, functional and ritual. Yet although textiles are part of our everyday lives, their very familiarity and accessibility belie a complex set of histories, and invite a range of speculations about their personal, social and cultural meanings. This ability to move within and reference multiple sites gives textiles their potency.

This journal brings together research in textiles in an innovative and distinctive academic forum for all those who share a multifaceted view of textiles within an expanded feld. Representing a dynamic and wide-ranging set of critical practices, it provides a platform for points of departure between art and craft; gender and identity; cloth, body and architecture; labor and technology; techno-design and practice—all situated within the broader contexts of material and visual culture.

Textile invites submissions informed by technology and visual media, history and cultural theory; anthropology; philosophy; political economy and psychoanalysis. It draws on a range of artistic practices, studio and digital work, manufacture and object production.

Berg Publishers is a member of CrossRef

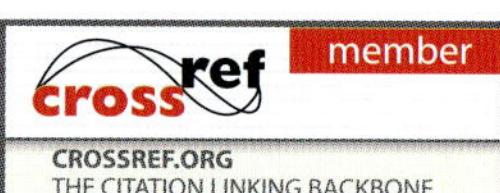

SUBMISSIONS

Should you have a topic you would like us to consider, please send an abstract of 300–500 words to one of the editors. Notes for Contributors can be found at the back of the journal and style guidelines are available by emailing kbruce@bergpublishers.com or from the Berg website (www.bergpublishers.com).

ISSN: 1475-9756

www.bergpublishers.com

Textile is indexed by Abstracts in Anthropology; AIO (Anthropological Index Online); ART Bibliographies Modern; British Humanities Index; Current Contents/Arts and Humanities; DAAI (Design and Applied Arts Index); IBR (International Bibliography of Book Reviews of Scholarly Literature in the Humanities and Social Sciences); IBSS (International Bibliography of the Social Sciences); IBZ (International Bibliography of Periodical Literature on the Humanities and Social Sciences); ISI Arts and Humanities Citation Index; Scopus; World Textiles.

Contents

EDITORS

Catherine Harper
School of Architecture and Design
University of Brighton
Grand Parade
Brighton BN2 4AY
UK
Catherine.Harper@brighton.ac.uk

Doran Ross
Fowler Museum at UCLA
308 Charles Young Drive
Los Angeles, CA 90095-1549
USA
dross@arts.ucla.edu

Announcement

The Editors of *Textile: The Journal of Cloth and Culture* would like to say a very sincere thank you to Jan Gilburt, Editorial Assistant for this publication over the last four years. Jan has been at the very center of the complex international activity that creates the journal and we are deeply grateful for her organization, commitment, wisdom, and good humor throughout. We would like to wish Jan the very best in future projects, and with her continued engagement with the Constance Howard Resource and Research Centre in Textiles, London.

Catherine Harper
Doran Ross

Textile, Volume 7, Issue 2, p. 147
DOI: 10.2752/175183509X460056
Reprints available directly from the Publishers.
Photocopying permitted by licence only.
© 2009 Berg. Printed in the United Kingdom.

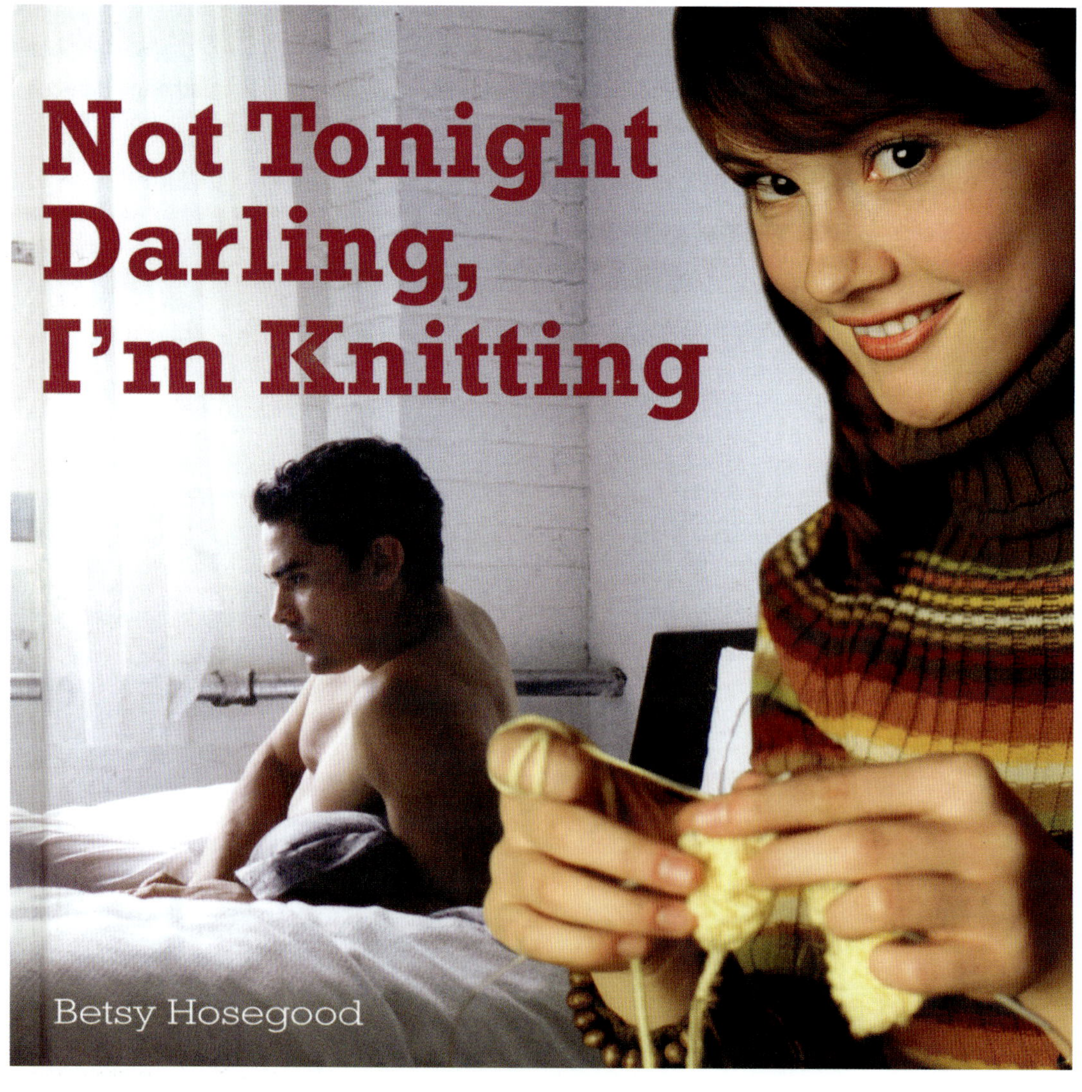
Not Tonight
Darling,
I'm Knitting

Betsy Hosegood

Abstract

In the last fifteen years, domestic hobbies especially needle and paper crafts have been revived and rediscovered in the English-speaking world. In the forefront of this renewed interest in old-fashioned hobbies is knitting. Contemporary proponents claim that this craft helps them to achieve balance between their busy lives and dedicate some time to themselves. They often take their project to public spaces such as coffee shops, pubs, and park benches. Publishing houses speedily cash in on the revival by providing increasing numbers of pattern books to local bookstore chains. Hence, knitting constitutes an ideal case study for redefining the role of craft in contemporary popular culture. This article argues that knitting participates in an opening up of the three binary oppositions, namely original vs. copy, public vs. private in relation to space, and heterosexual vs. homosexual.

Related to the past and conceived nostalgically through connection to our parents' and grandparents' domestic activity, knitting is rapidly being revitalized and repackaged by such groups as Debbie Stoller's *Stitch 'n Bitch* as hip and fun. Women of any age but especially younger women in their twenties and thirties see knitting as empowering hobby because it provides an opportunity to undertake something purely unpractical and inefficient. It provides a conceptual link and helps redefine the historical and contemporary significance of domesticity in society.

In the attempt to repackage and change the image of the craft several publications establish a connection between knitting and sexuality. These books construct knitting as not only a worthwhile and altruistic pastime but also as a decadent, self-indulgent, and subversive action. For example, *Domiknitrix: Whip Your Knitting into Shape* offers a bikini pattern as well as other edgy projects such as deep-décolleté tops and seductive hair and headpieces. Traditionally associated with home handicrafts, knitting had emerged into communal, activist practice. Contemporary popular media has also tied knitting to ideas of physical and spiritual love, peace amongst the nations, meditation, and rebelliousness against previous generations.

This research looks at the knitted objects and the images that appear in the media to explore how knitting as a phenomenon helps women and men negotiate their everyday lives. Dedicating time to such traditional, time-consuming activities promotes the idea of conscious choice, of being in charge of one's life and time. Participating in these activities provides an outlet for relaxation, slowing down and taking in simple life pleasures. My research builds on this argument and looks further at the knitted objects themselves to examine their roles in the lives of their makers and consumers. Using contemporary material culture scholarship, which underlines the importance of identity formation through agency, I try to determine how the knitted erotic objects differ from items purchased in stores. What is the role of the handmade and self-produced? How do hand-knitted items that become part of interior display help to negotiate the identities and individualities of their makers? Finally, this article looks at how the presence of knitters in different social contexts helps to blur the binary division between public and private space. It also discusses the gendered appeal of knitting books and the total omission of gay men and their interests from the literature.

Keywords: knitting, craft, feminism, domesticity, gender, queer, identity

ALLA MYZELEV

Alla Myzelev is an Assistant Professor of Art History at the University of Guelph. She is working on the book *Canadian Architecture and Design 1910–37: From Vernacular to Deco, From Rustic to Polished*. Myzelev is a co-editor (with Dr John Potvin) of the *Collecting Subjects in Britain, 1700–1914: The Visual Meanings and Pleasures of Material Culture* (Ashgate, 2009) and forthcoming *Fashion, Modern Identity and Interior Design since 1740* (Ashgate, 2010).

Textile, Volume 7, Issue 2, pp. 148–163
DOI: 10.2752/175183509X460065
Reprints available directly from the Publishers.
Photocopying permitted by licence only.

Whip Your Hobby into Shape: Knitting, Feminism and Construction of Gender

Desire, even when it is profoundly conventional, is at the same time the location of a resistance to convention. It demonstrates that people want something more.

Belsey 1994: 7

To be natural is such a very difficult pose to keep up.

Oscar Wilde 1895

As I am finishing my son's sweater and looking at the elephant intarsia pattern that he chose from one of those widely available pattern books, I am contemplating what knitting means to me. What does it provide? What makes me so drawn to the process? As my more practical and pragmatic friends mentioned several times, it is much easier and more reasonable to buy a good quality woolen sweater at a store. I can hardly find time to cook, clean, or file my papers, yet I leave a few minutes or more everyday to knit. It is the combination of creative efforts, repetitive tasks, physical movement, albeit very limited ones and the enjoyment of making something for someone special that constitutes my personal need to knit. It is from this understanding of and engaging with the craft that I wish to investigate its current place in the Western Society. Knitting makes for an ideal case study because in the last fifteen years it has gone through a tremendous revival and perhaps as no other craft at the present time is in the state of transition. The meaning of knitting as a traditional homespun craft is being redefined by the new generation of knitters who while recognizing its importance in the past also attempt to take it to another level of public awareness. Part of the renewed interest in DIY activities that overtook popular culture at the end of the millennium and still continues, knitting is being transformed to play an important part in haute-couture fashion, art installations and technology-based art and craft production. As such, knitting helps to redefine the meaning of craft practice in general.[1] In this article I claim that contemporary knitting circles and knitting literature build upon the traditional symbolism of handicraft, namely their communal aspect (knitting together), its ability to evoke an idealized past and the luxury of having time for manual labor. This, hopefully, will open up a larger debate of redefining the gendered roles in society (knitting books for men) and empowering women in the intimate sphere of sensuality and sex. There are three issues that I address: first, the meaning of contemporary craft revival in knitters' lives; second, the role of a knitted object in the interior décor of domestic space; and third, how knitting helps to construct and redefine gender in contemporary society.

The Meaning of a Pattern

While a variety of modernist narratives insist that the main value of the work of art or any creative endeavor lies in its complete originality, contemporary theoreticians had repeatedly asked: can we still create anything original (Barthes 1983; Baudrillard 1994)? Applying this question to knitting one might pose the question differently: what degree of creativity goes into working from a pre-designed pattern? Is the sweater worked from the pattern a result of the creative efforts of a maker, or is it a mere imitation of something that has been designed by someone else? In thinking of images and their copies Jean Baudrillard asks "what becomes of the divinity when it reveals itself in icons, when it is multiplied in simulacra? Does it remain the supreme power that is simply incarnate in images as visible theology" (1994: 97)? I suggest that we can substitute the notion of supreme power for the notion of originality and hence ask if the product created from the pattern constitutes an original creation. Hence, the pattern while resembling a simulacrum becomes "the concrete sign of the loss of representation power" (1994: 93). An object made from a pattern is not only the copy of the copy of a copy that substitutes reality because no one remembers or recognizes the original any longer, but it is also the product of our creative powers that becomes

the manifestation of nostalgia for something that has been lost:

There is a plethora of myths of origin and of signs of reality—a plethora of truth, of secondary objectivity, and authenticity. Escalation of the true, of lived experience, resurrection of the figurative where the object and substance have disappeared. Panic-stricken production of the real and of the referential, parallel to and greater than the panic of material production: this is how simulation appears in the phase that concerns us—a strategy of the real, of the neoreal and the hyperreal that everywhere is the double of a strategy of deterrence. (Baudrillard 1994: 98–9)

The uniqueness of the object comes through the choice of textures, colours, tension and more importantly by the unique touch of one's hand. The usefulness of the notion of simulacra for this discussion is that it allows opening up the binaries of the original versus copy, or pattern versus product. This omission of the restricting binary allows for creating and executing the patterns by the consumers as a unified open-ended creative process that allows for the joy of making. As Bruce Metcalf notes:

The hand molding clay, hand holding a mallet and chisel, the hand touching fabric, the object taking shape when before there was nothing but formless mud or wood or thread—craft diverts experience back to the physical. The choice of

craft is not anachronistic. It is a statement that we still live in a body rich in potential. In a sense, craft always tries to perform a metaphysical revision: the return of labour to equal status with thought. (Metcalf 2007: 7)

This description of the process of craft making demonstrates that the difference between the two notions, namely between the high craft (original, professional) and what is considered low amateurish craft (executed from a pattern) essentially require similar types of skills and the engagement of the mind and body.

According to Nikol Lohr, author of several knitting pattern books, "Knitting (or painting, or writing, or building furniture) is sexy because it fuses vision and skill into a creative superpower. Doing something resourceful and productive feels like magic because it is." She further continues to consider that because all people are essentially preoccupied by the same activities such as working, eating, sleeping and having some free time, "When you fill that time learning or perfecting something that not everyone can do, instead of just trudging to work or watching TV, you start to accumulate creative superpowers— and with them, a boost up on the human sexiness scale." Lohr ties knitting and sexuality through knitting's creative power and thus participates, perhaps inadvertently, in the century-old "is craft an art?" debate. Some academic literature has argued that work done from patterns is essentially just simple copying. Design and craft historian

Jo Turney, for instance, notes that the objects created from pre-made kits and patterns "are essentially copied and constructed from patterns produced largely by needlework designers" (Turney 2004: 270). Jennifer Stafford, like Lohr and others think differently, "I want you to experience the supreme satisfaction of creating a knitted piece that is well crafted and unhurried. A true Dominknitrix has no room for shoddy workmanship or uneven stitches," says Stafford to her readers (Stafford 2006: 2–3). She affirms the creative process is the supreme power of the producer whose creative efforts are the result of joy, imagination, and discipline.

The purpose of this section was to analyze the idea of the pattern and its role in contemporary craft debate to point the interrelationship between the creative processes that are involved in both work from a pattern and the design of one. The discussion of contemporary crafts often touches upon the role of designer and the maker and the problematics of privileging one over the other. The dichotomy of designer and maker prerogative is relevant to the contemporary knitting practice, a big share of which is amateur in nature. As my discussion in the following sections will show it is very important to realize that this binary (designer/maker) is in reality often blurred. The execution of a pattern involves choices, it allows for imagination to run as free as one chooses and more importantly it allows the agency, the decisions to be made by the amateur knitter on what pattern to make, what yarn to choose, when to follow the pattern, and when to mix and match the yarns or the patterns.

Nostalgia and Knitting

The analogous relations between knitting from a pattern and a simulacrum are also the result of nostalgia. Contemporary society does not know "how to manage its mourning for the real, for power, for the social itself, which is implicated in this same breakdown" (Baudrillard 1994: 46). In the discourse of craft, nostalgia is related to the handmade, to the process of using one's body and mind together, but it also goes back to the idea that any craft especially the making of textiles, such as weaving, embroidery, or knitting also involves countless repetitions. This "mindless" work of the body that allows for socializing with others or being able to contemplate or daydream is connected to the luxury of having free time, of being able to produce something inefficient in terms of the modernist understanding of the world as moving at a specific speed towards specific goals. Thus, the nostalgic feeling that often surfaces when knitting is discussed is related to the excess of time and space that allowed for the production of the objects that essentially could be produced more efficiently by machines. As John Potvin argues, excess can be seen as a "potent liminal condition that allows for creativity and empowerment."[2] Consequently, knitting affords a link between the past (perceived as calm, anachronistic, simple, and worry-free) and the present postmodern condition (a constant move forward and the lack of luxurious leisure time) that can be seen as a positive and empowering phenomenon.

Feeling of longing associated with knitting participates in three different yet interrelated discourses: as striving for leisure time, inclusions and exclusions of knitting within the social realm and finally, the tactile experiences and objects that evoke memory. Wendy Parkins addresses the nostalgic feelings associated with knitting by looking at the idea of the contemporary conditioning of time. Critics of the post-modern condition often note that we live between two extremes of either moving very quickly or spending great amounts of time waiting. "Only against the background of speed can slowness be determined and learnt," notes Helga Nowotny (1994). Yet, Thomas Hylland Eriksen (2001) argues, "That the conflict between fast and slow time in everyday life, exemplified by the fast time of work is a significant source of dissatisfaction and diminished quality of life" (quoted in Parkins 2004: 432). Knitting offers delayed pleasure, the opportunity to do something deliberately unrushed. This enjoyment and concentration of the process has always been important in women's craft production. According to one experienced Urban Knitter, "It's not instant gratification … It's methodical, process-oriented. That's what I find soothing" (Purloined Letter Blog 2006). This remark echoes George Simmel's comment on consumers' desires, which he made in the late nineteenth century, "We desire objects only if they are not immediately given to us for use and enjoyment; that is, to the extent they resist our desire" (quoted. in Miller 2005: 70). In the postmodern consumerist world where desire and not need drives consumption (consequently resulting in the production of sexually charged

items), slowly crafting such items acquires different connotations. Similar to the popular perception of feminism as the notion of women's choice, production and consumption of such objects become the manifestation of the desire to get away from the pressures of everyday life. Taking up knitting or another domestic hobby such as cooking or scrapbooking allows women to be "domestic goddesses" as British TV celebrity chef Nigella Lawson has revealed in her shows and books. Hobbies allow people especially women to become productive in contexts that are not driven by necessities of everyday life. "The knitting then is the resignification, not as domestic labour but as pleasure and care for the self, allows women to carve out time and space for themselves, despite proximity of caring responsibilities" (Parkins 2004: 434). It is about taking control of one's time when it is almost impossible because of the pressures of multifaceted lives.

For example, the *Stitch 'n Bitch* movement, loosely connected groups of women and men who like to knit and meet with others to socialize, exchange their craft knowledge and become part of the community of amateur craft people, may be understood as "a nostalgic, conservative response to a world no longer present" (Minahan and Cox 2007: 14). These types of gathering could be seen as an attempt to recreate "an idealized past when people belonged to a harmonious community and spent time chatting with friends and neighbors" (Wajcman 2004: 59). Yet there is difference between such aspirations and the desire

by some "young women to claim place and affiliation at a local level when they meet in Jazz 'n' Knit or *Stitch 'n Bitch* nights in pubs and clubs" (Minahan and Cox 2007: 15).[3] The main difference is the desire to be in public and yet be able to undertake a personal, intimate activity of creating craft objects. The nostalgia here then is transformed and revoked into the creative powers at establishing a public, active community of like-minded people. Such gatherings are part of the Craft Revolution as one of its leaders, Jean Railla, calls it. Her enormously popular website www.craftrevolution.com carries her "manifesto," a carefully worded essay on how she, a self-professed rebellious Third Wave feminist and bohemian, found deep satisfaction and profound meaning in cooking, fiber arts and domestic cleaning. "When I was younger, I saw crafts as sort of anti-intellectual. I think that's why I shunned them for so long," Railla explains, "I think this is one of the successes of feminism in fact, that young women feel so strongly about themselves that they can knit and be taken seriously." The New Domesticity according to Railla embraces traditional women's work, yet it is not traditional. "Just because I knit doesn't mean I do all the housework. The new domesticity is not conservative." Knitting then helps women to establish the progressive link between past and present where present allows for choice of which craft to take up while past signified the necessity to practice them all.

It is important to remember, however, that nostalgia is by

definition an exclusive entity. American political scientist Benedict Anderson thinks of the process of forging national consciousness as creating "imagined communities." Each such community creates a historical narrative to justify its right for independent existence. Usually these recounts of the past include nostalgic or pastoral scenes of happy premodern life. The nostalgic feelings that they evoke are usually exclusive as historian Angelika Bammer explains:

> Stories, the telling of which have the power to create the "we" who are engaged in telling them. This power to create not only an identity for ourselves as members of a community, but also the discursive right to a space (a country, a neighborhood, a place to live) that is due us, is—we then claim, in the name of the we-ness we have just constructed—at the heart of what Anderson describes as "the profound emotional legitimacy" of such concepts as "nation" or "home." (Bammer 1992: XI)

The limitations of nostalgia is in its claiming of others' territories and memories. Yet, there are other types of nostalgia that Svetlana Boym calls reflexive. This nostalgia does not aim at recreating place or time exactly as it was; rather, it looks at past events with irony and thoughtfulness attempting to recreate some aspects of the ambiance and mood of the past (Boym 2001: XVIII–XIX).

As Manahan and Cox argue, it is perhaps too often that the idea of handicraft comes into the discourse of Western cultural studies without the necessary acknowledgement that for many it has been and still is work, work that brings very little rewards either monetary or otherwise. "The 'digital divide' is very real for these women, and they are firmly placed on its 'have not' side. They live in a world of very basic and inadequate technology where there is no nostalgia for craft—it is a reality that brings income to the household" (Manahan and Cox, 2007: 15). Knitting according to them may or may not signify nostalgia. Stella Manahan tells her own story which the authors claim demonstrates that the practice of amateur knitting can be unrelated to nostalgia and be a reaction to the current cultural changes. For example, knitting in Manahan's case was facilitated by the fact that "knitting yarn was relatively inexpensive in Australia in the 1960s/1970s and provided lots of opportunities to knit and crochet the long vests and fringed ponchos of the hippie era" (Manahan and Cox 2007: 16). I would caution against such a proclamation of having singular economically driven motivations. In addition, the hippie movement and its fashions were tightly connected to the nostalgia for all-inclusive freedoms of the past (Neville 1995). This counter-culture movement itself was the product of the striving for a utopian idealized society and social changes that had precedents in the past centuries, for example the nineteenth century saw a bohemian movement opposing established bourgeois values (Shires 2007; Turner 2006). I would argue that similar to the inherited striving to look for an original substituted for simulacra, the desire to knit could not be completely divorced from nostalgia. Yet, the action of looking back to times gone by does not have to be regressive, rather it could help to create new communities, connections and opportunities to practitioners of knitting. Sherri Boggs describes the New Domesticity as providing people with the "sense of being part of something bigger" (Boggs 2005: n.p.). She continues that the "human element" may be the main reason for younger people to join in. Joe Wilcox, the creator of "Queer Joe's Knitting Blog" explains:

> One of the most appealing aspects of knitting is the throwback to a less high-tech tech and complex world, where it is possible to actually create fabric from thread. My next-door neighbour was showing me a custom-fabricated bolt he had made for his car on his meal lathe and I clearly understood the pride with which he discussed it. The combination of being able to create something by hand and the tactile experience of doing so can be an incredibly heady drug to some. (Wilcox 2005)

Knitting also provides the sense of belonging to something that feels a subversive, yet also inviting. Unlike other countercultural movements, contemporary knitting groups are about embracing rather than rebelling as noted by Railla, "This is different, edgier. In fact, it's kind of a punk rock version of Martha Stewart" (Purloined Letter Blog 2006). That sense of subversion of the normative nostalgia for old time is at the core of the new revival of knitting. Knitting creates a link between the past with its "reactionary claims for a return to something which of

course never quite was, or which at least is open to dispute" or "basis for the mobilization of emancipatory political change" (Massey 1995: 40). Yet, it helps to create new subjectivities in the younger generation of knitters. Interestingly, knitting as a communal activity lends itself particularly well to collective art projects that often blend nostalgic feelings with the concerns for current political and social issues.

Contemporary Knitting Culture: Process is What Counts

Presently, knitting books alone take up at least one bookcase in the larger bookstores. The number of publications on knitting increased more than twice starting from year 2000; 462 books were published between 2000 to 2007, while only 215 were published from 1980 to 1990.[4] These new publications offer a variety of knitting experiences from designs inspired by such staples of knitting patterning as Fair Isle and Nordic designs to books that explore knitting as therapeutic activity equal to meditation. The current trend is to take the craft outside of the traditional realm of home into the big world, which includes subways, restaurants, bars and other social gatherings. No longer is knitting a predominantly female craft either. Men (although still a minority in the knitting circles) are often equal participants in knitting circles, including in the Chicago-based *Stitch 'n Bitch*, and in celebrity circles including those of Julia Roberts, Hilary Swank, Sandra Bullock, Jennifer Aniston, and Brad Pitt (Parkins 2004: 427).

Along with the patterns, many books provide inspirational quotes and descriptions free flowing train

of thought of a knitter while she/he works. For example, a reader of *Knitting into the Mystery: A Guild to the Shawl-Knitting Ministry* notes:

> A warning—this is not a pattern book or a technique book, it does not teach how to knit or provide instructions for any shawls. This is a book about the process of making shawls to help and comfort others in times of need, in times of celebration, or simply to mark the strength of the relationship between the knitter and the recipient. (Amazon.com review)

The reviewer of *Zen and the Art of Knitting: Exploring the Links Between Knitting, Spirituality, and Creativity* claims: "For me, my time to craft (I crochet, knit, cross stitch) is my time to reconnect with myself and my inner dreams of spending my days making things for other people to wear and enjoy" (Amazon.com review). These and many other titles indicate the turn from the craft that is oriented toward the product to the process-oriented enjoyment of handiwork.

Interestingly, contemporary popular psychology, which calls for being completely immersed in this moment's existence and the traditional craftsperson's aspiration for experiencing the process of making merged together in the knitting revival. Attempting to borrow some of the communal experiences from past generations can be seen as a "remedial theme" (Manahan and Cox 2007: 10) that helps to get away from loneliness while pursuing one's hobby. As Manahan and Cox argue, "The return of women to basic crafts is not simply a rejection of technology, for in many cases *Stitch 'n Bitch* may be a unique cyber-feminist phenomenon one of women expressing their own thought and reflecting their own circumstances and environment." The gathering in what Richard Florida (2002) terms a "third space," outside of house and work spaces allows for a different outlet of their individuality.

The main result of the empowerment that nostalgic knitting brought to contemporary practitioners is the ability to knit in a public place:

> It's Wednesday night at the Spike. Despite the fresh snow and freezing cold, seven women have made it downtown and are now claiming the best corner of the coffee shop ... Tonight's *Stitch'n'Bitchers* are young—most are in their 20s and 30s. And lest you mistake this for some sort of old-fashioned knitting circle complete with polite chit-chat and doilies-in-progress, it should be mentioned that many members are fond of the 'f' word and apply it liberally while, say, untangling a hissing snarl of yarn or realizing one's scarf has a big ugly drooped stitch. (Boggs 2005: n.p.)

It appears that contemporary knitting proponents ultimately are trying to change craft's image on a number of different levels including social class, gender-orientation and design production. Interestingly, while attempting to change the craft and to make it more acceptable for middle-classes, they also re-enforce stereotypical attitudes towards the role of needle crafts in history. As Turney has shown, needle crafts have a particular place in British popular culture, "Frequently the butt of jokes (Granny's hand-knitted jumpers), home needlecrafts are deemed largely kitsch (crinoline lady toilet roll covers), 'homey' (cozies of all kinds) and old-fashioned, requiring little skill or design flair (kits), they are seen as being inexpensive to make and prolific in number" (Greenhalgh 1997: 20–25; Turney 2004: 267–8). Throughout the twentieth century, women were encouraged to take up the needle arts for employment and leisure. The skills acquired through understanding the craft were seen as useful in life. The emphasis was on discipline and obedience. Moreover, craft activities as taught in schools were often determined by social and cultural definitions of gender, educational ability and future role in society (Berlo 2006: 205). Knitting was usually associated with thriftiness, making due and saving money; therefore, it was related to poverty and lower classes. It was also representative of a sense of pride, joy, self-discipline and aesthetic sensibilities of the producers. Soetsu Yanagi also mentions that craft has been considered the preoccupation of lower and working classes (1989: 38). Rejected by the upper middle classes, hand-knitted objects enjoyed special attention within particular social groups. The New Domesticity and the knitting Renaissance then attempt to transplant knitting from, to use Bourdieu's term, *habitus* of lower classes to the contemporary urban culture of the middle classes.

Knitted Objects in the Interior

A blog on the Internet named "Knitting and Feminism" (2006)

attempts to reconcile being a feminist and practicing fiber arts. The anonymous writer of the blog offers the following defense of making objects:

> The objects that were made afforded warmth to those who used them, but they also offered comfort and pleasure to those making them. What a shame it would be to detach all our everyday objects from the process of their creation. When we buy a blanket or shirt or scarf at Wal-Mart, we've done just that. The consequence of this process of detachment seems to be that we care less and less about our world. ("Knitting and Feminism" 2006)

Over and over again women who knit wrestle with their positions in society as either feminists or homemakers. Yet another important aspect that one can see in the above quoted passage is creating intimacy through making things. What is the role of objects, handmade objects, in creating a house, a home? How does making it change its relevance? These issues *vis-à-vis* knitting and handicrafts in general are yet to be explored. A Russian émigré writer, Nina Berberova (1901–93), reminisced that while living in exile in Paris in the 1920s she had an embroidered tea cozy that she received as a gift from a female friend who remained behind in the Soviet Union and ended up in Siberian exile because she had communicated with friends abroad. When another Russian writer, Ivan Bunin, came to visit Berberova and her husband Vladislav Khodasevich, the former was appalled by the presence of the embroidered

rooster on the teapot in the writer's house. "For Bunin, it was an example of domestic kitsch that compromised the purity of Russian nostalgia. It was the betrayal of the purity of suffering and a pervasive attempt to come to terms with the temporary condition of dislocation" (Berberova 1991: 338; Boym 1998: 498–9). The objects created with love and given to a friend were supposed to help create an intimacy in the new place where Berberova and Khodasevich settled. Boym further notes that "while intimate experiences are personal and singular, the maps of intimate sites are socially recognizable; they are encoded as refuges of the individual" (Aries 1989: 15, quoted in Boym 1998: 500), The home then is prescribed by society to be one of the intimate spaces. Yet, when knitters claim public spaces, such as bars and subways, as the places to practice the craft, one can argue they also claim these spaces for more intimate relations. The spaces that in normative society serve public socialization become stages for traditionally domestic practices. The gathering of groups such as *Stitch 'n Bitch* undermine very core function of public spaces by blurring the binary between private and public.[5] Naturally, such transformations of spaces are temporary. Once, the knitting groups finished, the spaces such as coffee shops, go back to their original function. The residues sometimes remain. For example, some of the Second Cup coffee shops in Guelph, Ontario, which houses knitting group Knittaphon decided to enhance its support of the handmade undertaking by commissioning to some members

of the group and other knitters to create coffee cup cozies and tea cozies which the shop sold as part of their holiday offerings. As Parkins notes:

> The urban café, as a space of vibrant and visible sociality in modernity where the exchange of (the latest) ideas can take place, is represented as a site for (new) knitting which takes on a public dimension not traditionally associated with the craft. Like the visibility of celebrity culture, the new knitting is performed publicly; it is something one is seen doing. (Parkins 2004: 430)

To that one can add that not only the craft is transformed into a public spectacle but the café is also transformed into a more intimate space. Knitting is often credited by its practitioners as providing more intimate and solid relationships between people. Spaces, such as cafés, become intimate, domesticated stages for craft production.

Knitting and Sex? The Gendered View

If knitting contributes to creating intimacy within a public space, then taking knitting to the bedroom or creating objects for the bedroom would only intensify the notion of intimate relations. Yet, seemingly, it is hard to think of more opposing notions than knitting and sex. What could knitting possibly have to do with sex, sexual desires, and fantasies? There are a few books on the shelves of North American bookstores that invite their largely female readership to think of knitting as a gender-conscious, tactile, fantasy-ridden, escapist activity. The first one is *Naughty Needles: Sexy, Saucy Knits for the Bedroom and Beyond*, which professes to be "fun and feisty knitting adventure filled with designs that can go from bedroom to costume party and back again" (jacket). Among the seductive creations are the cave girl bikini, kinderwhore socks, and crisscrossed laced corset, garters, and gloves. The author Nikol Lohr, according to the book jacket, "is the thirty something creator of DisgruntledHousewife.com and ThriftyKnitter.com, as well as the co-author of cooking site OutoftheFryingPan.com. Lohr, a champion of domestic creativity, can cook, sew, crochet, knit, needlepoint, embroider, decoupage, print, grow things, fix things, and generally craft her ass off. A longtime resident of Austin, Texas, Lohr recently moved to rural Kansas, where she works on transforming four old school buildings into a secluded arts retreat" (http://www.subversivecrossstitch.com/query5.htm).

The second book *Domiknitrix: Whip your Knitting into Shape* by Jennifer Stafford teaches knitters to take control of their yarn, technique and projects to make sure that the results are beautiful and wearable. For the author the success of the garment is contingent on how many times it has been worn and if it was ever confused with a store-bought item. The projects include Valentine Candy Pillows, a Devil's Hat, and The Sling. Stafford proposes the following definition for a Domiknitrix: "a woman who dominates her knitting; broadly: a badass knitter" (Stafford 2006: 7). The premise of the book is to create the items that showcase their creator and her (his) personality. The author asks, "Are you sick of wishy-washy knitting books with vague patterns and a total of three pages covering techniques?" And since the answer is undoubtedly yes, and this is what possessed us to buy this book in the first place, she offers, "Let me take you under my wing and whip you into shape" (Stafford 2006: 9–10).

The two publications discussed above appeal to female knitters and claim that this craft can enrich one's sexuality and alter women's subjectivity. Creating sexualized objects by way of knitting creates yet another level of escapism. *Naughty Needles* and *Domiknitrix* offer an escape into solitude and into the pleasures of sexuality. These creative efforts also provide pleasure and satisfaction of the different kinds, namely, the needleworks help their creators to produce items and objects that could be taken to the bedroom. Both Lohr and Stafford invite their followers to experiment with creating toys and gadgets that have sexual and erotic connotations. Similar to the romance novels, eroticized knitting literature is "a principal site for the struggle over feminine subjectivity and sexuality" and as Janice Radway claims, by extension, "over feminism as well" (Radway 1998: 139).

One cannot help but wonder if the knitters are invited to be in the bedroom alone? Or, are they knitting garments and toys that could be used by couples? Although some of the items definitely suggest the idea of sex for couples, most of the designs and descriptions are geared to women. Moreover, the enjoyment of these items also presupposes women's pleasure rather than men's. In other words, women are invited to create designs that are sexual in nature to enjoy themselves. The choice of having a partner in play or not is theirs! Both books definitely offer a place for women to rule. The images offer suggestions for

creating ties, gags, straitjackets along with other bondage and S&M (light sadomasochism) paraphernalia. Interestingly, when the pattern is for a women's straitjacket sweater, the woman is photographed by herself, enjoying listening to the CD player (Figure 1). The restraining costume shows a woman but no men in sight. The Dirty Secrets section includes the pillows with hidden compartments so her favorite bedroom toys can be hidden in plain sight (Figure 2).[6]

These popular publications illustrate that Western women can now exercise freedom of self-expression of their sexuality. Knitting helps to create the intimate world where women are in charge of their bodies and their pleasures. In a world where most birth control pills have been shown to significantly reduce women's libido, where Viagra and similar drugs have been tested and approved for men, but there is hardly any advancement in producing a libido-boosting drug for women, where scientific articles talk about impotence and infertility as if they were parallel and gender-specific problems, taking control of one's sexual pleasure is indeed no less important than

ensuring one's creative freedom. These images and the description in these books equate women's sexual and creative powers to bring attention to the new type of women. Contemporary women, instead of going back to the mythical traditions of our mothers and grandmothers who found solace, support, and joy in the company of other crafty women, know how to enjoy their sexuality, craftiness, and everything else alone or in the company of others. They are not afraid to be spinsters or lonely souls; they embrace it as a choice that they make for themselves. Such knitting literature "marks the first appearance of a large and coherent body of sexual literature for women, providing the opportunity to learn to use sexual fantasy and to explore an aspect of their identities that patriarchal society has long denied women" (Thurston 1987: 88).

Some of the knitting books present women as preferring the process of knitting over sensual engagement with their partners. Betsy Hosegood's *Not Tonight Darling, I'm Knitting* (2006) presents a happily knitting woman with her undressed partner lying on the bed waiting for her (Figure 3).

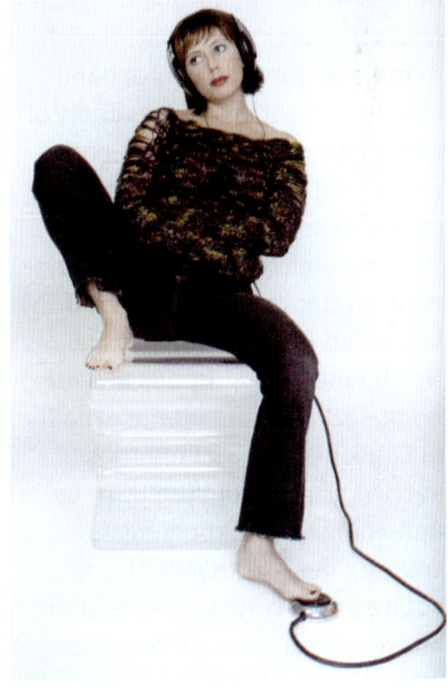

Figure 1
Robyn Eden, photo of a model in Straightjacket. Courtesy of Potter Craft.

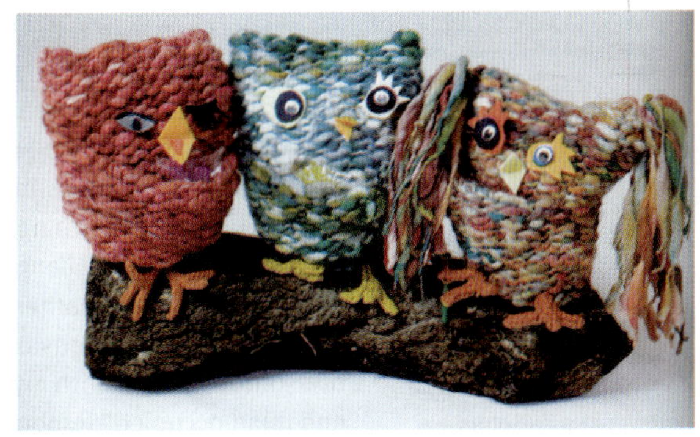

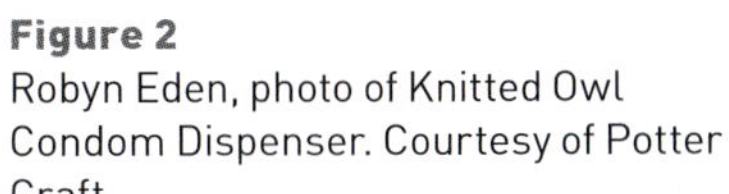

Figure 2
Robyn Eden, photo of Knitted Owl Condom Dispenser. Courtesy of Potter Craft.

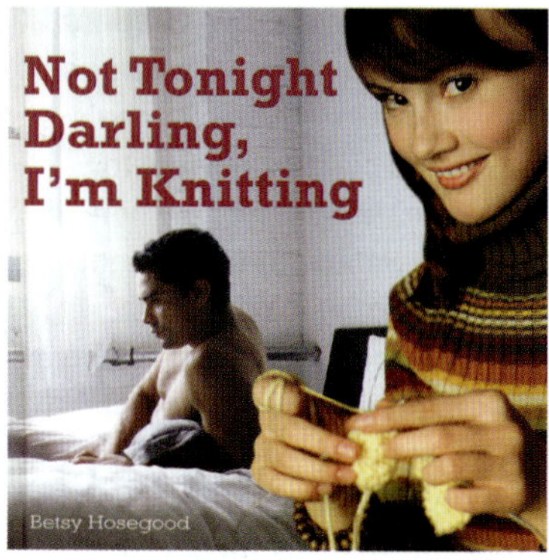

Figure 3
Cover of *Not Tonight Darling, I'm Knitting* (Hosegood 2007). Courtesy of David and Charles Publishing.

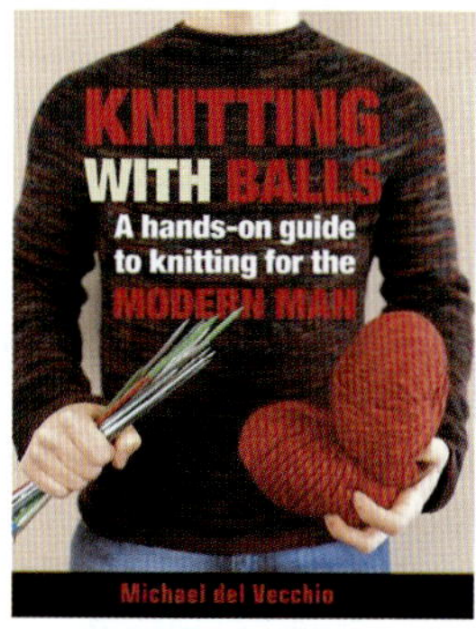

Figure 4
Cover of *Knitting with Balls: A Hands-on Guide to Knitting for the Modern Man* (Del Vecchio 2006). Courtesy of DK Publishing.

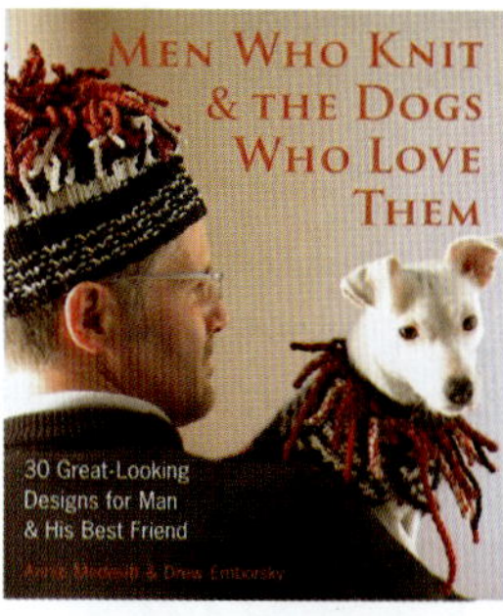

Figure 5
Cover of *Men Who Knit and the Dogs Who Love Them* (Emborsky and Modesitt 2007). Photography by Keith Wright. Courtesy of Lark Books.

Nothing in the content of the book refers to the sexual frustrations of the abandoned partner, but is dedicated to an overview of knitting as a cultural phenomenon and as a great way to entertain and sooth oneself. Hosegood celebrates the experience of knitting, "What could be more alluring than the silky feel of yarn between your fingers ... and the satisfaction of watching your beloved ball of boucle transform into a sensational creation" (2006: book jacket). This popular culture selling gimmick also implicitly suggests that knitting could provide an alternative emotional connection with friends or other knitters.

Knitting and Sexuality

Not all knitting books appeal to women alone. *Knitting with Balls: A Hands-on Guide to Knitting for the Modern Man* renders the gendering of craft to the extreme by providing patterns for men only (Figure 4). The book is a reaction to the fact that, according to its author Michael Dell Vecchio, "men knit ... and have for centuries" (2006: back jacket). Yet although the perception is that many men who knit are gay, the literature on the subject attempts to make it very clear that it reaches out to straight men. The authors of *Men Who Knit and the Dogs Who Love Them* (Emborsky and Modesitt 2007) ask, "Men Golf, Men Fish, Why Can't Men Knit?" (Figure 5). The emphasis here is on traditionally straight male hobbies such as golfing and fishing. Another male knitter is quoted saying, "I like things to be perfect, which is a challenge with knitting. Being very mathematical, determined and a bit obsessive, I find knitting keeps both my hands and mind occupied" (Emborsky and

Modesitt 2007: 7). The connection of knitting to characteristics that are stereotypically male—assertiveness, determination, and inclination to mathematics—gives knitting legitimacy for straight men. However, some readers who reviewed the book had different opinions. Some complained that, "most of the patterns seem to be geared towards gay men. Not that there is anything wrong with that, but it doesn't suit me at all." While another reader noted that: "I wish that the author would have done more to appeal to a wider variety of men" (http://www.amazon.com/review/R2JX0NOE22660E/ref=cm_cr_rdp_perm, May 9, 2008).

The publications that feature male knitters raise a number of important questions regarding North American attitudes towards homosexuality and metrosexuality in English-speaking countries such as Canada and the USA. By appealing to straight men and creating designs that mainly fit a young urban crowd, this literature misses the audience that is really interested in knitting, namely gay men. In fact many users and reviewers of male knitting books are women; they still constitute the largest share of the interested constituency because they are not afraid to change the pattern to make it suit the men in their lives. For example, eight out of the nine reviewers on Amazon.com of *Men Who Knit and the Dogs Who Love Them* are women and according to one of them, "a few of the patterns have potential if you change yarns from those suggested" (http://www.amazon.com/review/R2BA8LG9L6R8VG/ref=cm_cr_rdp_perm, May 2,

2008). While reviewing *Knitting with Balls* one female knitter mentioned: "I can see it in all kinds of yarn/fabric lining combos" (http://www.amazon.com/review/R24IV3LMSL36GX/ref=cm_cr_rdp_perm, May 2, 2008). While men tended to look at the patterns without visualizing the changes. One reviewer thought that the patterns "came in ridiculously bright colors and were suited to the super-trendy urban man" http://www.amazon.com/review/R2JXoNOE22660E/ref=cm_cr_rdp_perm, May 4, 2008). These books also force us to reconsider and analyze the role of the metrosexual male in contemporary culture. The phenomenon of the metrosexual attests to our new understanding of the role of men in the society. This well-groomed, psychologically aware, and emotionally intelligent male takes care of his appearance, health, and public presentation. Behind these positive attitudes, however, is the desire of consumer society to boost economic gains by promoting men's cosmetic surgery and use of beauty products.[7] In addition to promoting certain normativity in society such as adequate weight and appearance, the construct of a metrosexual male poses a range of questions. Seemingly a cross-pollination between a traditional homosexual and heterosexual, a metrosexual embodies the threats of both, namely aesthetic sensibilities and emotional awareness of gay men and the normative sexuality of the straight man. Unlike the "country bumpkin," metrosexuals such as David Beckham are not intimidated by their erotic appeal to homosexuals. They embrace their attractiveness and use it to their advantage. The problematic issue with all this is the notion of sexual norm that is still embedded in this definition of the metrosexual. The word sex that is inscribed in all three descriptors (heterosexual, homosexual, metrosexual) emphasizes the importance of sexual demarcation. Although the metrosexual is gay-friendly, he is definitely straight, normal, and heterosexual. The appeal to metrosexual males in the knitting books helps to obscure homosexuals, making sure they are invisible to the untrained eye, as has often been done in the past. Carefully avoiding photographing two men together the illustrations concentrate on male bodies, demonstrating mainly sweaters that reveal fit masculine torsos. Interestingly, the illustration on the front jacket of *Knitting with Balls* shows a slim, fit, male body dressed in the ubiquitous, trendy sweater holding balls of yarn and very phallic-looking knitting needles. The head of the figure is cut off so that the viewer concentrates on the aesthetically pleasing, trendily fit body, and attractive hands holding yarn and (popular with urban knitters) bamboo needles. This example of a sexualized image attracts one's attention in the visually overloaded environment. The problem with such images, much like with the example of feminism, is that it attaches themes of liberation to sexuality, "which may eventually dilute equality issues in favor of commodification" (Rohlinger 2002: n.p.). Following this logic, affiliating knitting with homosexuality will not sell as successfully as presenting it as a metrosexual phenomenon that is digestible by both straight and gay men. Paradoxically, while much knitting literature empowers women to be independent and embrace their interests, the same activity obliterates gay men and further problematizes the notion of gay and lesbian liberation.

In conclusion, the revitalization of knitting in contemporary culture brings to the forefront several issues related to craft in general namely the notion of originality and the meaning of pattern making. Contemporary knitters often choose to blur the boundaries between the original and the copy by combining their own ideas, such as choice of colors, with those set by the designer's parameters. Another important notion that knitting underlines is the use and function of space. Similar to other activities such as embroidering, crocheting, and breastfeeding, it allows women and in some instances men to bring their private hobbies to public spaces and thus reformulate even if temporarily the function of public areas such as cafes, buses, and libraries. My research shows that contemporary knitters mainly consist of heterosexual women and gay men while the literature on knitting mainly appeals to heterosexual men and women. Although the internet blogs and other discussion groups indicate an increasing presence of male craftspeople who identify themselves as gay, no publication acknowledges that particular group. In this sense knitting helps to identify the stereotypical understanding of masculinity and perhaps will help to address that void in appropriate literature in the future.

Notes

1. By craft practice I understand any practice that includes the four main characteristic discussed by Larry Shiner in "The Fate of Craft": hand, material, mastery, and use.

2. For more on excess and empowerment in the context of interior design, collecting, and craft making, see Myzelev and Potvin (2009).

3. Although Minahan and Cox (2007) describe the knitting phenomenon in Australia, the same has been reported in the UK, USA, and Canada.

4. Knitting appears to be the most popular, widely consumed, and most widely published upon craft. My local Toronto library has 1,162 books on knitting, 728 books on quilting, and 310 books on crocheting. Similar proportions are kept in other public libraries in large cities such as San Francisco, Montreal, and New York. Amazon.ca offers 2,323 books on knitting, 4,184 on quilting, 2,302 on embroidery, and 921 on crocheting.

5. Knitting is not by any stretch of the imagination the only activity that undermines public space. Breastfeeding, an activity that is normally prescribed as private and suggests intimacy between mother and infant, functions in the same way.

6. The women depicted are seemingly all heterosexual although the authors and photographers do not make their targeted audience explicitly clear.

7. For example, between 1996 and 1998 male cosmetic surgery increased by 34 percent, mostly because of liposuction and 15 percent of plastic surgery in 2001 was performed on men. From 1999 to 2001 hair transplants increased by a staggering 316 percent (Miller 2005: 115).

References

Bammer, Angelika. 1992. "Editorial: The Question of 'Home.'" *New Formations* 17: IX.

Barthes, Roland. 1983. *The Fashion System*. New York: Hill and Wang.

Baudrillard, Jean. 1994. "The Precession of Simulacra." *Simulacra and Simulation*. Trans. Sheila Faria Glaser. Ann Arbor, MI: University of Michigan Press.

Belsey, Catherine. 1984. *Desire: Love Stories in Western Culture*. Oxford: Blackwell.

Berberova, Nina. 1991. *The Italics are Mine*. London: Chatto & Windus.

Berlo, Janet Catherine. 2006. "Chronicles in Cloth." In Deborah Cherry and Janice Helland (eds) *Local/Global: Women Artists in the Nineteenth Century*, pp. 201–23. Aldershot and Burlington, VT: Ashgate.

Boggs, Sheri, "Crafty Revolution." *The Pacific Northwest Inlander Online*, January 27, 2005. http://www.inlander.com/topstory/282474543224104.php, accessed December 31, 2007.

Boym, Svetlana. 1998. "On Diasporic Intimacy: Ilya Kabakov's Installations and Immigrant Homes." *Critical Inquiry* 24(2): 498–524.

Boym, Svetlana. 2001. *The Future of Nostalgia*. New York: Basic Books.

Del Vecchio, Michael. 2006. *Knitting with Balls: A Hands-on Guide to Knitting for the Modern Man*. London, New York: DK Publishing.

Emborsky, Drew and Annie Modesitt. 2007. *Men Who Knit and the Dogs Who Love Them*. Asheville, NC: Lark Books.

Eriksen, Thomas Hylland. 2001. *Tyranny of the Moment: Fast and Slow Time in the Information Age*. London: Pluto Press.

Florida, Richard. 2002. *The Rise of the Creative Class: And How it's Transforming Work, Leisure and Everyday Life*. New York: Basic Books.

Greenhalgh, Paul. 1997. "The History of Craft." In Peter Dormer (ed.) *The Culture of Craft: Status and Future*, pp. 20–53. Manchester: Manchester University Press.

Hosegood, Betsy. 2006. *Not Tonight Darling, I'm Knitting*. Newton Abbot: David and Charles.

"Knitting and Feminism." 2006. *The Purloined Letter*. April 12. http://thepurloinedletter.blogspot.com/2006/04/knitting-and-feminism.html, accessed January 4, 2008.

Lohr, Nikol. 2006. *Naughty Needles: Sexy, Saucy Knits for the Bedroom and Beyond*. New York: Potter Craft.

Massey, Doreen. 1995. "Space–Time and the Politics of Location." In James Lingwood (ed.) *House*, pp. 34–49. London: Phaidon.

Metcalf, Bruce. 2007. "Replacing the Myth of Modernism." In Sandra Alfoldy (ed.) *NeoCraft: Modernity and Craft*, pp. 4–33. Halifax: NSCAD Press.

Miller, Toby. 2005. "A Metrosexual Eye on Queer Guy." *GLQ: A Journal of Lesbian and Gay Studies* 11(1): 112–17.

Minahan, Stella and Julie Wolfram Cox. 2007. "*Stitch 'n Bitch*: Cyberfeminism, a Third Place and the New Materiality." *Journal of Material Culture* 12(1): 5–21.

Myzelev, Alla and John Potvin 2009. "Introduction." *Material Culture in Britain, 1750–1920: The Visual Meanings and Pleasures of Collecting*. Aldershot and Burlington, VT: Ashgate (in press).

Neville, Richard. 1995. *Hippie Hippie Shake: the Dreams, the Trips, the Trials, the Love-ins, the Screw ups … the Sixties*. London: Bloomsbury.

Nowotny, Helga. 1994. *Time: The Modern and Postmodern Experience*. Trans. Neville Plaice. Cambridge: Polity Press.

Parkins, Wendy. 2004. "Celebrity Knitting and the Temporality of Postmodernity." *Fashion Theory* 8(4): 425–42.

Purloined Letter Blog [Internet]. 2006. The Takoma Park, Maryland. http://thepurloinedletter.blogspot.com/2006/04/knitting-and-feminism.html, accessed January 7, 2009.

Radway, Janice A. 1998. *Reading the Romance: Women, Patriarchy, and Popular Literature*. Chapel Hill, NC: University of North Carolina Press.

Rohlinger, Deana. 2002. "Eroticizing Men: Cultural Influences on Advertising and Male Objectification." *A Journal of Research*, February 2002. http://findarticles.com/p/articles/mi_m2294/is_2002_Feb/ai_90888979, accessed May 2, 2008.

Shires, Preston. 2007. *Hippies of the Religious Right*. Waco, TX: Baylor University Press.

Stafford, Jennifer. 2006. *Domiknitrix: Whip Your Knitting Into Shape*. Cincinnati, OH: North Light Books.

Thurston, Carol. 1987. *The Romance Revolution: Erotic Novels for Women and the Quest for New Sexual Identity*. Urbana, IL: University of Illinois Press.

Turner, Fred. 2006. *From Counterculture to Cyberculture: Stewart Brand, the Whole Earth Network, and the Rise of Digital Utopianism*. Chicago, IL: University of Chicago Press.

Turney, Jo. 2004. "Here's One I Made Earlier: Making and Living with Home Craft in Contemporary Britain." *Journal of Design History* 17(3): 267–81.

Wajcman, Judy. 2004. *TechnoFeminism*. Cambridge: Polity Press.

Wilcox, Joe. "Queer Joe's Knitting Blog." 2005. http://www.queerjoe.blogspot.com/, accessed January 10, 2009.

Wilde, Oscar. 1895. *An Ideal Husband*, http://www.online-literature.com/view.php/ideal_husband/1?term=very%20difficult%20pose%20to%20keep%20up, accessed January 10, 2009.

Yanagi, Soetsu. 1989. *The Unknown Craftsman: A Japanese Insight into Beauty*. London: Gillingham House.

Red Shoes: Linking Fashion and

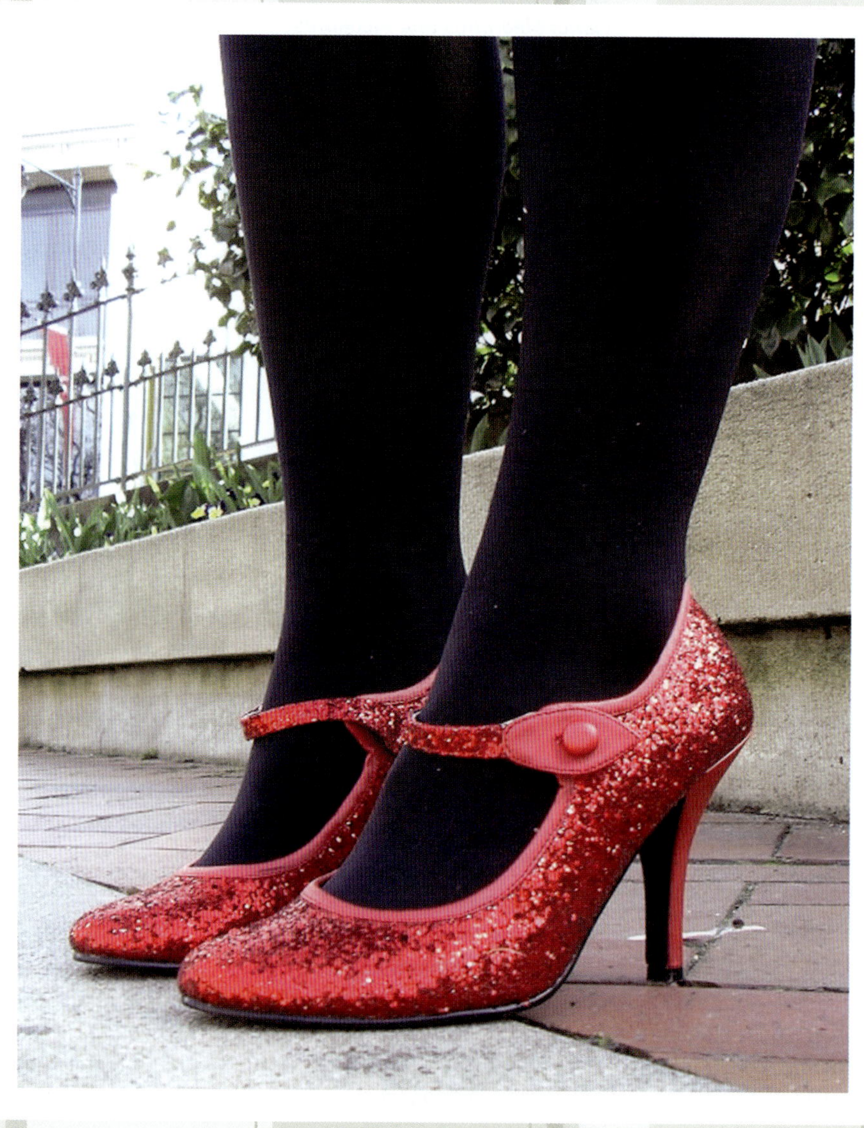

Abstract

What is it about red shoes? Conjuring multiple images and responses like black or blue shoes never could, red shoes connect literature, fashion, and dress through meanings that are uniquely personal yet resonant across wider cultural and social groups. These symbolic meanings of red shoes are powerful, partly because they are encountered in childhood stories, partly because they are reiterated by fashion, which capitalizes on and reinterprets these meanings, and partly because we can choose to wear them, contributing both to their vitality and our self-image, in ambiguous but evocative ways. Red shoes are never neutral. Glass slippers are quite different, being never obtainable in the material world, and also somehow lacking as a metaphor for wish fulfillment, which is suggestive when we consider the content and intentions of their stories. The red shoes by Hans Christian Andersen and the much older story of Cinderella with her glass slippers demand commitment from their wearers to a course of action, one leading to wild and willful dancing which ends in terrible suffering and death, the other to union and recognition. Both red and glass shoes have a place in our shared childhood libraries and in the wardrobes of our imaginations. Their stories are about desire, envy, transformation, and sin, so have a clear relationship with the impulse and character of fashion. By exploring these themes I hope to discover more about the symbolic meanings of these shoes, and their links through myth to fashion, style, and the self.

Keywords: red shoes, myth, fashion, transformation, self

ELAINE WEBSTER

Elaine Webster is writing a book about red shoes following widespread interest in an earlier version of this article presented at "The Fashion in Fiction Conference," University of Technology, Sydney, in May 2007. She has published several papers on dress and symbolic meanings and works at University of Otago, Dunedin, New Zealand.

Textile, Volume 7, Issue 2, pp. 164–177
DOI: 10.2752/175183509X460074
Reprints available directly from the Publishers.
Photocopying permitted by licence only.
© 2009 Berg. Printed in the United Kingdom.

Red Shoes: Linking Fashion and Myth

Perception has this inexhaustible profundity, because what we perceive is tacitly understood by us to be an aspect of reality, and aspects of reality are tacitly believed to be clues to boundless undisclosed, and perhaps yet unthinkable experiences.

Polyani and Prosch (1975: 188)

Introduction

What is it about red shoes? Conjuring multiple images and responses like black or blue shoes never could, red shoes connect literature, fashion, and dress through meanings that are uniquely personal yet resonant across wider cultural and social groups. The symbolic meanings of red shoes are powerful, partly because they are encountered in childhood stories, partly because they are reiterated by fashion, which capitalizes on and reinterprets these meanings, and partly because we can choose to wear them, contributing both to their vitality and our self-image, in ambiguous but evocative ways. Red shoes are never neutral.

They are also not new, yet in 2006 in the small southern city of Dunedin, New Zealand, red shoes were suddenly everywhere. They appeared in shop windows, in magazines, and on the feet of not only young and fashionable women, but women of all ages.

Prominent in fashion again, yet red shoes do not conform to the usual trajectory of fads but instead show a curious and disruptive longevity and are almost a classic form. Described by their wearers in unusually affectionate terms, and featuring in other cultural forms, red shoes clearly draw on a rich symbolic source. Neither fleeting nor empty, red shoes as fashion items challenge simplistic notions of fashion participation and processes, raising questions of meaning and interpretation.

What do these shoes mean to their wearers and how are such meanings created? Tempting as it is to rely on existing scholarship for these meanings, I wanted to find out what they mean to the people wearing them. So I started asking the question "what is it about red shoes?" Over a period of two months I asked virtually all the women I even vaguely know, and any woman wearing red shoes who seemed approachable, including strangers at bus stops and in supermarket queues. I also asked a number of men. Their answers provide the basis of the interpretations that follow.

Nearly all the women who love red shoes love them for their color, and many also made a connection with stories and films. "I love a bit of colour" (Figure 1). "They are about dance! That movie, the red shoes,

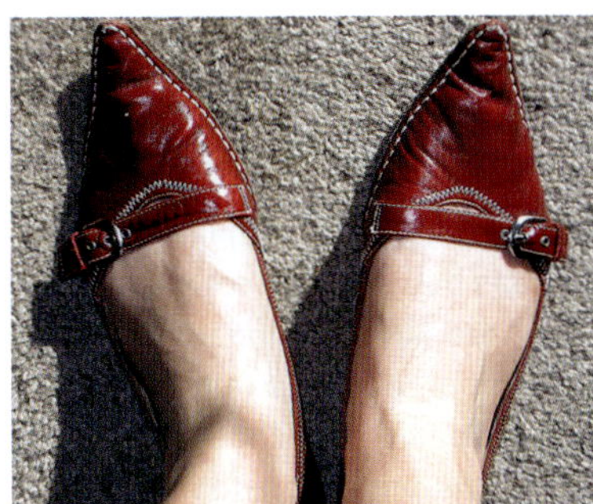

Figure 1
"I love a bit of colour." Photograph by
E. Webster.

I loved that as a child and took up
ballet." "Something about Dorothy?"
(clicking her heels together with a
laugh). "They are like Dorothy; I had
to have them!" (Figure 2). "I love
red shoes; like in the story." Linking
red shoes with color, life, vitality,
and dance, many of these women
made a deeper connection, recalling
cherished stories from childhood,
stories that lived in memory, that
vast and imperfect store. In these
stories red shoes were the central
motifs, almost reified, and always
powerful in their connection to life,
vitality, and the self.

For a smaller group, the
associations were quite different.
Red shoes for them always meant
illicit sex, and although most
obviously related to red high heels,
this meaning overshadowed all red
shoes. "Red shoes, no knickers!"
"My father always said that only
prostitutes wear them ... so I have
never been able to wear them." "I
don't want men thinking that I am
asking for it." All those linking red
shoes and sexuality interpreted red
shoes as worn or seen by others,
taking an external viewpoint and
reading this meaning as a fixed
property of the shoe. Men in

particular associated red shoes
with sex, with lust and danger. For
them, red shoes were the costume
par excellence for female sexual
passion and fetishism. This theme
of eroticism has been explored
elsewhere (see, for example,
Davidson 2006). Yet how can red
shoes mean such different things?

A major difference between
these groups was that so many of
the former group made an explicit
link with childhood stories and
film. Nourished by these stories,
red shoes had become a potent
symbol of the self and self-making,
of integration, connection, and
transformation. To explain the
power of these symbolic meanings I
turned to myths and stories, having
first looked at various approaches
to them.

There are many ways of looking
at stories and myths. These include
the historical materialist approach
of Jack Zipes, the literary and
social history approach of Marina
Warner, and the universalizing
anthropologies of Mircea Eliade and
Sir James Frazer. Hilary Davidson
(2006) analyzes red shoe stories
and films taking a literary and socio-
historical approach, foregrounding
Andersen's biography as context and
exposing the sexual undertones,
his obsessions, and extreme social
unease. But this explanation is only
partial, offering insight to the story
as a text, but shedding no light on
the diverse symbolic meanings
people have actually taken from
the story. Rationalizing the origin
of meanings and limiting them to
texts and social contexts neglects
the domain of symbolic meaning
itself, the unconscious. Social and
historical approaches also focus on
group processes and thus external

forces in meaning-making, while
I want to stress agency and the
personal. So for my analysis, I rely
on psychoanalytic treatments of
myth and stories, following Carl
Jung, Marie-Louise von Franz, Bruno
Bettelheim, and Joseph Campbell.
Through this approach, differences
in personal interpretations of myth
and story can be explained without
excluding or denying social and
historical contexts. The enchanting
vitality of red shoe stories and their
meanings is also preserved.

Disenchantment

To Sigmund Freud, father of
psychoanalysis, myths were public
dreams and dreams were private
myths, both being manifestations
of the compulsive fears and
delusions of the infant mind
(Campbell 1972: 12).[1] Freud, like his
contemporary the anthropologist
Sir James Frazer, judged the world
of myth and magic negatively, "as
errors to be refuted, surpassed, and
supplanted by science" (Campbell
1972: 13). While this great march
of scientific rationalism has
made both the best and worst of
modern life possible, Max Weber
described this process as one of
disenchantment (Giddens 1971),
which implies a loss.

During the twentieth century
myths have been treated as fables,
inventions, and fictions, if not
outright lies (Eliade 1998[1963]).
Eliade credits Xenophanes with
being the first of the Greeks to
reject the myths, emptying them of
metaphysical value and contrasting
mythos with *logos* and *historia,* until
mythos came to denote "what cannot
really exist" (1998[1963]: 2). Roland
Barthes discusses myth in the
sense of contemporary bourgeois

fictions, as ideologies without history posing as unchanging and unquestionable truths (1972). Myths do involve stories and stories can be lies, but not all myths are lies. Myths are fictions in that they are made (and remade) but are not "fictional" in relation to truth. Myths are another way of knowing (Eliade 1991[1952]) and knowing is self-truth (Kaiser 2001). Myths are cultural phenomena, occurring everywhere and in every time, and what is more, they are living. Myths disclose creative activity and the self, transform and transcend chaos and time, and reveal the sacred, i.e. that which really matters (Eliade 1998[1963]).

Re-enchantment

Departing from Freud, Carl Jung interpreted mythology as serving positive, life-furthering ends, offering us instead a re-enchantment. Appreciation of mystery and the numinous is a tonic for the outwardly oriented consciousness demanded by daily life (Campbell 1972). The symbolic images of myth offer reconnection with our innermost psyche, bringing us back in touch with our inward self through symbols, the language of imagery. In this way "the symbol is an object pointing to the subject" (Campbell 1972: 265). Myths are another way of knowing, and through symbols reveal certain aspects of reality otherwise unknowable, showing the world to be full of meaning (Polyani and Prosch 1975). The reality that symbols bring to light cannot be reduced to concrete references; by thinking of symbols as images we can see them as multivalent, just as reality is (Eliade 1991[1952]).

Myths and stories reconnect us to accumulated human wisdom weathered through time, as points of connection with others but also accessed through internal dialogs between the conscious and unconscious mind. Jung was not proposing a return to archaic patterns of thought and feeling inappropriate to modern life (Campbell 1972; Jung 1990), but instead, through continual interplay, the tapping of a rich and refreshing stream. Myths and stories can show what cannot be shown directly, supply models for human behavior without being didactic, and give us access to a time outside time. For Eliade (1998[1963]), myths evoke a different sense of time, the fabled time of the beginnings, explaining for us how a reality came into existence, establishing the world. To know myth is to know the secret origin of things. Myths awaken and maintain consciousness of another world, another possible reality, a world accessed through ritual and dialog (Eliade 1998[1963]).

Delight

The great Indologist Heinrich Zimmer describes story telling (which encompasses myth) as "both serious and light hearted," likening stories to seeds "blown across the generations" (Zimmer 1971[1948]: 1). Most of our literary heritage comes to us in this way, from "remote epochs and different corners of the world" (p. 1). This great scholar describes himself as a dilettante, which, in its less encumbered meaning, is one who takes delight in something. He recommends a dilettante approach to the images of myth and folklore

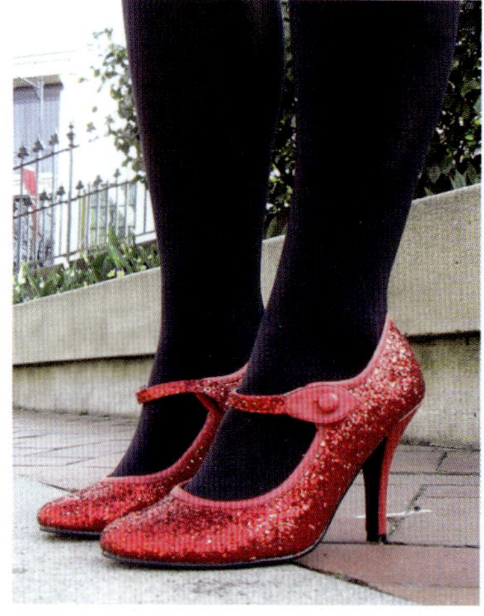

Figure 2
"They are like Dorothy, I had to have them." Photograph by E. Webster.

and avoidance of the concrete and the systematic, because at the moment we begin to feel certain of our interpretation "we deprive ourselves of the quickening contact, the demonic and inspiring assault that is their intrinsic virtue" (Zimmer 1971[1948]: 2).

The symbols and images of myths have a miraculous property: they are inexhaustible. "With every draft taken by our imaginative understanding, a universe of meaning is disclosed" (Zimmer 1971[1948]: 6). There is fullness yet fullness remains. For Zimmer, the images of myth and story are alive and potent, ever renewing, unpredictable yet self-consistent. To study them requires an open-ended dialog, allowing them to provoke a creative reaction involving an encounter with our imaginative understanding. Delight is the best way. " ... [A] cupped handful of fresh waters of life is sweeter than a reservoir of dogma" (Zimmer 1971[1948]: 5). With delight and re-enchantment in mind then, I invite you to explore the following interpretations with me.

Red Shoes

The tale of the red shoes was written by Hans Christian Andersen in 1845 (Wullschlager 2004). The son of a cobbler and a seamstress, it is not surprising that so many of Andersen's stories involve shoes. Although his writing was always influenced by a childhood steeped in folk tales, "The Red Shoes," like many of his earlier stories, contains mythic elements yet is not a myth (Wullschlager 2004).

In this story, a beautiful child, Karen, is left orphaned by the death of her mother. On the day of the funeral the old shoemaker gives her red shoes made of scraps sewn together. While not really appropriate for mourning, these shoes save her from going barefoot. When on that same day a rich old woman notices Karen and kindly offers to take her in, thereby rescuing her from destitution, Karen attributes this act to her red shoes. Soon afterwards the queen travels through the land and brings her little daughter along for all to see, and what is the princess wearing? Red shoes, of course! Then the time comes for Karen to be confirmed in the Church, and she must have new clothes and shoes. Since the old woman is almost blind, she doesn't know that Karen has chosen for herself red shoes just like the princess's. Everybody in the Church looks at her with disapproval while all she can think about is her red shoes. And so it goes on. Again and again she chooses red shoes, against the wishes and approval of everyone, and eventually she wears them to the dance instead of staying home to care for the old woman. Once Karen starts dancing she cannot stop. "Dance she did, and dance she must, right out into the dark forest" (Andersen 2004[1845]: 209).

Exhausted, she eventually begs the executioner to chop off her feet, which he does. She is crippled, but still the red shoes dance on: they have a life of their own. Suffering, repenting, chastened, she struggles for acceptance back into the Church, the community, and dies forgiven, having come to know the depth of her sin.

Red Ballet Shoes

Rank, Powell, and Pressburger's 1948 feature film *The Red Shoes* continues the theme of punishment for choosing dance over duty, but first seduces us with a sumptuous ballet and a dream lifestyle. The ballet at the core of the movie has a plot loosely based on Andersen's story, outlined by the impresario as: "The story of a girl devoured by her need to dance in a pair of red shoes, shoes that never tire but dance her through fields and forests, through day and night ... and in the end she dies" (Rank *et al.* 1999[1948]). The film repeats this theme in depicting the ambitions of the talented young ballerina played by Moira Shearer. Torn between love and ambition, she is forced to choose between the composer who loves her and the owner of the ballet company who has made her a star. She marries and leaves the company, but finds she cannot accept a satellite role of wife, and so returns to the dance (how could she not?). But this is a fatal choice, and her red shoes dance her first off a cliff and then under a train. Her husband tenderly removes the red shoes then she dies in his arms. What do we learn from this brutal tale? Red shoes seem so tempting yet so dangerous—why do we still want them?

"I Have a Feeling We're Not in Kansas Anymore"

Perhaps more famous still are the red shoes worn in the classic feature film *The Wizard of Oz* released in 1939 and based on the book by L. Frank Baum. Dorothy is transported by tornado from a dreary and distressing Kansas to the colorful Land of Oz. After accidentally killing the Wicked Witch of the East, Dorothy gets to wear her fabulous ruby slippers, gleaming their sequined wattage straight into our hearts. Transformed from powerless and threatened she is suddenly famous and heroic, and sets out along the yellow brick road with her little dog Toto and three friends she meets along the way. In no time she begins a little skipping dance, and it carries her along. After all, ruby slippers are red shoes, and red shoes must dance.

The ruby slippers are (naturally) coveted by the Wicked Witch of the West, not because they look fantastic, but for their great power. Plotting to take the shoes, the witch finds she cannot remove them but must kill Dorothy first: they have become so integral to Dorothy they cannot be taken off. Dorothy then saves her shoes, herself, and her companions by killing the witch (in yet another accident). After missing her ride by hot air balloon back to Kansas, she finds out she has had the power on her feet all along. Clicking her heels together she recites "There's no place like home" over and over until there she is, waking up in dreary old Kansas again.

Dislocations

Those ruby slippers were really something: beautiful, powerful, transporting, wish-fulfilling. Even Barbie has a pair (Figures 3 and 4). The pair worn in the film by Judy Garland sold at auction in 2000 for US$450,000 (Blanchard 2000). But Dorothy's shoes nearly were not red at all: in the book the slippers were silver (Scarfone and Stillman 2004). Noel Langley, one of the scriptwriters, is credited with introducing the idea of the "ruby shoes," creating one of the most

enduring symbols in this (or any) film (Rushdie 1992).[2] By making these shoes red an existing symbol was accessed and amplified, breaking through into the rich world of myth, and taking us with them. Dorothy's ruby slippers were stars in their own right, constellating all that we love about red shoes.

So it is interesting to consider in this movie, as in the previous stories, the problem of the ending which runs counter to imaginative truth. Do we really want those red shoes to take us home again? As Rushdie asks: why would anybody want to go back to Kansas? And why would a brilliant dancer want to give up the dance to be a stay-at-home wife? And would Karen or any young and beautiful girl, already made conscious of her potential social mobility, choose a life of domestic work and piety over dancing? Rushdie points out, and I agree with him, that *The Wizard of Oz* is more about the archetype of *escape*, the human dream of *leaving* (Rushdie 1992). This makes the red shoes more about going over the rainbow than back to Kansas. Red shoes are about finding your feet and going somewhere else.

Symbolic Shoes and Redness

Shoes are so personal, they carry us, we stand in them, we go places in them, and find our feet in them. Walking in someone else's shoes is to know what they know. Shoes symbolize being in and with your self. Perhaps this is another interpretation of "no place like home."

But it is their redness that really gives these shoes their potency,

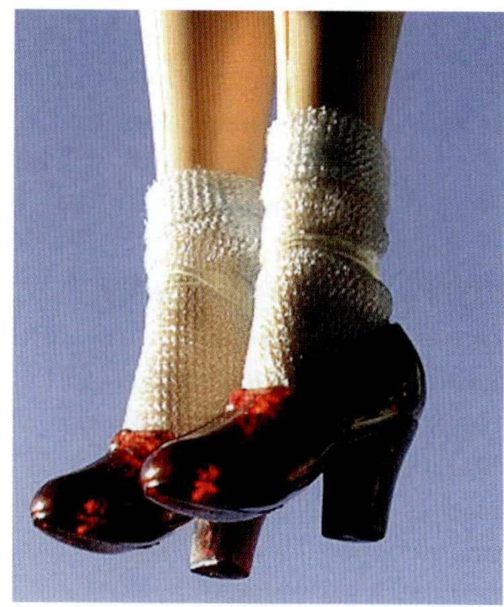

Figure 3
Barbie wearing her ruby red slippers; the shoes light up when you press down on them! Photograph by E. Webster.

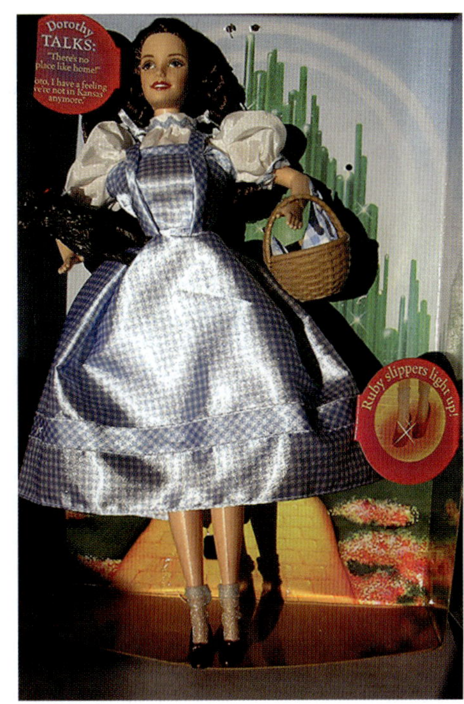

Figure 4
Barbie as Dorothy. Photograph by
E. Webster.

their transforming potential, their enduring symbolic power. Red suggests opulence[3] but more importantly the color red is dynamic, vibrant, and dangerous, so stands against the safety of propriety and convention. Perhaps this is why so many people also associate red shoes with "loose women" who also live outside conventional society. In this context redness symbolizes choice, the dynamic of agency running counter to the social group. In this light, the tragic endings in the story and the film of the Red Shoes seem an expression of outraged morality, the group triumphing over the desires of the individual dreaming of escape. Selfhood is presented as sin, so fails to convince us, although we may heed the warning that in a patriarchy, the agency of women is transgression. We already know that to be oneself is to be in some ways outside the group, that there is a cost. Yet the truth about red shoes is that as soon as they are on, we are dancing in the mythic, we are over the rainbow already. The desire that gives birth to the action embodies the myth: it is ritual, breaking through into sacred time.

The Glass Slipper

The more famous story of shoes is Cinderella, one of the oldest fairy stories (Bettelheim 1989). It is useful here as a comparison. There are hundreds of versions of this story which all contain two essential elements: the ill-treated heroine and her slipper.[4] An early story written down in China in the ninth century revolves around a tiny foot of unusual beauty and distinction, and a shoe of precious materials (Bettelheim 1989). An even older version from Egypt is told by Strabo, and involves the search for the wearer of an extraordinarily delicate sandal that had been carried away by an eagle then dropped at the feet of the pharaoh. The story that we know today is derived from Charles Perrault's seventeenth-century version, differing in some important respects from *Aschenputtel*, the version collected and retold by the Brothers Grimm (Bettelheim 1989; Crick 2005; Grimm and Grimm 2005; Opie and Opie 1974). Drawing on existing material and refining it for the French court, Perrault discarded many of the symbolic elements in the older stories, and introduced some new ones. Most important of these was his substitution of gold shoes with the slippers made of glass. This innovation serves to emphasize luxury, purity, and a transparently unique fit (Bettelheim 1989).

Perrault's Cinderella is young and beautiful but mistreated by her stepmother and ugly stepsisters. Dressed in rags and tatters, she does all the work and sleeps among the ashes. When everyone else goes to the ball, her fairy Godmother helps her to go too, by magically transforming pumpkins, rats, and mice into coach and coachmen, and her rags into a golden dress and glass slippers, "the loveliest slippers ever seen" (Perrault 1999[1697]: 9). Unrecognized by anyone, including her stepsisters, she dances all night with the prince, but must leave before midnight when the spell wears off. Just before midnight she departs, leaving the prince in love but in the dark. The next night it is the same again, but this time she loses one glass slipper as she hurries away. The prince seeks far and wide to find the mysterious and beautiful one who fits the slipper, finally coming to the home of Cinderella. Although the ugly stepsisters try very hard, they cannot fit the slipper, which fits only Cinderella. She must be The One, and so she marries the prince.

That the pair is broken up is an important feature of the story. One slipper is left behind to enchant and finally guide the Prince to his bride, and this one slipper must also find its corresponding other, contributing to the overarching theme of marriage and union, which is extended through the metaphor of fit. And what better than unflinching glass to resist all but the most precise of fits, and to do this "transparently?" (Bettelheim 1989). While glass shoes have the added luster of novelty, glass as the material for shoes also reminds us the story takes place in a world of enchantment and magic. Glass also has that telling property of reflection, which shines her perfection back at her like a mirror (Warner 1994).

Although the glass slippers carry Cinderella into marriage, union, and triumph over her envious sisters, Perrault makes her almost too sweet and obedient (Bettelheim 1989; Ulanov and Ulanov 1998). Glass slippers make her an object, emphasizing her dependence and passivity,[5] while her status as outright winner in the envy drama leaves us uncomfortable about her prospects for happiness, since she does not seem to have either the strength or awareness to fully enjoy it. Perhaps she is too preoccupied with her own reflection, the image of herself in her own mind.

The meanings of these shoe stories are quite distinct: the red shoes are everything that Cinderella is not. Dangerous, disobedient, and willful, the red shoes dance their wearers into another reality. This shows us that the vitality of red shoes cannot be explained simply through their connection to childhood stories, since glass slippers, for all their magic, fail in this way. Their meanings count. Red shoes carry and perpetuate an important archetype, conveyed through the red shoe stories and resonating well beyond their context, their literary and textual existences, far beyond the intentions of their writers, collectors, moviemakers, and fashion appropriators.

Linking Myth and Fashion

Fashion is a complex system, a social phenomenon, an effusion of images. Participation in fashion involves desire, envy, sin, and transformation: the desire that reaches out, the envy that stimulates emulation, competition, display, and consumption. Fashion shamelessly disregards (like most modernity) the other sins of pride and vanity (Ribeiro 2003[1986]; Steele 1985). Fashion transforms us into knowing participants in a social system, assists membership of multiple groups and statuses, and locates us in time (Blumer 1969; Davis 1992; Kaiser 2001; Stone 1962). Fashion is a mechanism of power, an art of consumption, a multi-billion dollar global industry (Entwistle 2000; Kaiser 2001; Martin 1997). Fashion is both monster and facilitator: as an archetype, fashion is probably the devil.

Fashion's children are uniformly well-dressed, in a sense making everyone the same, but style is fashion made personal (McDowell 1989). Style is part of who I am and who I could be (Kaiser 2001). Style is part of dress, which is always an embodied, situated practice (Entwistle 2000). In making selections individuals are interacting and interpreting from within these contexts as a self, while also participating in the world of material culture. As new dress objects are encountered, new meanings must be generated for them and these meanings are symbolic (Kaiser *et al.* 1995; Mead 1967[1934]). Style, fashion, and dress involve symbolic expression (McCracken 1988), and through this symbolic communication fashion is linked to myth, and to culture. Symbols suggest and offer meaning: meaning is not inherent

in objects, although the capacity for meaning is. Meaning is a property *we* give to things through a social process of interaction, through interpretation, and sometimes transformation, but also by drawing on symbols whose meaning is already suggested (Kaiser 2001; Mead 1967[1934]; Wilson 1985). Symbols accrue meaning for each of us over time, activated through what we do, through a process of interpretation, enactment, and ritual. The symbols of shoes, of redness, combine and resonate with remembered tales from childhood, fed by alluring fashion images, nourished by our own articulations of a desire to leave, to have more life, more color. Red shoes are about style and style is a vehicle for becoming (Kaiser 2001).

In Practice, and in Conclusion

Perhaps understanding this, the principal of a girls' high school in Southland, New Zealand, introduced red shoes into the school uniform during the 1940s, enlivening an already rather stylish uniform (Figures 5 and 6). Although all other aspects of their uniform have since changed, red shoes remain the distinctive feature of the uniform and the school, as has that principal's vision of success for these girls (Figure 7). Artists such as Megan Jenkinson (1997), Sharon Peoples (Figure 8), and Lynda Cullen have used red shoes to symbolize transformation, mobility, or a selfhood which may be dangerous or precarious but is nonetheless worth striving for, and their red shoes are always for women. Many women when interpreting red shoes to me, spoke of desire,

change, risk, and movement, always in terms of enlarging the self or becoming more one's own self. For these women red shoes embody journeying, knowing the self, and agency. Others told me that they chose red shoes because they "wanted a bit of colour." What is this if not a metaphor for an enriched life?

Red shoes offer a vivid ritual, a symbolically rich participation in the desire for more life, a bigger life than the one we currently have, a life somewhere or somehow different. The appeal of red shoes lies in their mobility, their embodiment of choice, the *act of being* and becoming one's self. In contrast, Cinderella's glass shoes offer objectification, impossible desires, and immobility. They seem the ultimate in high-status display, with the added allure of being mysterious, iconic, and novel, seeming to exemplify fashion at its best. Yet fashion *is* a fiction. It is a tale of envy, passivity, and objectification. Fashion as myth is empty; glass shoes have inspired few contemporary manifestations, few ritual enactments. Silver or gold shoes, their closest imitators, enter daywear fashion every few years but fade quickly, striking a note but not a chord. Fashion can only try to access myth, to create symbolic meanings and to convince us of its vitality.

Fashion however, does provide us with agency's wardrobe. Red shoes are almost continually available. Through red shoes and their links to mythic time we access the source of vitality, and it is through the ritual of wear that their symbolic value is activated. It is our participation in myth rather

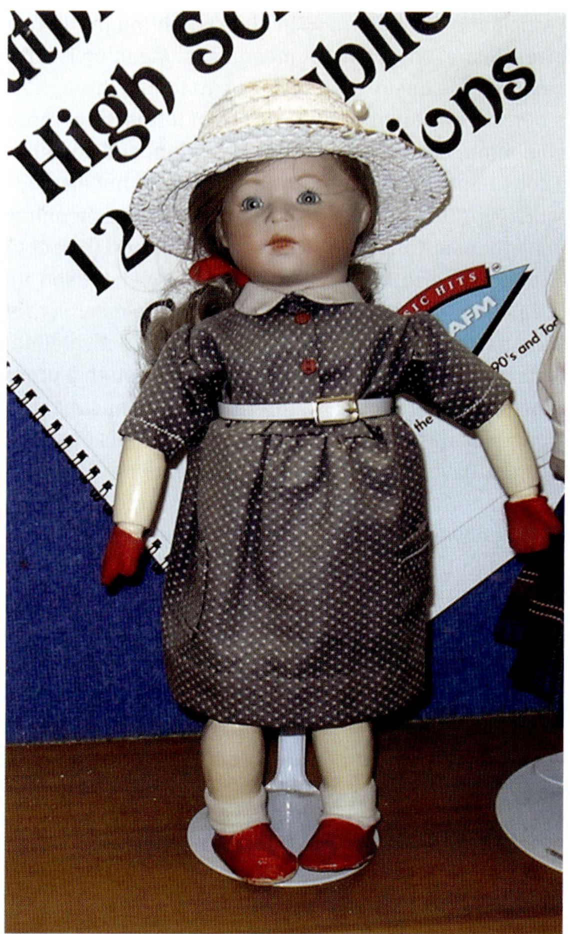

Figure 5

Red shoes were first introduced during the 1940s to enliven this school's summer uniform of dark blue and white spots, and have continued as the most distinctive feature of the uniform. This doll is dressed in the uniform as part of a centennial display, although the dark blue cotton has faded to gray. Photograph by E. Webster.

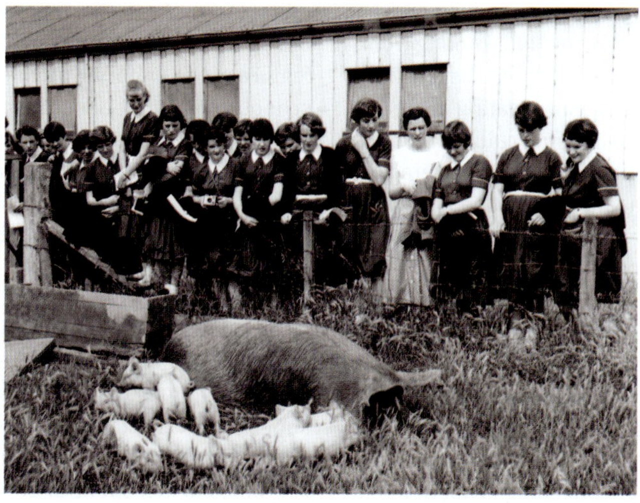

Figure 6

Girls wearing the uniform on a class trip, 1962 Photograph from the collection of Southland Girls High School.

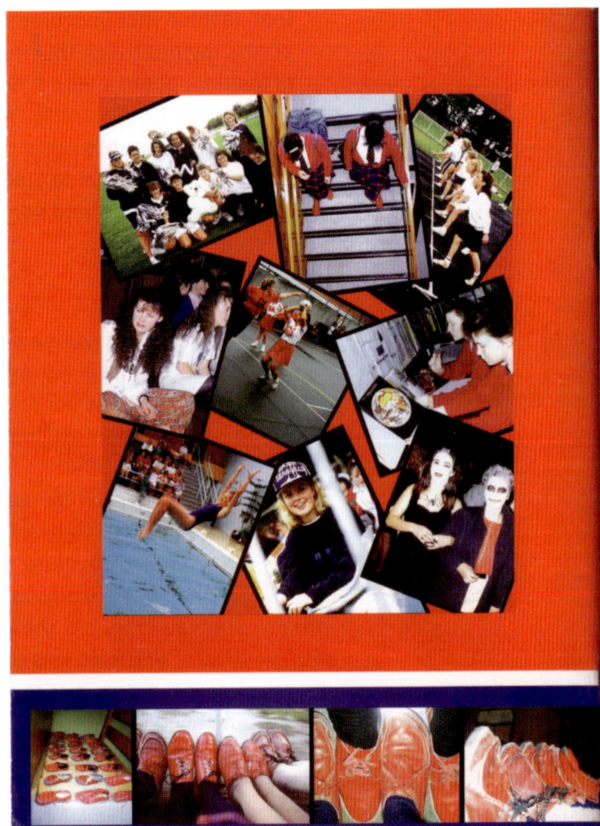

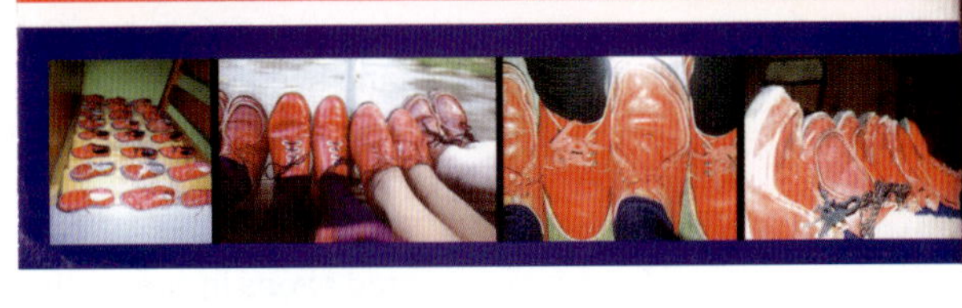

Figure 7
Back cover of the 1991 Southland Girls High School Magazine (Invercargill, New Zealand). Red shoes continue to operate as the defining motif for this school. Reproduced with permission from the school.

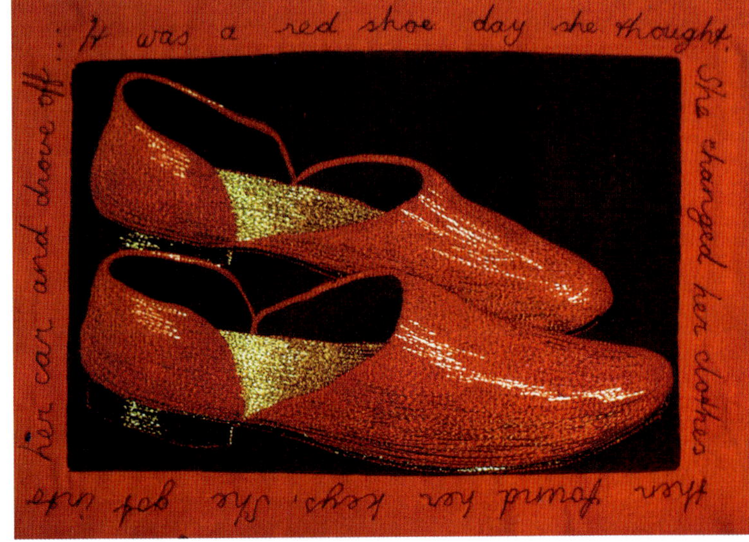

Figure 8
"Red shoes." Embroidery by Sharon Peoples, reproduced with permission from the artist.

than fashion that invigorates us. We access myth through the ritual, not of fashion, but of style.

Acknowledgments

Special thanks to Lynda Cullen for her art, her insight, and some key references.

Notes

1. For Freud, civilization itself is a pathological surrogate for unconscious infantile disappointments (Campbell 1972: 12).

2. I do not believe that red was chosen only to contrast with the Technicolor yellow road, as claimed by Scarfone and Stillman (2004) in *The Wizardry of Oz*. The choice was probably also influenced by the dynamic and symbolic properties of red, and directly or indirectly, by Andersen's story.

3. There are many stories of red shoes in connection with monarchy and aristocracy. Shoes with red heels were favored by Louis XIV and his courtiers in the seventeenth century, explaining some associations with opulence and high status (Blanchard 2000; McDowell 1989). The history of red as a textile colorant underpins this association, since prior to the development of cheap chemical dyes in the 1870s, good strong red was an expensive color (Butler Greenfield 2005; Chenciner 2000).

4. Marina Warner links Cinderella with the myth of Cupid and Psyche, which although it lacks the shoe motif has the characteristic themes of deprivation and sibling envy (Warner 1994)

5. In the Grimms' version she must *work* for transformation. Her slippers are not glass but golden, indicating value. When the prince recognizes her in her tatters, he values her beyond her appearance. By fitting the shoe onto her own foot she demonstrates the felicity of being true to oneself, thus providing a more satisfying ending (Bettelheim 1989).

References

Andersen, H. C. 2004[1845]. "The Red Shoes." In *Hans Christian Andersen: Fairy Tales*. Trans. T. Nunnally. Ed. J. Wullschlager. London: Penguin.

Barthes, R. 1973. *Mythologies*. Trans. Annette Lavers. New York: Hill and Wang.

Bettelheim, B. 1989. *The Uses of Enchantment: The Meaning and Importance of Fairy Tales*. New York: Vintage Books.

Blanchard, T. 2000. *The Shoe: Best Foot Forward*. London: Carlton Books.

Blumer, H. 1969. "Fashion: From Class Differentiation to Collective Selection." *Sociological Quarterly* 10: 275–91.

Butler Greenfield, A. 2005. *A Perfect Red*. New York: Harper Collins.

Campbell, J. 1972. *Myths to Live by*. New York: Bantam Books and Penguin.

Chenciner, R. 2000. *Madder Red: A History of Luxury and Trade*. Richmond: Curzon Press.

Crick, J. 2005. "Introduction." In *Jacob and Wilhelm Grimm: Selected

Tales, pp. i–lix. Trans. J Crick. Oxford: Oxford University Press.

Davidson, H. 2006. "Sex and Sin: The Magic of Red Shoes." In G. Riello and P. McNeil (eds) *Shoes: A History from Sandals to Sneakers*, pp. 272–88. Oxford: Berg.

Davis, F. 1992. *Fashion, Culture and Identity*. Chicago, IL: University of Chicago Press.

Eliade, M. 1998[1963]. *Myth and Reality*. Trans. W. R. Trask. Long Grove, IL: Waveland Press.

Eliade, M. 1991[1952]. *Images and Symbols: Studies in Religious Symbolism*. Princeton, NJ: Princeton University Press.

Entwistle, J. 2000 "Fashion and the Fleshy Body: Dress as Embodied Practice." *Fashion Theory* 4(3): 323–48.

Giddens, A. 1971. *Capitalism and Modern Social Theory: An Analysis of the Writings of Marx, Durkheim, and Max Weber.*Canbridge: Cambridge University Press.

Grimm, J. and Grimm, W. 2005. "Ashypet." In *Jacob and Wilhelm Grimm: Selected Tales*. pp. 78–84. Trans. J Crick. Oxford: Oxford University Press.

Jenkinson, M. 1997. *Under the Aegis: The Virtues*. Auckland: Fortuna Press.

Jung, C. G. 1990. *The Archetypes and the Collective Unconscious*, 2nd edn. Trans. R. F. C. Hull. Princeton, NJ: Princeton University Press.

Kaiser, S. B., Nagasawa, R. H. and Hutton, S. S. 1995. "Construction of an SI Theory of Fashion Part 1. Ambivalence and Change." *Clothing and Textile Research Journal* 14(2): 162–83.

Kaiser, S. 2001. "Minding Appearances: Style, Truth, and Subjectivity." In J. Entwistle and E. Wilson (eds) *Body Dressing*, pp. 79–102. Oxford: Berg.

Martin, R. 1997. "A Charismatic Art: The Balance of Ingratiation and Outrage in Contemporary Fashion." *Fashion Theory* 1(1): 91–104.

Mead, G. H. 1967[1934]. *Mind, Self, and Society: From the Standpoint of a Social Behaviorist*. Ed. C. Morris. Chicago, IL: University of Chicago Press.

McCracken, G. 1988. *Culture and Consumption*. Bloomingdale, IN: Indiana University Press.

McDowell, C. 1989. *Shoes: Fashion and Fantasy*. London: Thames & Hudson.

Ribeiro, A. 2003[1986]. *Dress and Morality*. Oxford: Berg.

Opie, I. and Opie, P. 1974. *The Classic Fairy Tales*. Oxford: Oxford University Press.

Perrault, C. 1999[1697]. *Cinderella*. Trans. A. Bell. New York: North-South Books.

Polyani, M and Prosch, H. 1975. *Meaning*. Chicago, IL: University of Chicago Press.

Rushdie, S. 1992. *The Wizard of Oz*. London: British Film Institute.

Scarfone, J. and Stillman, W. 2004. *The Wizardry of Oz: The Artistry and Magic of the 1939 M-G-M Classic*. New York: Applause Theatre and Cinema Books.

Stone, G. P. 1962. "Appearance and the Self." In M. E. Roach and J. Eicher (eds) *Dress and Adornment and the Social Order*, pp. 216–45. New York: John Wiley and Sons.

Steele, V. 1985. *Fashion and Eroticism: Ideals of Beauty from the Victorian Era to the Jazz Age*. New York: Oxford University Press.

Ulanov, A. and Ulanov, B. 1998. *Cinderella and Her Sisters: The Envied and the Envying*. Einsiedeln: Daimon Verlag.

Warner, M. 1994. *From the Best to the Blonde: On Fairy Tales and Their Tellers*. London: Chatto and Windus.

Wilson, E. 1985. *Adorned in Dreams: Fashion and Modernity*. London: Virago.

Wullschlager, J. 2004. "Introduction." In J. Wullschlager (ed.) *Hans Christian Andersen: Fairy Tales*, pp. i–xlvi. Trans. T. Nunnally. London: Penguin.

Zimmer, H. 1971[1948]. *The King and the Corpse*, 2nd edn. Ed. J. Campbell. Princeton, NJ: Princeton University Press.

Zipes, J. 1983. *Fairy Tales and the Art of Subversion: The Classical Genre for Children and the Process of Civilization*. London: Heinmann.

Filmography

Rank, J. A., Powell, M. and Pressburger, E. 1999[1948]. *The Red Shoes* (DVD). UK: Criterion Collection.

Rank, J. A., Powell, M. and Pressburger, E. 1999[1948]. *The Red Shoes* (DVD). UK: Criterion Collection.

Iconic Images and Jade Textile Tools for Neolithic and Bronze Age China's Silk Industry

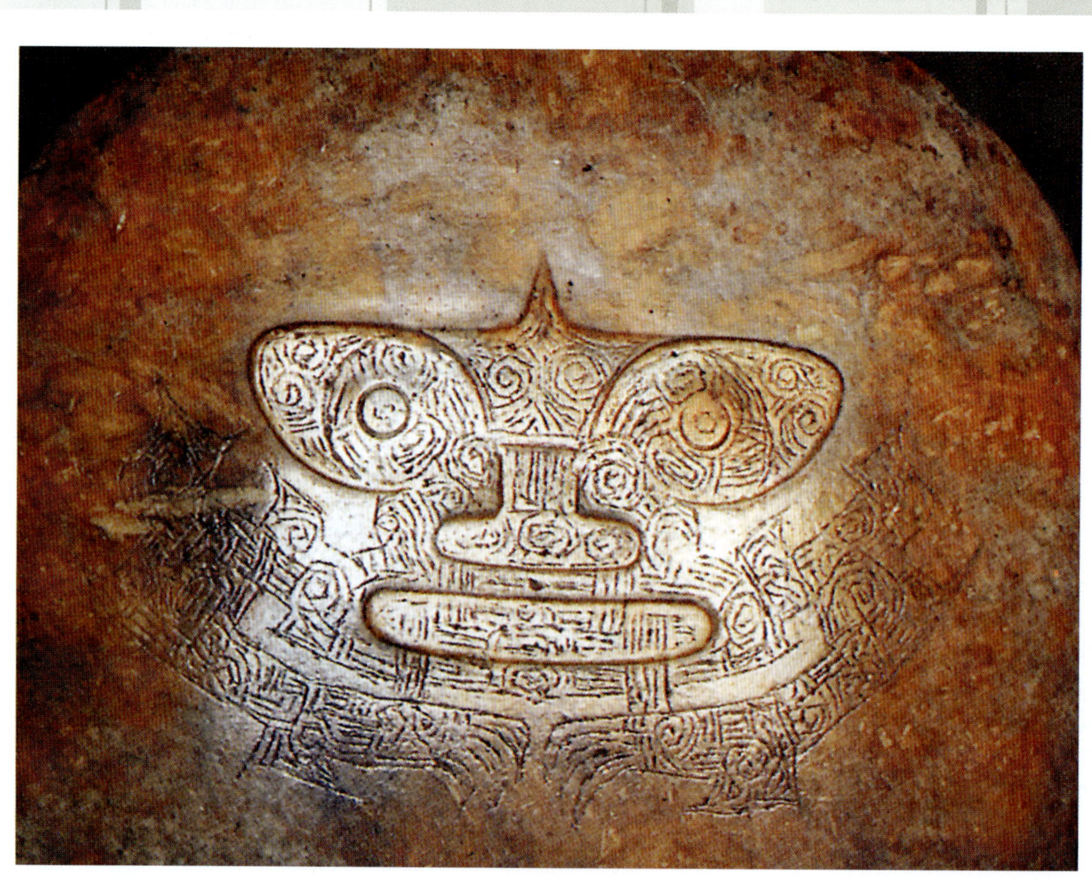

Abstract

China's Neolithic cultures were the originators of silk thread production. I propose that this development is represented by a ubiquitous iconic image, the silkworm–silk moth life cycle motif, commonly called a *taotie* or "monster mask." Silkworms are also portrayed in small Neolithic jade carvings. Subsequent Shang bronzes show that the "life cycle motif" had evolved. Increasingly abstract, decorative patterns, derived from intricate silk textiles, were often combined in this period with new images depicting silkworm egg and larvae motifs. These images are indicative of advances in sericulture and silk textile production. By the end of the Shang, China's textile industry had a new iconic image: the Chinese Dragon, a chimera that I propose is a composite of the silkworm, silk moth, coiled Hongshan forms, and Shang tiger images. The silk textile industry was of such great importance, I contend that tools from its operations have survived in many jade artifacts. Because their original purpose has not been recognized, they are usually described as pieces of adornment or "ceremonial" objects. Many of the jades seem likely to have been tools that assisted in the chores of spinning, reeling, and twining thread for silk fabrics.

Keywords: life cycle, dragon origins, mechanical technology, textile tools

MARY BELLE L. O'BRIEN

Mary Belle L. O'Brien has a BA (Biology major), from Manhattanville College, New York, and an MA in History of Art, Columbia University, New York. Additional study, creative arts, San Francisco Art Institute, College of the Arts, Oakland. A practicing artist (watercolor, oil pastel, stained glass design), O'Brien is also an independent scholar.

Textile, Volume 7, Issue 2, pp. 178–203
DOI: 10.2752/175183509X460083
Reprints available directly from the Publishers.
Photocopying permitted by licence only.
© 2009 Berg. Printed in the United Kingdom.

Iconic Images and Jade Textile Tools for Neolithic and Bronze Age China's Silk Industry

Part One: Iconic Images
Introduction

The textile and basketry designs decorating Chinese Neolithic artifacts (5000–1700 BC) show a complexity that indicates textile arts had taken firm root during the Paleolithic era. The earliest evidence for weaving practice is from a site dated 27,000 BC in what is now the Czech Republic (Soffer and Adavasio 1995: 276). The astonishing cave paintings at Chauvet, France, were created about the same time. Seven thousand years later, concurrent with bast fibers found at sites of this period, more visual evidence for weaving came in the form of the Paleolithic figurines called "goddesses or Venuses" which have string skirts with woven waist bands incised on their bodies (Barber 1991: 15–19).[1]

The first evidence of spinning and weaving in China is seen in artifacts of the Hemudu culture (5000 BC) discovered near present day Shanghai. Some artifacts appear to be textile working tools (Wu Hung 1985: 21, Fig. 3). Pottery incised with geometric designs may reflect Hemudu textile patterns (Ebrey 1999: 16–17).

Two Yangshao pottery bowls from Banpo (3500–2500 BC) depict a nearly identical image that I interpret as an anthropomorphized spider. The body shape is similar to some arachnids and the figures have eight appendages. On the wall opposing the spider motif, each bowl has a different image: One appears to represent what might be a square ground-loom (Nelson Gallery–Atkins Museum Catalog 1975: 29); the other image (Chung 2005: 73, Fig. 18) that some see as a fish, I would interpret as a primitive rendering of a back-strap loom.[2] The message seems to be "spiders weave; people weave too; this is how our people weave." The interest of this Neolithic culture in spiders as spinners and weavers would surely have been extended to silkworms spinning cocoons.

Ancient images point to a thriving and widely dispersed tradition of textile arts in Neolithic China. The Liangzhu jade artifact (3300–2250 BC) from Yao Shan seen in Figure 2 (below) has images incised in the upper left and right corners that may represent rolled, woven fabric tapes. These rolls have the appearance of fabric bands woven on a back-strap loom. A petroglyph in the Amur River Valley shows a female figure with what appears to be a forked distaff above her head (Okladnikov 1981: Pl. 9).

The Silkworm–Moth Life Cycle: Neolithic Icon for Silk Thread and Textile Production

A single cut cocoon preserved in a Yangshao excavation is the earliest direct evidence for awareness of the silkworm (Barber 1991: 31). Larvae are a traditional source of food in many cultures, which may account for its presence. Ancient textile experts had agreed that no Neolithic artifacts could be cited that depicted silkworms or that showed an "awareness" of the silkworm's importance as a source of silk thread. A Hemudu bowl with images said to portray silkworms, however, has been cited by several historians recently (Vainker 2004: 22).

I propose in fact that a profusion of Neolithic artifacts exist depicting images of the silkworm–silk moth life cycle; that these images of metamorphosis became the icon of Chinese Neolithic cultures and the symbol for their discovery of silk and the creation of silk textiles. Recognition of the silkworm life cycle motif and its iconic status in Chinese Neolithic cultures has remained blocked because images or artifacts tend to be perceived in terms set by their traditional description.

A substantial body of literature classifies and names artifacts on the basis of Zhou and Han Dynasty texts which many historians now realize cannot be relied on to interpret the purpose of Neolithic and Bronze Age artifacts, but those names and classifications are still applied to objects being discussed and studied. Images inevitably described as "animal" or "monster" masks or a *taotie* as seen below in

Figures 2a, b, and 5a may not be properly named. Craig Clunas says descriptions in later Zhou texts call the *taotie* a greedy monster that devours everything (Clunas 1997: 21). The texts postdate the Neolithic *taotie* images by almost 2,000 years. I propose that the Zhou definition does give a clue to their original meaning, which relates to the identity I suggest for the *taotie*.

While studying the image of a Liangzhu jade plaque in the Freer Gallery to interpret it for a painting, I realized the incised image was the representation of a moth that had emerged from its cocoon, rising above its cocoon and larval stage. The forms of the three stages are connected by vertical parallel lines, an ancient convention used by artists to indicate motion or unfolding of connected serial events. A fine linear design, resembling a fabric pattern, is incised over the entire motif and brackets the central form with what appears to be an arrangement of silkworms heraldically opposed. Comparing the Freer moth icon to the wild oak silk moth supports this interpretation (Figures 1a and b). The "*taotie* as greedy monster" also fits with the fact silkworms are voracious feeders prior to spinning the cocoon from which the silk moth will emerge. Cultivated moths do not have the eyespots found on

wild moth's wings which evolved to deceive predators. The eyespots have also deceived historians, who interpreted the eyespots, cocoon, and larval shape as eyes, nose, and mouth, perceiving the motif to be an animal mask.

It appears to me the Neolithic creators of this motif deliberately exaggerated the eyespots, and often anthropomorphized it, adding a stereotyped human face to the icon to personify what may be a silk deity (Figures 2a and b). The icon is repeated in many recognizable versions, too numerous to cite, on Neolithic artifacts: *cong*, plaques, rings, and blade-like artifacts. A few examples are cited here (d'Argence 1983: Pl. VI, 72, Fig. 8; James 1991: 102–10, Figs 2–24; Lawton and, Merrill 1993: 205, Fig. 140).

My identification of the coupled silkworm–silk moth motif occurred prior to Chung's reference to some historians who suggested silkworms and moths are "modeled" [represented] on many artifacts from Chinese sites and who speculated those images are symbols of death and rebirth (Chung 2005: 76). This supports my original identification.

When comparison is made between a small, three-dimensional Hongshan sculpted jade amulet in the Shanghai Museum (Figure 3a) and Isao Kishida's photograph

Figure 1

(a) Life cycle motif (Lawton and Merrill 1993: 205, Fig. 139). Courtesy of the Freer Gallery of Art, Smithsonian Institution, Washington, DC. Gift of Charles Lang Freer, F1916.511. (b) Oak silk moth (Johnson and Kishida 1982: 28). Courtesy of photographer Isao Kishida, Hokuto City, Japan.

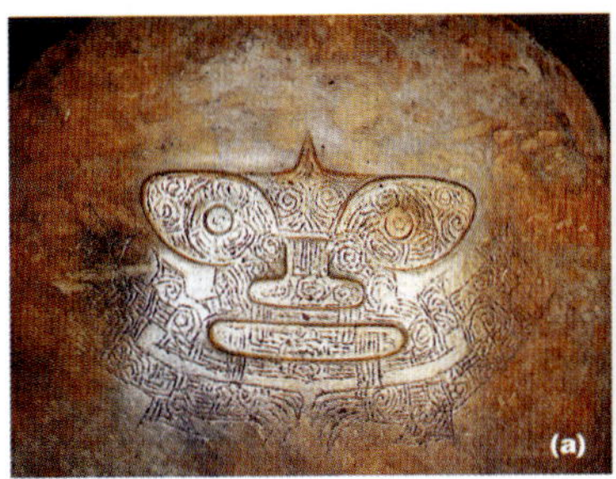
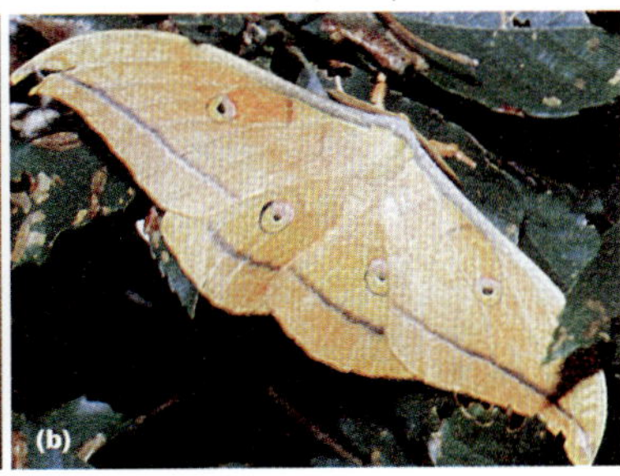

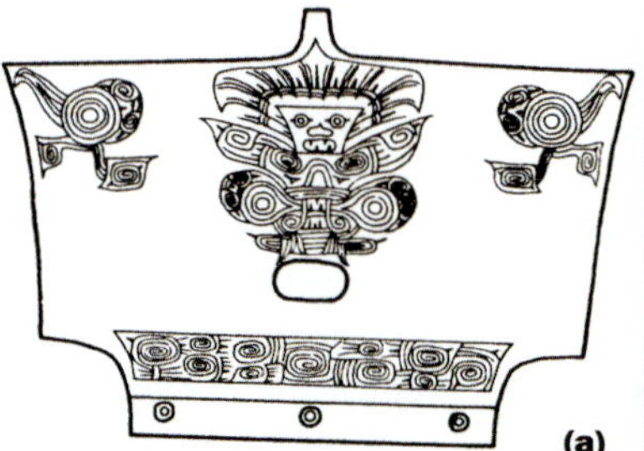
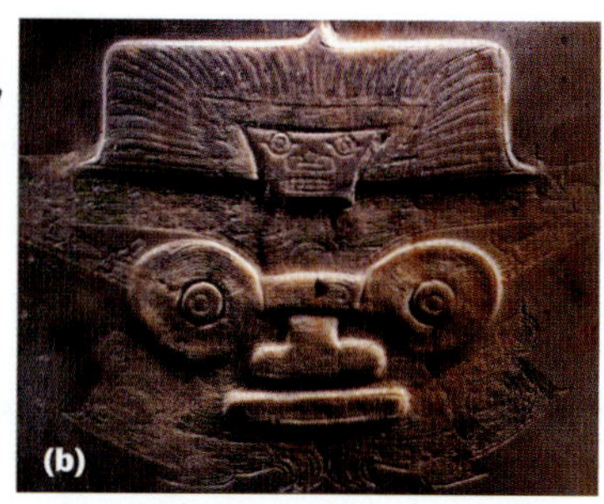

Figure 2
(a) Drawing: Anthropomorphized life cycle motif, or *"taotie"* (James 1991. 104, Fig. 9b). (b) Jade relief carving: Anthropomorphized life cycle, or *"taotie"* (James 1991: 104, Fig. 10a). Both courtesy of *Orientations.*

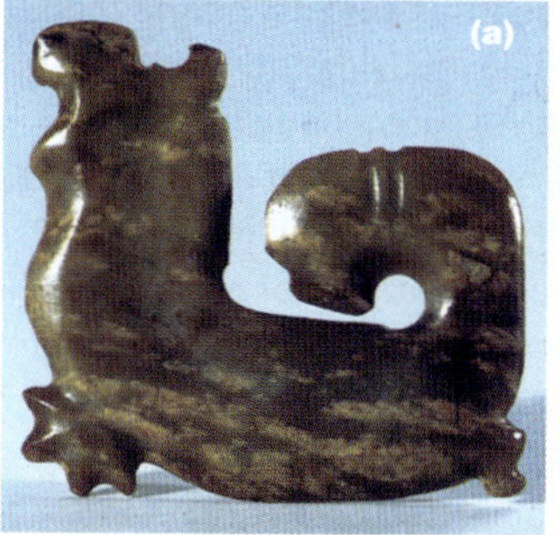
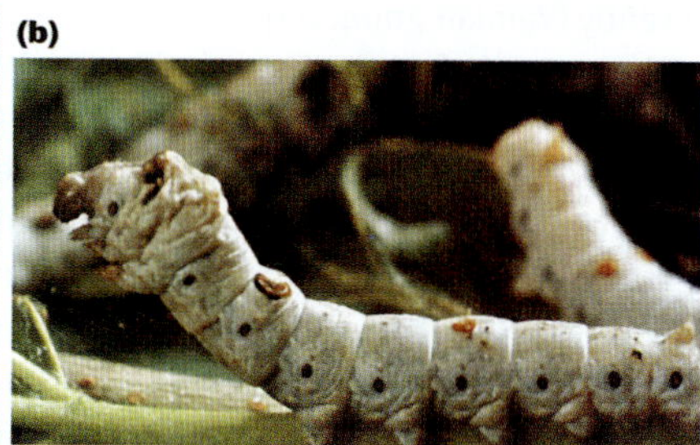

Figure 3
(a) Hongshan jade, silkworm amulet, or "bird," Shanghai Museum (Shanghai Museum: Ancient Chinese Jade Gallery n.d.: 3, left-center). Courtesy of the Shanghai Museum. (b) Photograph: silkworms (Johnson and Kishida 1982: 20). Courtesy of photographer Isao Kishida, Hokuto City, Japan.

of a silkworm (Figures 3b, 6a), it is hard to deny that the amulet shows characteristics of a larval silkworm. A jade amulet in the Paul Singer collection in New York (Childs-Johnson 1988: 52, Fig. 8), likewise, seems to resemble the wild mulberry silk moth (Johnson and Kishida 1982: 6). These jades are not literal representations but have identifying characteristics of their live counterparts.

Other uncommon, small three-dimensional Hongshan jades, usually identified as "cloud scrolls" (Salviati 1995: 164, Fig. 1; So 1993: 128, Fig. 10), appear to me to depict tangles of silkworms (Figure 4). The tangle motif was developed further in the Shang period.

Silkworm Imagery in China's Bronze Age: Shang and Zhou Periods
Shang artisans (1650–1050 BC) continued using the *taotie* icon (Ebrey 1999: 36), but manipulated its elements, developing more abstract designs filling the object's surface as in the Freer Gallery Hu (Figure 5a) and other examples (Shanghai Museum: Ancient Chinese Bronze Gallery 1995: 5, 8). Eventually, the motif lost its iconic status and became a decorative device. Shang artisans introduced decorative elements that reflected advances in sericulture. Intricate textile patterns, indicative of skillfully woven silk fabrics, became common decorative motifs on Shang bronzes (Geijer 1979[1972]: 110–11). Silkworm larvae and eggs became recurring decorative devices, exemplified by the Shang Ting (Figure 5b) and other artifacts (Shanghai Museum: Ancient Chinese Bronze Gallery 1995:19, 20, 21).

The "open jaws posture" for the silkworm began to appear as a common motif, which seems to portray its voracious feeding habits (Shanghai Museum: Ancient Chinese Bronze Gallery 1995: 15; Wen Fong 1980: 130, Fig. 43).

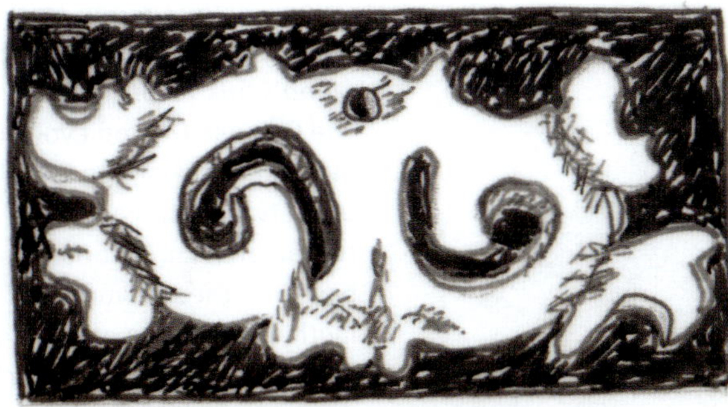

Figure 4
Drawing: Hongshan jade, silkworm tangle or "cloud scroll" (Fu Zhongmo Collection, People's Republic of China). Author's rendering.

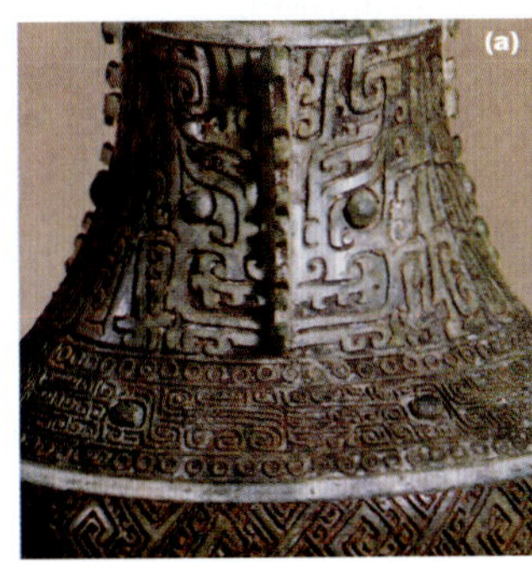
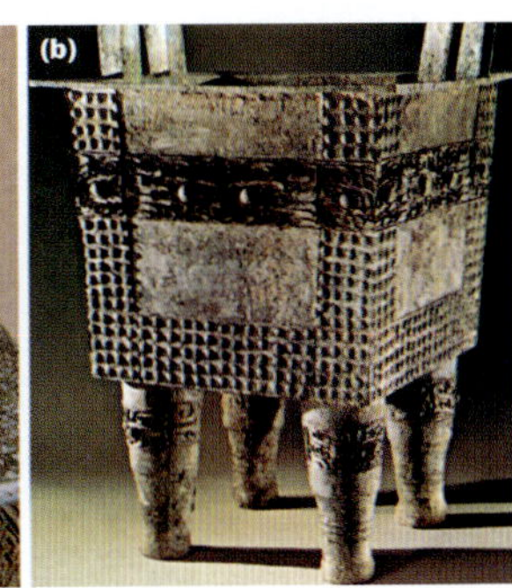

Figure 5
(a) Shang bronze Hu (detail) with silk textile motifs (Pope n.d.: Pl. 2). Courtesy of the Freer Gallery of Art, Smithsonian Institution, Washington, DC. Gift of Charles Lang Freer, F1916.511. (b) Shang Ting with silkworm egg motif (Wen Fong 1980: Pl. 11). Courtesy of Henan Museum, Zhengzhou, Henan Province.

The profusion of larvae, the jaws posture, and egg motifs indicates that domestic cultivation of silkworm larvae and eggs had begun, supplanting the earlier Neolithic practice that relied solely on gathering wild cocoons to obtain silk. It is likely that wild eggs were still gathered for indoor cultivation. Sericulture was highly developed by the end of the Shang Dynasty and was a fiercely guarded secret kept by Chinese cultures. In her correspondence with me, Eleanor Guralnick (personal communication, 2006) called my attention to the silk cocoons that have been excavated in a Bronze Age Aegean house at Akrotiri (*circa* 1630 BC) and at similarly dated sites in Israel. Women in the frescoes at Akrotiri and other Minoan sites on Crete are portrayed wearing very sheer garments that appear to be made of silk. Excavations, as of yet, show no evidence for widespread practices of sericulture.

Following the Shang Dynasty, sericulture attained higher levels of accomplishment in the Western and Eastern Zhou cultures (1050–425 BC). During this period, some artifacts are completely covered in bas-relief figures that appear to be little silkworms (Rawson 2002: 63, Pl. 46; Wen Fong, 1980: 258, Fig. 89), or are brocaded with egg dots (Rawson 2002: 62, Fig. 45, 252, 5:1, 253, 5:2, 254, 15:3).

Eleanor Guralnick (personal communication, 2006) also noted in her correspondence that she sees a relationship between the mass production of silk introduced by Chinese cultures and the mass production of food developed by Neolithic farmers in the Fertile Crescent. It seems that Chinese cultures were among the originators of mass production concepts.

These curlicue worm forms that appear to depict masses of silkworm larvae and eggs can actually be seen in sericulture practice (Dinkum 2004; Johnson and Kishida 1982: 13). Mass production of cocoons made mass production of silk thread and fabrics possible, generating wealth for the acquisition and commission of gold and jade objects. These luxury items were often based on the forms of much earlier Neolithic jades, which originally may have had a utilitarian purpose. Decorative motifs were also developed from the earlier artifacts. Rawson depicts examples (Rawson 2002: 63, Pl. 46, 64, Fig. 45).

Origins of the Dragon Traced in Shang Artifacts: New Symbol for China's Silk Textile Industry
The Chinese Dragon evolved piecemeal during the Shang Dynasty. The dragon's core characteristics, I propose, are based on the silkworm and silk moth, evident in a comparison of the silkworm and Chinese parade dragons of today (Corbis 2004: #NL005836, #TS002792, #VV11703, #U7247961NP).

Key characteristics of the silkworm are posture, segmented body, tail spike, and knobby protuberances on silkworm heads and bodies (Figures 6a, b). The silk moth contributes its large eyes, wooly body and beard, and feather-like antennae to dragon representations (Johnson and Kishida 1982: 13; Corbis 2004: #AAEZ001112). Chinese New Year "Lion" dancer masks have notable features that relate to the silk moth (Corbis 2004: #YMO12916; iNetours 2004: 2, "lion head close-up").

Two other forms contributed to the silkworm based dragon: the first is the form of a tiger with a mushroom crown exemplified by a Shang jade musical chime (Figure 7a). The tiger attributes were combined with an evolving silkworm form seen in an example of a jade the Min Chiu Society acquired from the Salmony Collection (Figure 7b). The Min Chiu jade exhibits both silkworm and tiger characteristics. The tiger's claw, reverse tail curl, and mushroom crown have been combined with a silkworm-like body. The backward gesture of an actual silkworm's head and the tail spike (Johnson and Kishida 1982: 29) is echoed in this "chimera." Its reverse side is inscribed with a diamond textile design. The voracious open jaws of silkworm and tiger are a shared attribute. I suggest the tiger contributed the size and ferocity the silkworm needed for the stature to become China's new icon for the silk industry. Melded

Figure 6
(a) Photograph: Silkworms (Johnson and Kishida 1982: 22). Courtesy of photographer Isao Kishida, Hokuto City, Japan. (b) Chinese parade dragon with inset of caterpillar, "hickory horned devil." Mary Belle O'Brien, original watercolor; caterpillar inset rendered by author from Hilary Nelson photograph of the "hickory horned devil." Courtesy of http://hilarynelson.com.

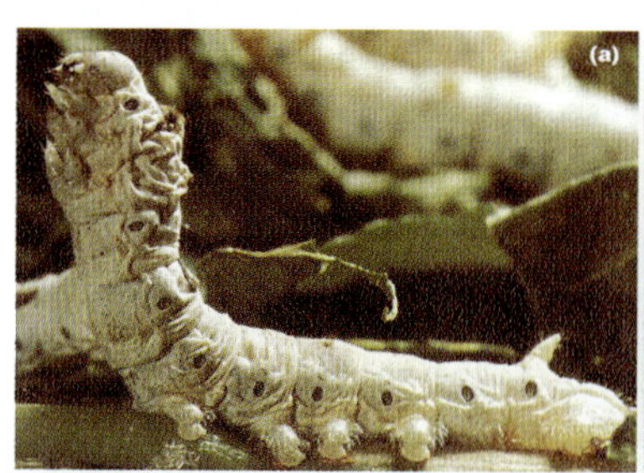
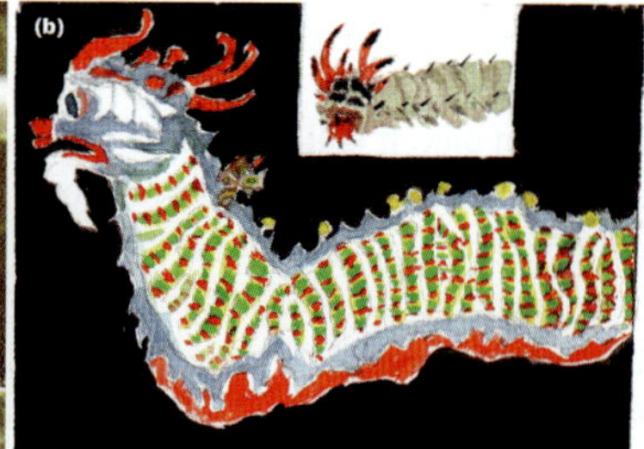

Figure 7
(a) Shang jade tiger chime (Hajek and Foreman 1996: 116). Private collection (undocumented). (b) Shang jade, silkworm–tiger chimera or "dragon pendant," Collection of the Min Chiu Society (Rawson 2002: 213, 12:5). Courtesy of the Hotung Collection, British Museum, London.

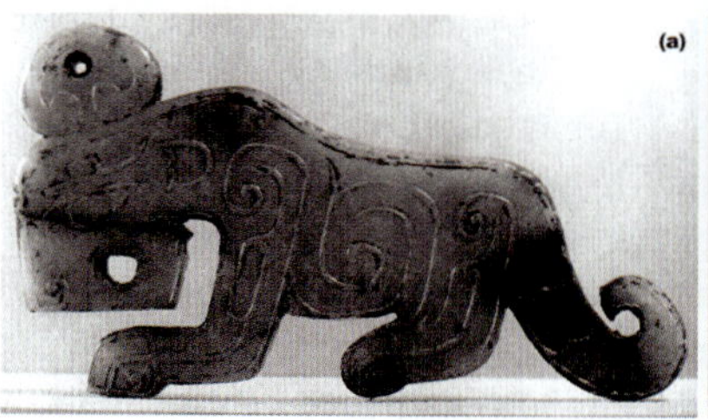
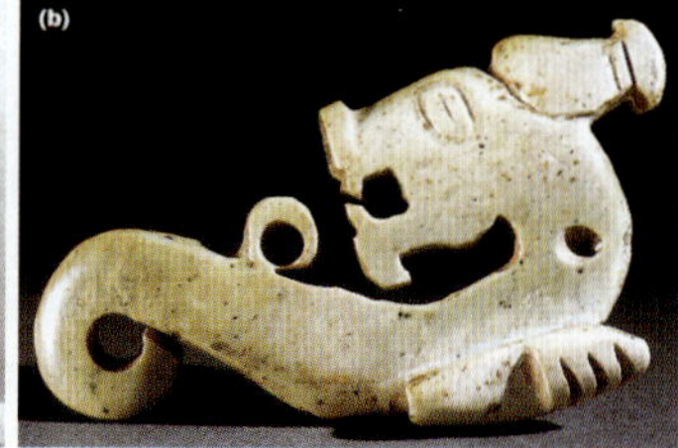

forms of silkworm/tiger images are found through the Shang and Zhou Dynasties (Shanghai Museum: Ancient Chinese Jade Gallery n.d.: 17, 19; Rawson 2002: 208–11, 12:1–12:4).

A group of coiled jade forms some call "dragons" (Childs-Johnson 1988: 50, Figs 2, 3, 7; Shanghai Museum: Ancient Chinese Jade Gallery n.d.: 3) contributed a coiled posture to evolving dragon images. Close examination of these

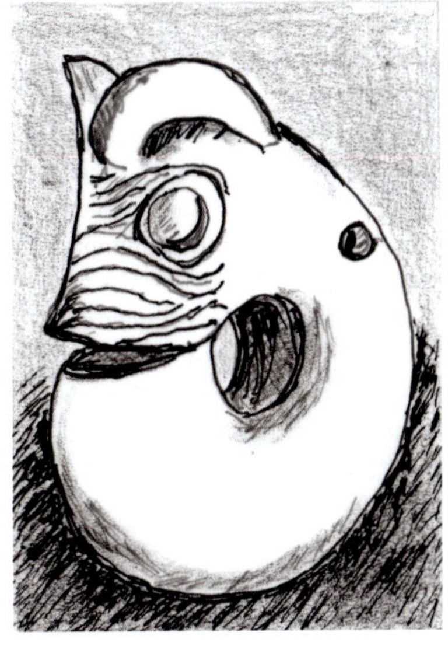

Figure 8
Drawing: Hongshan funerary jade, coiled fetal water buffalo, or "dragon" (Liaoning Provincial Institute of Archaeology, Shenyang). Author's rendering.

burial artifacts, specific to the Neolithic Hongshan culture, reveals a likeness, in my view, not to a "dragon," but to a water buffalo, particularly the features of its head, horns, and wrinkled muzzle (Figure 8), or possibly, in some examples, a pig's head, as Jao thinks (Jao 1988: 62–3, Figs 1–3).

Reptilian traits are not evident in the Hongshan artifacts. The coiled posture might well represent a farm animal in the fetal stage. If so, these funerary objects could have conveyed hope the deceased farmers would be reborn with their farm animals, the water buffalo and pig. These ancient jades subsequently resurfaced to influence later forms, and were then probably seen as "dragons." None of the Hongshan Neolithic jades have the mushroom-shaped horns, apparently derived from the tiger's mushroom crown, that are seen later in the Shang jade dragon from Fu Hao's tomb (Figure 9a).

The tiger's mushroom attribute, probably associated with healing and hallucinatory states, is the link that makes it possible to trace transformation of the earlier silkworm and tiger chimeras into the jade dragon form of the late Bronze Age, from Lady Fu Hao's tomb (Figure 9a). The mushroom motif establishes the connection

between the artifacts shown in Figures 7a, b, and 9a and another dragon prototype also from Fu Hao's burial (Rawson 2002, 209, Fig. 2). The mushroom motif, portrayed as a pair of horns on the prototype dragons from Fu Hao's tomb, is a clear indication of this connection.

Worm-like characteristics in early forms may have led to the perception millennia later that these figures were reptilian. Eastern Zhou artisans (770–475 BC) began to depict the dragon as a reptilian image (Rawson 2002: 269–71, 17: 9:10–9:12), although the Shang dragon jades from Fu Hao's tomb (1200 BC) were clearly derived from non-reptilian elements. Eastern Zhou images of the tiger often have reptilian postures. A tiger Rawson depicts retains a silkworm hook on its back (Rawson 2002: 276, Fig. 1). During this period, reptile-like chimeras began to dominate the way dragons were portrayed. Representations ultimately evolved into classic Chinese Dragon images. I propose this chimera was originally seen as the new icon for China's silk industry during the latter part of the Shang Dynasty.

Chinese scholars and scientists say they do not know the origins of dragon figures because their origins preceded written records. Some scholars assert its origins

Figure 9
(a) Shang jade Dragon figure. (b) Shang jade figure of kneeling woman (Wen Fong 1980: Plates 38 and 39). Both courtesy of the Institute of Archaeology, Chinese Academy of Social Sciences, Beijing.

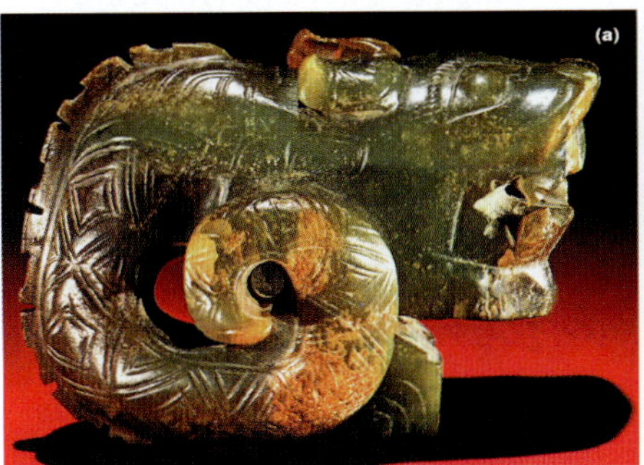
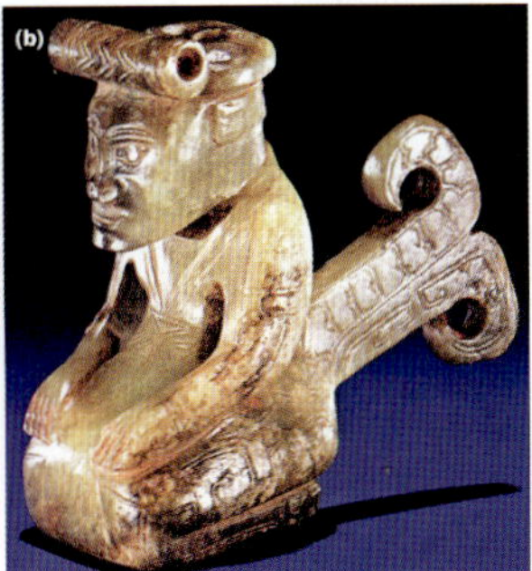

are undoubtedly reptilian while others say the origins are totally imaginative.[3] I suggest that they have failed to recognize the Dragon as the icon that evolved during the Shang Dynasty more than 3,000 years ago to symbolize Chinese dominance in sericulture and silk textile production.

Part Two: Jade Textile Tools of Neolithic and Bronze Age China
Introduction

Silk goods, among the most treasured commodities in the ancient world, were produced by China's flourishing textile industry without competition from other ancient cultures. China's hegemony was probably the main source of its economic power and wealth that began with the benefits reaped by its Neolithic and Bronze Age leaders.

I propose that not all of the tools used by this important industry were made of perishable materials. Jade was the most durable, frictionless material available for making tools and parts for early mechanical devices before the age of metal. It was a material especially suitable for working with silk as it takes a smooth polish and has a low friction interface (low wear) with other materials.

Artifacts for which the original purpose is not understood are often classified "ceremonial" or decorative by generations hundreds and thousands of years later. Neolithic people had a difficult time surviving, even those of royal rank. Producing food, clothing, and tools, it seems, would have taken precedence over creating personal adornment or ceremonial objects of jade, a time-consuming material

to shape. I suggest that jade was not the exclusive property of the wealthy during the Neolithic era and that many Neolithic artifacts had a practical purpose in China's early cultures and were not ceremonial.

Silk Production and Jade Textile Tools in Ancient Feudal Systems

Neolithic tombs of the Liangzhu (3200–2900 BC) at Yao Shan and Fan Shan appear to be burials of high ranking persons. Numerous carefully worked jade artifacts were excavated from these graves: *cong*, rings, awls, spindles and crescent forms, three-pronged arcs, trapezoids, and D-shapes (James 1991: 101–8). Many could have been working tools for producing silk and other textiles. These burial artifacts suggest silk textile production of the Neolithic and Bronze Ages may have been controlled by the wives of local potentates, a proposition consistent with the traditional view that spinning and weaving is women's work. Two legendary royal women of the Bronze Age, Queen Penelope, Odysseus's wife and Ariadne, King Minos's daughter, are associated with textile weaving in ancient literature. Barber cites the Queens of Mari whose transactions in textile production and trade are documented in cuneiform. She describes ancient settlements along the Euphrates River where numbers of women, both royal and common, were actively engaged textile enterprises (Barber 1994: 175–84).

Those royal weavers have a counterpart in Bronze Age China, the Lady Fu Hao, wife of Bronze Age warlord Wu Ding (1200 BC). One of the most significant burials of the Shang period (1600–1050 BC) was Fu Hao's tomb at Anyang. Over 700 jade artifacts were buried with Fu Hao, in addition to a great quantity of bronzes and other valuable objects, which attested to her high status and wealth. She may have directed an important textile enterprise in her husband's stronghold at Anyang. Perhaps Wu Ding traded the silk as he traveled making war. Another indication Fu Hao may have been the head mistress of silk workshops at Anyang is a kneeling jade figurine from her tomb (Figure 9b) that may represent Lady Fu Hao, herself, cast as Xiwangmu, Queen Mother, who was an early Daoist cult goddess.[4] The figure has a spool of thread above her forehead, a spindle whorl lies on the crown of her head, her garment is incised with fabric patterns, and silkworm-like images protrude from her back as a decorative sash.

Burials of women at Songe and Yao Shan, as well as Anyang, contain a concentration of jade artifacts that may be textile tools. Most appear to be tombs of high-ranking women, which indicates that silk production in ancient China may have begun as a cottage industry but soon came largely under the control of powerful local leaders.

Shared Technology
As there was a cross fertilization of ideas between the arts of basketry and weaving, an exchange also occurred among ancient mechanical technologies developed for textile, lapidary and farm work. All used technology that was derived from the primitive mechanics of the whorl and spindle. Thread spinning and winding devices, winnowing machines, drills and grinders, and

the foot-treadle incorporated into early looms and grinding lathes were all based on it. Chinese cultures are conservative and utilize the same shapes, motifs, and methods in many variations of application over millennia. It is tempting to suppose that later mechanical devices for which records exist could reflect features of much earlier ones. China's use of the same decorative motifs can be clearly traced back over four thousand years. Joseph Needham compared a photograph of a spinning machine taken at Shansi in 1942 with one in a Chinese painting dated *circa* 1220 AD, showing the device to be virtually unchanged in over seven hundred years (Needham 1965: Plates CL, CLI).

Needham supports the idea that Chinese cultures had a need early on for mechanized devices to handle the vast amount of reeling, winding and twining that the early silk industry entailed, a position with which I agree. He documented existence of such machines from the first millennium BC to the second millennium AD. Needham suggested the devices were in use long before they were documented (Needham 1965: 2, 102–8, 266–9). Mary Schoeser (Schoeser 2007: 22) notes use of a spindle wheel in the Zhou Dynasty (1050–475 BC).

Whorls: The Most Ancient Example of the Flywheel
The function of the jade discs called *bi* should not have become obscure. They are used in spinning to this day. Whorls are weights that assist circular momentum, not just in spinning thread but in many other mechanical operations. The whorl functions in conjunction

with the spindle, which is the axis for its rotation. These round discs with a central hole have been found in great numbers in Neolithic and Bronze Age burials. Near the end of the first millennium BC, ancient Chinese scholars viewed these discs buried with the dead as symbolic, ceremonial objects (Zhao 1989: 65–9) though originally, they may have had utilitarian purposes.

Whorls for spinning thread, especially silk, were small, usually 3.5 to 7 cm. (Rawson 2002: 112, Fig. 2; Nelson Gallery–Atkins Museum Catalog 1975: 25). Silk thread from broken cocoons was spun in addition to plant fibers, according to Hecht, Needham, and others (Hecht 1989: 18; Needham 1965: 105).

Larger whorls probably powered drills for piercing, incising, and grinding jade, or to operate mechanical farming devices that required the weight of a large flywheel to assist the spindle's rotation. Discs that I propose are flywheels to power this equipment range in diameter between 10 and 35 cm (Rawson 2002: 131–6, Figs 1, 2, and 4:1–4:6).

Whorls provided force and momentum for the work of the living. Perhaps that is the reason they were ubiquitous grave offerings. In a Liangzhu burial at Sidun (3300–2250 BC), jade discs were positioned over the heart and belly of the corpse (Zhao 1989: 68, Fig. 6). Whorls may have signified hope that *qi* (energy) would be imparted for the journey into afterlife, or rebirth.

Spindles, Axles, and the Mechanics that Keep Them Turning
The spindle, either vertical or horizontal, is the axis for a

mechanical operation involving rotation weighted by a flywheel. Neolithic flywheels or whorls were often ground from jade. The circular form and the weight assisted the spindle's rotation. Spindles in a variety of sizes and forms have been excavated (Pearlstein 1993: 134, Fig. 16d; Rawson 2002: 143, 5:6, 5:8, 5:9) and were used for numerous tasks including drilling jade, spinning and reeling, and as axles for primitive winnowing machines.

A Neolithic jade spindle, 3.4 cm (Figure 10a), is quite similar to the one used by a contemporary spinner in Mexico (Figure 10b) with a spinning bowl. Perhaps the ivory bowl cited by Vainker (2004) served the same purpose.

Needham published the photograph of an extant primitive Chinese spinning wheel with a foot-treadle drive directly connected to the wheel (Needham 1965: Plate CXLIX). It is not known when the principle of the treadle drive was first applied to equipment for spinning and weaving. Palmer shows a lathe powered by a foot-treadle for grinding jade illustrated in a late-nineteenth-century drawing (Palmer 1967: Frontpiece). The primitive spinning wheel and lathe may reflect mechanical principles of ancient machines for reeling, grinding, twining, spinning, and weaving that might have existed three or four millennia earlier.

The treadles of the grinding lathe in the nineteenth-century illustration do not operate a continuous belt drive run on pulleys (see discussion of belt drives below). The treadles turn the wooden spindle (axle) by means of cords wrapped around the spindle that attach to the treadle bars. Jade was also drilled with a hand-operated, whorl-weighted spindle with the cord wrapped in a way that is similar to the cord wrap in the print. The weight of the grinding wheel on the end of the spindle acts as the flywheel. The abrasive slurry poured onto the wheel does the grinding, not the wheel itself.[5] Such abrasive slurries would have gouged circular groove marks onto jade and stone grinding wheels.

Similar grooves are seen on the artifacts Rawson and others refer

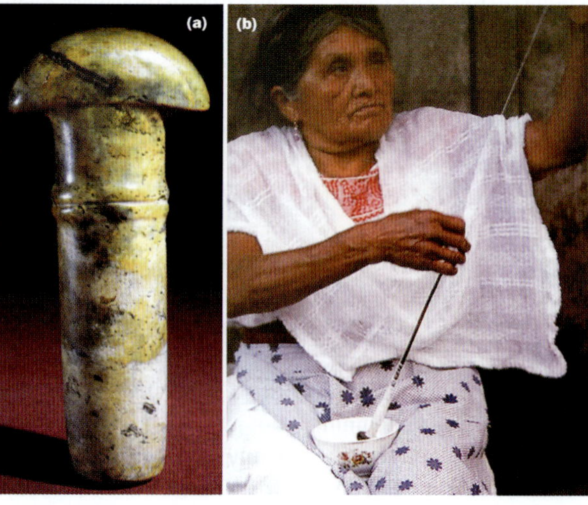

Figure 10
(a) Neolithic jade spindle, or "finial" (Rawson 2002: 196, 10:28). Courtesy of the Hotung Collection, British Museum, London. (b) Photograph: Mexican woman spinner Courtesy of Chloe Sayer and the British Museum Press.

to as "collared discs" (Rawson 2002: 164, 165–6, 9:1–3; Shanghai Museum: Ancient Chinese Jade Gallery n.d.: 16). The Asian Art Museum in San Francisco displays several examples in its jade gallery. Palmer's nineteenth-century image of the lathe grinding wheels suggests to me a possible identity for these "collared discs" (Figure 11). Circular grooves scored into most of the discs (some may have been reground and polished by later owners) are an indication abrasive slurries might have been used with them. The collar rim formed around the central hole, the thinned condition of some discs, and the scored surface are consistent with their use as grinding wheels to shape jade and stone objects.

Rawson supposes that "collared discs" are a form of bracelet. Their size, weight, and shape do not appear to be suitable for a piece of jewelry worn on the arm. A more practical suggestion might be that the discs were grinding wheels. They have been excavated from Shang and Western Zhou tombs. Some may have Neolithic origins (Rawson 2002: 164). Diameters range from 9 to 21 cm.

Pulleys, Gears, and Cogs for Mechanical Drive Systems

If jade artifacts in Fu Hao's tomb are textile tools, they indicate that the Bronze Age textile industry continued to use traditional implements fashioned by Neolithic textile workshops. Fu Hao's tomb, like the Neolithic tombs of her high-ranking predecessors, contained many jade rings, *cong,* and other artifacts that might be textile tools or parts for intermittent and continuous drive pulley systems used for winding and reeling operations in textile workshops. The rings Rawson identifies as bracelets (Figure 12a) are dated late Neolithic and Shang (Rawson 2002: 146–9, 6:1, 6:2, 6:5). The open centers

measure 7–9 cm, a diameter more suited to fit on a wooden pole (axle) than a woman's arm. "Notched discs" (Figure 12b) also could have fitted onto a wooden pole or axle and may have functioned as a gear to control reeling speed.

The notched discs may be related to a more complex artifact that I suggest may also have been part of a pulley-driven system (Rawson 2002: 42, Fig. 29). The artifact has a flange similar to the "notched" jade disc in Figure 12b. Researchers do not agree on the purpose of Neolithic and Shang jades called "notched discs" (Rawson 2002: 163, 8:1, 8:2). Many sources identify the jades as "circumpolar templates" to chart star positions. Rawson rejects the idea while suggesting that the discs may have had a decorative purpose (Rawson 2002: 160-63). In my view, the notched discs appear to be primitive gears or pinions for regulating mechanical operations

Figure 11
Drawing, top: Shang jade disc, or "collared" disc (British Museum). Drawing, bottom: Grinding wheel on spindle (Palmer 1967: frontpiece). Palmer notes his frontispiece is reproduced from *Investigations and Studies in Jade* (1906). Author's renderings.

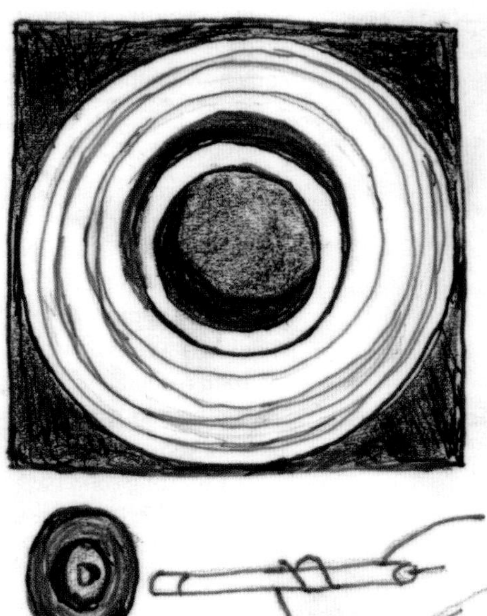

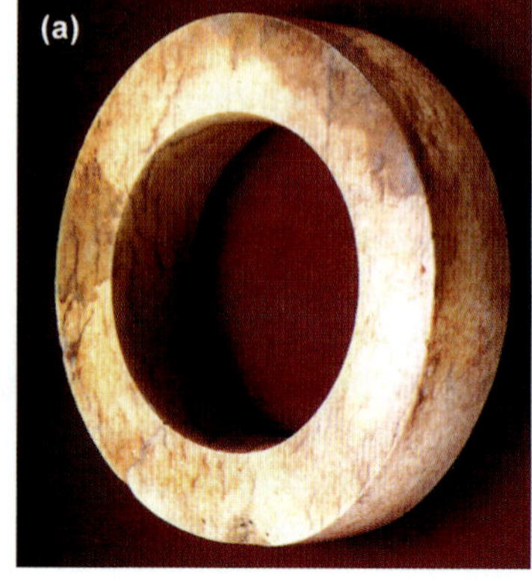
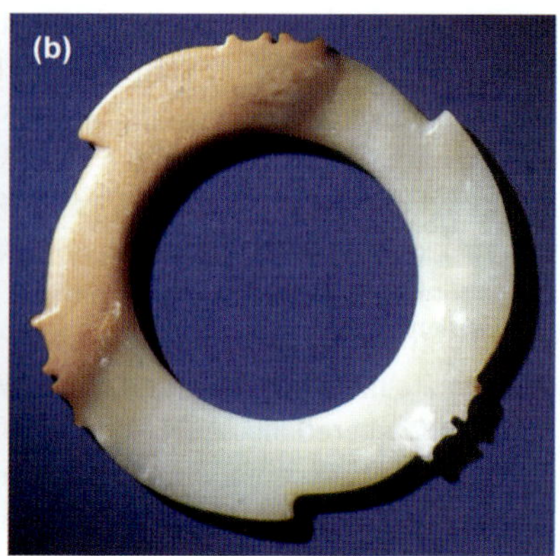

Figure 12
(a) Liangzhu jade ring, or "bracelet" (Rawson 2002: 148, 6:4). (b) Neolithic, possible jade gear, or "notched disc" (Rawson 2002: 163, 8:1). Both courtesy of the Hotung Collection, British Museum, London.

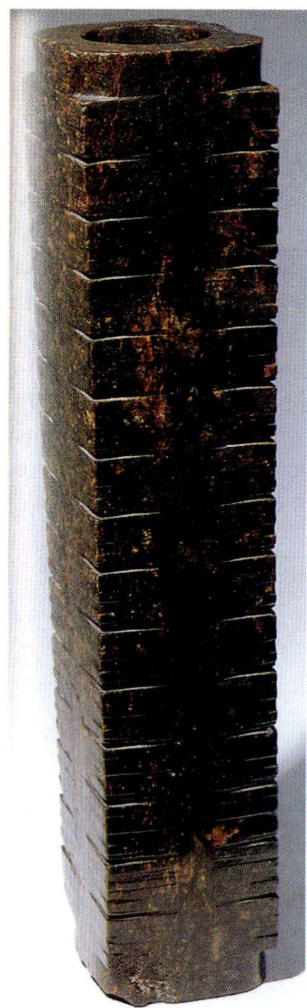

Figure 13
Neolithic jade (long tapered type) *cong* (Rawson 2002: 128, 3:6). Courtesy of the Hotung Collection, British Museum, London.

in a pulley system or transferring rotation to a second drive. I consulted a mechanical engineer, Bertrand Boutte Jr (July 8, 2007), who agreed with my proposals for the purpose of the concave surface rings and notched discs. He said that small notches in the discs, when spaced between large ones, would function like the treads on a tire, and that the configuration definitely suggested a gear.

Both of these jade forms provide evidence that hints at the possibility that pulley-driven mechanical systems might have been in use as early as Neolithic times.

The "Cong" as a Spool on Neolithic Reeling Machines and/or as a Loom Warp Beam
Whatever the *cong*'s original function, it seems evident it was made to be slipped onto a pole or spindle (Figure 13). Ancient texts say the *cong* resembles a "*chegong*": "being the hole through which the axle of a vehicle is fixed" (Zhao 1989: 66). Long *cong* have sizes ranging from 17–23 cm x 8 cm to 29–49 cm x 8 cm. The outside shape is square. Inside, a round center hole has been ground out, usually 7.5–8 cm. The shape is

tapered, reminiscent of some thread spools. A series of grooves girdle the four-sided surface that is also decorated with repetitions of the silk moth motif, which wrap around the corners. This suggested to me that threads may have been wrapped around it, such as the threads by which a fabric litter bed was bound to its pole. I speculated that *cong* might have covered wooden litter poles as a decorative finish, thinking this might explain the large number of *cong* found in a Neolithic burial arranged along both sides of the skeleton (see Zhao 1989: 68, Fig. 6).

However, Ann Hecht describes the *jibata* loom's warp beam as having a "narrow square-sectioned center part, on which the warp is wound … " (Hecht 1989: 132–3, Fig. 114). It seems to me that she is describing the shape of the *cong*. The *jibata* loom's use in Japan can be documented from the year 202 AD and is thought to have come from China (Hecht 1989: 132). That its origins are much more ancient is suggested by the fact that it does not employ more advanced technology such as a foot-treadle or drive belt, but used a cord attached to the weaver's ankle to lift a heddle bar for the counter-shed. The *jibata* may have had a predecessor during the Chinese Neolithic or Shang periods that had a jade *cong* warp beam. Liangzhu and Hongshan are sites where the most *cong* have been excavated, but they have been found all over China. Fu Hao was buried with an array of *cong*, which could have been contemporary, or relics she collected and used.

An article in *Orientations* by Chang (1989: 70) explored his view on the symbolic role of the *cong* in shamanism. A surprise was tucked in his article: Chang's reference to the 1949 speculation by the historian Gou Baojun that the "ancient *cong* was originally made of wood and was a mechanical part of the loom serving to lift the warp." It gave imperfect support to my idea of the *cong* as a warp beam or loom part. [Did Gou mean carry or "hold" the warp instead of "lift" it or confuse a warp beam with a heddle?]. The author made no comment on these issues.

The wood prototypes Gou Baojun suggests are not likely to have existed. It seems that Neolithic artisans skilled in working jade would have found it less difficult to produce a *cong* from jade than to make one in wood without using iron blades and saws (Iron Age, *c.* 750 BC). In correspondence, Barber (2009, personal communication) suggested an alternative: the *cong* may have been a heddle bar, serving to space the heddles, and not a warp beam.

The bulk and square shape of the *cong* seems to me to be more consistent with its function as a warp beam, which is subjected to a lot of tension. The warp beams on looms that I have observed are constructed as a cage of wooden rods in a square configuration. Images of extant primitive technology show thread being reeled onto or wrapped around square cages made of

wooden dowels (Conway 1992: 67; Crockett 1977: 196), and those from early in the second millennium AD, show silk being reeled onto square frames whose structures echo the four-sided *cong* (Needham 1965: Plate CLIII, CLIV; Schoeser 2007: 45). Barber (2009, personal communication) describes a square caged device for reeling silk kite string, which came with a Chinese kite she bought in 1974. Many traditions in textile production seem to survive for millennia, including designs derived from textile weaving.

Possibly, warp threads could have been reeled onto a *cong* before it was installed on a loom. This suggests that it might have been a spool in a reeling apparatus, such as the Thai machine (Figure 14), discussed further below, which has a removable spool (Conway 1992: 66–7). The *cong*, full of reeled silk thread,

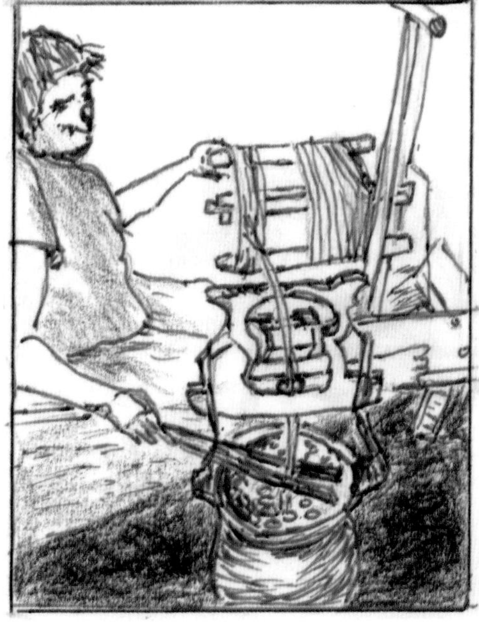

Figure 14
Thai Silk Reel. Author's rendering after the Gordon Conway photograph (Conway 1992: 67).

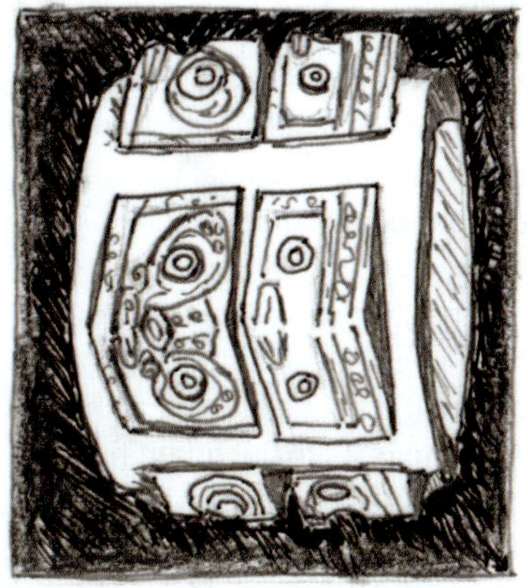

Figure 15
Drawing: Neolithic jade *cong* (short type). Proposed silk conducting reel. Nanjing Museum. Author's rendering.

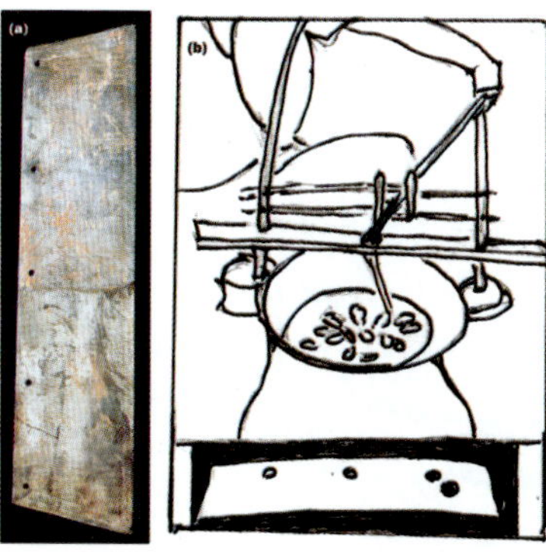

Figure 16
(a) Shang, Erlitou period, trapezoidal jade bar, or "jade knife" (Rawson 2002: 37, Fig. 23). Courtesy of the British Museum. Bequeathed by Oscar Raphael (1a, OA 1945, 10-17-144). (b) Laotian silk reel (Wormspit 2007). Author's rendering of silk reel.

could be removed and installed as a warp beam.

The "Short" Cong as a Conducting Reel
Those *cong* characterized as "short" by Rawson have average lengths of 5–7 cm, with diameters of 7 or 8 cm (Chang 1989: 70–6, Fig. 6, Fig. 7; Rawson 2002: 125–7, 3:1–3:4). They resemble smaller sections of the long *cong*, but are not tapered and are more highly modeled and also decorated with the moth motif. I speculate these artifacts may have had a function in textile workshops that involved reeling and would have been fitted onto a wooden cage or an axle that rotated (Figure 15). The traditional silk reel from Thailand, depicted by Conway in Figure 14, has a rotating drum-like part she calls a "conducting reel," which assists in reeling the thread onto the square cage spool above, after it is drawn through a hole in the bar placed across the kettle of cocoons. This image and Figure 16b suggest the "short" *cong* may have functioned as a conducting reel. In both silk reeling machines (Figures 14 and 16), the conducting reel is positioned above a bar with a hole, through which the silk thread is drawn (further discussion below). The extant Thai reeling assemblies in Figure 14 and 16 exhibit simple parts and mechanical operations that could have been well within the reach of Neolithic cultures.

Another variant of *cong* are block-like, undecorated jades, which may have functioned as counterweights in mechanical operations (Rawson 2002: 129, 3:7, 151, Fig. 2).

Since these enigmatic *cong* are part of very ancient, unwritten history, the only hope for understanding their purpose is to strive for the "best guess."

Broad, Flat, Trapezoidal Jade Bars with Drilled Holes
Rawson and others identify these jade artifacts as "ceremonial blades in the shape of reaping knives" (Figures 16(a), (b)), said to be evolved from reaping implements of stone (Rawson 2002: 184–7). Flint stone and obsidian are among the common geological formations that have a sharp cutting edge, when flaked from a core. Implements created by this method are not necessarily large. I am not aware of any implements made of flint or obsidian that are crafted in the shape or size of these jade bars. In any case, such bars would not be effective reaping tools, not having a curved edge. Barber (2009, personal communication) described to me Neolithic reaping tools of the Middle East that were made from animal jaw bones with flaked obsidian points fixed in the tooth sockets.

Early cultures did extract jade slabs from core rocks. Their methods probably resulted in a thinner edge along one edge of the slab, which could account for the blade-like taper seen in these jade bars. (Antique jades were often reshaped and polished by later generations who acquired them, another factor that must be taken into account.) A great number of these broad, flat, trapezoidal artifacts originated in Neolithic cultures of northern China where rice is not grown, and the main crops cultivated were probably leafy vegetables, roots, and legumes which, when harvested, are not "reaped." It seems unlikely that the trapezoidal jade bars were based on stone prototypes of reaping implements. These puzzling artifacts beg for a reasonable guess that suggests another purpose.

My speculation is that the "blades" may have been textile tools, though it is hard to imagine how they might have been used. The weavers I consulted did not think the blades were beaters for a loom,[6] but had no suggestions for their purpose as textile tools. These bars, mostly of jade, occur in great numbers in Neolithic and Bronze Age excavations and have variations in their form and the number of drilled holes. Lengths range from 24 cm to 70 cm; average widths are 6–9 cm. A stone "blade" dated 5000 BC from Chinglienkang has seven holes (Nelson Gallery–Atkins Museum Catalog 1975: 39) and is similar to another early Neolithic stone blade with thirteen holes (Rawson 2002: 182, Fig. 1). The ends of these artifacts are all ground at an angle, creating a trapezoidal shaped bar. This stone prototype is repeated in later Neolithic jade bars, which may have been used in the process to produce silk thread. Some bars have three holes along the top edge, others five or seven, such as one from Erlitou (Rawson 2002: 184, Fig. 2, 185–7, 10:17–10:19). The sloped, notched ends are a clue that the bars could have been fitted in slots between two upright posts and possibly have been used with the Asian loom Hecht describes below.

Rawson discusses a variant type of the Neolithic flat jade bar she describes as "tablet-shaped sceptres" or "ceremonial blade"

(Rawson 2002: 178–83, 10:14–10:16). These artifacts have a range of measurements comparable to the "reaping knives," but dimensions are more regular and nearly rectangular. Most have just two drilled holes and some are inscribed with the silk moth motif. These also might be candidates for textile work, and fit with several suggestions made below.

Traditional methods still used by non-industrialized cultures provide avenues for conjecture (Birrell 1953; Crockett 1977; Hecht 1989; Wormspit 2007).

Birrell reported on a device used by Indians along the Yukon River in Alaska to spin (twine?) thread. She sketches a vertical frame with a horizontal cross beam that has three holes drilled in it, spaced apart, from which are suspended broad, rectangular boards with a hole in the top. The suspended "spindle" boards, when twirled, wound drawn threads and freed both hands for more control of the thread being spun (Birrell 1953: 34, Fig. 13). This seems to describe a crude method for making thread. Some stone artifacts Rawson calls "axes" (see Rawson 2002: 174–7, 10:8–10:13.) might have functioned as weights for twining or spinning thread when used with a bar such as the stone bar with thirteen holes cited above.

Some wide jade bars (Figure 16a) also might have functioned as a warping beam on a loom with a non-continuous warp, one that does allow the warp to circulate freely over the loom beams. A South-East Asian loom, that Hecht refers to as "the discontinuous warp loom," has a flat rectangular warp board onto

which a long warp can be wound, which drops into a slot between vertical uprights on the loom (Hecht 1989: 106–7, Fig. 95). It appears that the board can be lifted out to unwind more warp. However, the extant warp board, a true rectangle, is usually used with a reed to order the threads (Hecht 1989: 106), and no drilled holes are apparent. The imperfect, trapezoidal shape of the jade bars and their widths may be unsuitable for this function.

I see another possible function for some of these jade bars, suggested by the traditional Laotian way of reeling silk from cocoons as in the Thai silk reel (Figure 14), and the Laotian reel (Figure 16b). The Lao woman's kettle, full of heated cocoons, shows a flat smooth wooden bar, having a central hole, attached above the kettle; a conducting reel is mounted above that. The woman is pulling silk strands from several cocoons in the kettle through the hole, over the conducting reel by hand and onto a separate small spindle wheel at her side (not shown). It is reasonable to suppose that the Neolithic jade bars might have functioned in the same way as shown in Figures 16 and 14. Alternatively, the bars could be mounted on edge, between vertical upright slots, attached to the sides of a cocoon bucket (Hecht 1989: 133, seventeenth-century print, 114, depicting bucket with uprights).

Forefinger Guard Ring
Another device that may be associated with reeling operations is the so-called "archer's thumb ring" (Rawson 2002: 286–8, Figs 20, 20:2). Center openings are approximately 2–2.5 cm (based

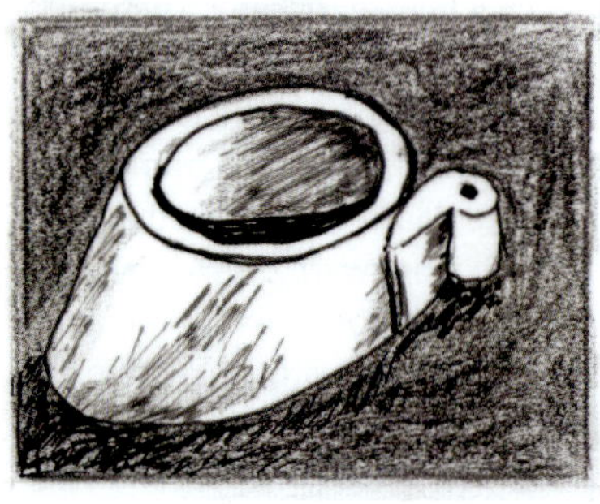

Figure 17
Drawing: Zhou jade forefinger guard ring, or "archer's thumb ring," British Museum. Author's rendering.

on total measurements of object). I propose that such a ring, worn on the forefinger, would serve to protect the finger that guides the silk thread in the reeling process (Figure 17). Such a ring in my jade collection has a 2 cm opening which fits onto the forefinger, not the thumb. Fu Hao's tomb contained an "archer's ring."

The Huang as the Basic Silk Throwing Device
I propose the earliest Neolithic tool for twisting or "throwing" silk thread must have been the *huang,* and that it was not a piece of jewelry, originally. James reports that at Songe and Yao Shan, *huang* were found "only in what are believed to be women's graves" (James 1991: 109). An early Neolithic example from Songe appears to be made from a piece of damaged jade whorl (Figure 18a), while a later example shows deliberate

sectioning of a whorl into three *huang* (Rawson 2002: 158, Fig. 7).

I realized *huang* had a functional relationship to the "flyer" artifact discussed below. Both seemed to apply the mechanical principles of a flywheel, and each might be used to twist and ply thread.

To test this concept, I made a facsimile of a jade *huang* from a lead strip. After threading it with two strands, I attached one end and turned the bundled threads like a jump rope. The lead crescent, acting as a flywheel, caused the two single threads to twist around each other. In effect, the threaded piece is thrown in an arc, which may account for the term "throwing silk," that is, twisting a number of silk threads together. When I threaded the arc thus—one strand threaded through the front side of the right hole and out through the back side of the left hole; then threaded the second strand in the

Figure 18
(a) Songe jade *huang,* Shanghai Museum (Shanghai Museum: Ancient Chinese Jade Gallery Catalog, n.d.: 3, left-bottom). Courtesy of the Shanghai Museum. (b) Liangzhu jade flyer, or "pronged ornament" (James 1991: 106, Fig. 14). Courtesy of *Orientations.*

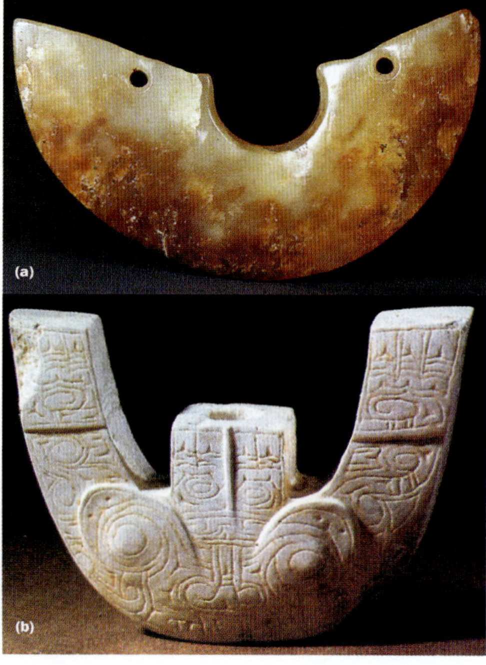

reverse—I discovered the twisted threads were less susceptible to unraveling because of the complex twist that resulted. Threading each strand the same way resulted in a simple twist that unraveled easily. A number of twists were probably devised by Neolithic textile workers. Schoeser describes the variety of twists produced by the modern silk industry (Schoeser 2007: 236–7).

The Prototype Flyer as a Winding and Twining Tool

When Neolithic arch-shaped artifacts, described as "three-pronged" jades, are rotated into a position so that the arms are oriented horizontally, pointing right, (Figure 18b) the form has a striking resemblance to the flyer on the traditional spinning wheel, which spins thread and winds it onto a bobbin by continuous drive in the same operation. Leonardo de Vinci is usually given credit for inventing the flyer spinning wheel. However, Needham says that Leonardo's drawing was an almost exact copy of earlier Chinese illustrations of the machine, that there is no reason to insist everything Leonardo sketched was original, and that ancient Chinese textile machine designs reached Europe in the time of Marco Polo (Needham 1965: 103). Many Chinese inventions were based on the principle of the whorl or flywheel. The arched fly arm advances this principle with a new configuration.

The flyer-like artifacts illustrated by James and Rawson are incised and sculpted with the silk moth icon, but James sees the *"taotie"* image as a "power mask," not a silk moth (James 1991: 101–10).

Many flyer jades seem to have been reshaped to remove damage. Rawson believes the "pronged" jade from Liangzhu originally had a center prong (Rawson 2002: 141, Fig. 5:4). She describes its "complex holes" at the ends of the two remaining prongs (Rawson 2002: 142).[7] Yao Shan "flyers" also appear to have been reshaped to remove damage (James 1991: 103–6). The center prongs of the Yao Shan artifacts are intact, while the ends of the arches with the holes Rawson describes are missing.

Each "flyer" has a hole drilled through the center of its arch, an indication it may have been mounted onto a spindle. James reports that in Yao Shan burials, many spindles were found in association with the "three-pronged" jades (James 1991: 104). These flyer-like forms may be evidence that the flyer arm was invented in the Neolithic period. Testing a facsimile of an intact original could answer questions about whether it merely wound, twined, and plied thread or could also spin thread. Leonardo's drawing of the Chinese flyer showed it was used with a pulley and belt drive system.

Huang Associated with the Spindle Wheel

After discovering how *huang* could twist threads manually, I realized that late Shang and Zhou *huang* (Figure 19a) had the right shape to have been attached to spindle wheels, such as those Schoeser says existed in the Zhou period. Rawson depicts a number of *huang* from the Zhou Dynasty (Rawson 2002: 241–2, 260–7). These *huang*

resemble the shape of a device that is illustrated in a Chinese print dated 1313 AD, reproduced by Needham (Figure 19b). The device holds three spindles of thread, and is attached to a wheel. It appears that the woman seated at the wheel is plying three spindles of thread. *Huang* might have been used with Zhou wheels in the manner depicted in this much later Chinese print.

Schoeser explains that the "spindle" wheel was adapted for use with silk in the Zhou Dynasty. She says, "this wheel which merely twists the thread, should not be confused with the spinning wheel … " (Schoeser 2007: 22). It would be interesting to know what the similarities and differences might have been between the Zhou wheel and that of the early second millennium Chinese wheel seen in Figure 19b.

Comb-like Artifacts

Broken silkworm cocoons result in masses of broken silk threads that cannot be reeled from damaged cocoons and would need to be combed to untangle the threads the way other plant fibers need to be straightened prior to spinning. This jade toothed artifact (Figure 19c) may have been a tool to comb out tangled silk threads, or it might have functioned as a thread guide in reeling or twining operations. It does resemble a wood beater comb that Mexican weavers sometimes use with looms, but when I asked several weavers if they thought this jade comb-like artifact served as a beater, all replied that it was not likely (see note 6).

Jenny So suggests that the Hongshan artifact in Figure 19c is an

Figure 19
(a) Jade *huang,* possibly for use with spindle wheel (Rawson 2002: 265, 17:4). Courtesy of the Hotung Collection, British Museum, London. (b) Woman at spindle wheel (Needham 1965: Pl. CXLVIII, Fig. 402). Courtesy of Cambridge University Press and Joseph Needham. (c) Hongshan jade fiber comb or thread guide, or "toothed pendant" (So 1993: 124, Fig. 1a). Courtesy of the Freer Gallery of Art, Smithsonian Institution, Washington, DC. Gift of Therese and Erwin Harris. F1991.52.

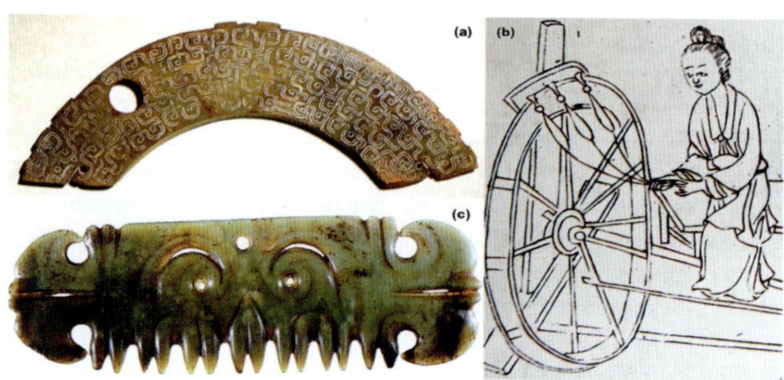

"ornamental jade pendant," as well as other examples she cites (So 1993: 126, Figs 4–6). She believes the jades may have been based on "functional stone prototypes," and that the decorative motif may relate to the boar or pig and a landform called "Boar Mountain" (So 1993: 124–9). The jade combs seem too refined to have been derived from rough stone prototypes and are of a size (17.2 cm) and weight not well suited to jewelry. Furthermore, the motif appears to me to be a version of the ubiquitous silk moth icon (Rawson 2002: 34, Fig. 18).

Spools
Though not a typical spool form, this curious Hongshan jade of 3500 BC, might be a simple tool on which to wind thread (Figure 20). Rawson considers it an ornament, calling it a "three ring pendant" (Rawson 2002: 111–2, Fig. 1; 112, Fig. 2). It might be fitted onto wooden pegs or the last three fingers of a woman's hand.

A group of "beads" in the Sackler Collection (Rawson 2002: 239, Fig. 1) resemble various thread spool types. All have holes drilled lengthwise through them, and

several resemble the spool or sheng worn as an attribute by the kneeling woman in Figure 9b. Rawson notes that many "beads" in Fu Hao's tomb may belong to a much earlier time (Rawson 2002: 239, Fig. 2). By the same token, the spool Rawson cites from a Zhou burial is the same type as the "beads" found in earlier Shang burials (Rawson 2002: 240, 14:3). Rawson suggests that "beads" in burial vessels seem to have been handed down through many generations and that similar spool-like artifacts, cached in bronze burial vessels as late as the seventh century BC, are dated much earlier than the burials.

Rawson is especially puzzled by a small triangular form, 5 × 1.3 cm (Figure 21) that she considers an "oddity," and which suggests to her an insect. The tapered, grooved artifact dated early Zhou (Rawson 2002: 225, 12:24) has the appearance of a small thread spool to me. Rawson comments, "We can only hope that future excavations will reveal the significance of the piece" (Rawson 2002: 225).

Jessica Rawson's extensive assembly of photographs and illustrations in *Chinese Jade*

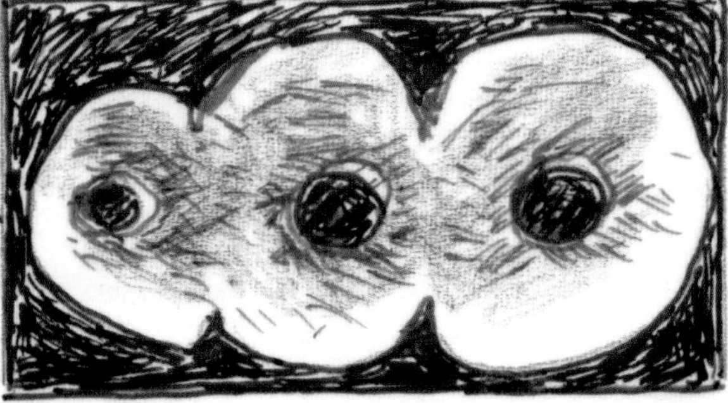

Figure 20
Drawing: Hongshan jade. Thread reeling hand device, or "three ring pendant" (Hutougou Fuxin, Liaoning Province, Rawson 2002. 111, Fig. 1). Author's rendering.

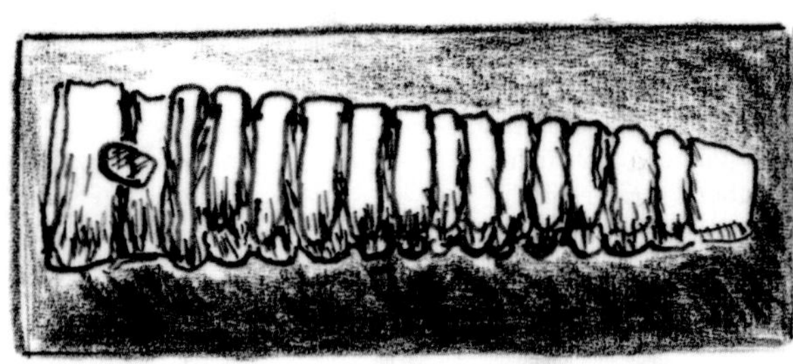

Figure 21
Drawing: Small thread spool, Zhou jade, or "insect" (British Museum). Author's rendering.

makes it possible, without further excavation, to see some Chinese jades in a new light.

Stone Jacks
Rawson discusses artifacts from the Neolithic that she calls the "stepped axe" or "adze," which is exemplified by a Liangzhu stone artifact dated 3000 BC, 24.8 × 3.6 cm (Figure 22). According to Rawson, their occurrence was common at many later Neolithic sites (Rawson 2002: 171, 10:3). A similar artifact comes from Chinglienkang dated 5000 BC (Nelson Gallery–Atkins Museum Catalog 1975: 40). Neither bears a functional resemblance to a chisel (adze) or an ax head. The shape of this artifact makes me think it would function like a jack or levering device. These artifacts were usually made of stone, not jade, and have a "prop ledge" on one end, and on the other, an angled bottom under which a wedge could be inserted to

tighten the implement into position. The set-up can be disassembled easily by knocking out the wedge to release tension. I would imagine Neolithic farmers and trade people would have put such an implement to many uses (I have used them myself).

If the image on a Yao Shan pottery bowl from Banpo (see earlier and note 2) does represent a Neolithic ground loom, such a "jack" might have been used by weavers to prop up heddle bars on their ground looms the same way Winlock illustrates their use with an Egyptian ground loom (Barber 1991: 82, 3:2). The broad, flat bottom on the Egyptian heddle jacks would have made them more difficult to dislodge than their Neolithic predecessors.

Bobbins
The weavers I consulted (see note 6) all seemed to agree that the artifacts cited here might have

been bobbins that held weft thread (Rawson 2002: 115, 1:1; 143, 5:7; 202, 11:1; 202–3, 11:2; 203, Fig. 1). According to Rawson, the bird figure, a common form for bobbins, was found at many Neolithic sites. A similar artifact was also found in Fu Hao's tomb (Rawson 2002: 202–3). A scoop-shaped bobbin, 12.7 × 1.8 cm (Figure 23) from the 4000 BC Neolithic site at Chahai, Liaoning, seems to be a singular example of its type (Rawson 2002: 115, 1:1).

Jade Blades in the Form of Bronze Swords and Daggers
I question the supposition that jade objects, in the form of Shang bronze swords and daggers, only had a ceremonial purpose. The discovery of how to produce bronze metal for making tools, weapons, and vessels surely generated excitement and awe in the Shang Dynasty, so it would seem that metal objects should have had

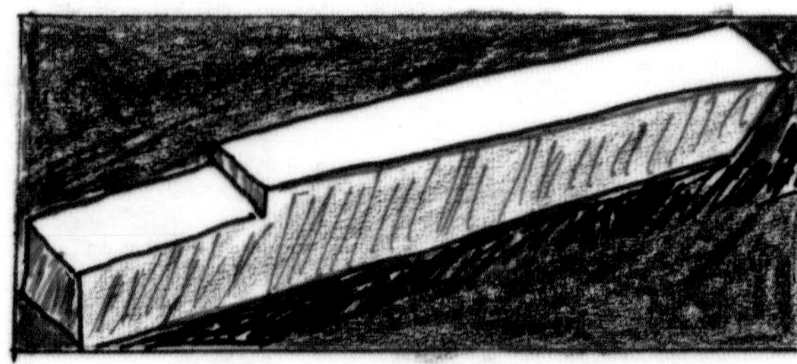

Figure 22
Drawing: Liangzhu, pale green stone
levering device, or "stepped axe"
(British Museum). Author's rendering.

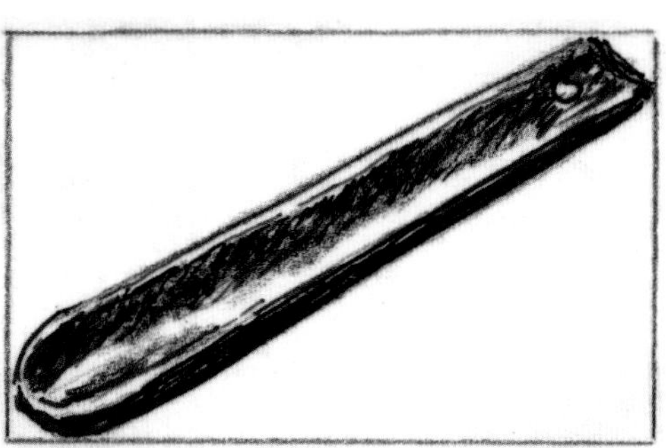

Figure 23
Drawing: Neolithic Chahai culture.
Possible bobbin, or "scoop-shaped
jade, function unknown" (British
Museum). Author's rendering.

more ceremonial significance than jade in that particular time period. Shang jade blade forms appeared almost simultaneously with bronze blades called *ge* and apparently imitated the bronze forms (Rawson 2002: 192). Shang textile artisans probably recognized that if the less refined metal forms were re-created in jade, they would make excellent textile tools.

It is not likely that Lady Fu Hao was buried with ceremonial weapons of war. Thirty-nine jade blades were excavated from her tomb. The great variety of the blade forms found in Fu Hao's tomb puzzle Rawson (Rawson 2002: 192). The explanation might be that Fu Hao's warrior husband captured women and brought them back with their textile tools to be slaves in the textile shops run by his wives. Ebrey refers to the use of captured slaves by Shang kings (Ebrey 1999: 24). Syrian kings engaged in the same practice during the Middle Bronze Age (Barber 1994: 176).

The dagger and sword blades range from 14 × 2 cm to 36 × 4 cm in length (Rawson 2002: 192–6, 10:23, 10:25). The long sword-like jades could have been used as sword beaters on the loom, while others appear to be picks to lift selected threads or separate groups of threads (Figure 24) as Rachael Brown illustrates (Brown 1998: 88, Fig. 127).

Blades with a Concave End Suggestive of a Pair of Horns
These jade artifacts, deemed to be ceremonial, are sometimes called *zhang* (Yang 1995: 141–8). Yang describes their physical characteristics in detail but cannot relate them to stone prototypes or a function. Rawson discusses the distribution of these forms but views their meaning and purpose to be an enigma (Rawson 2002:

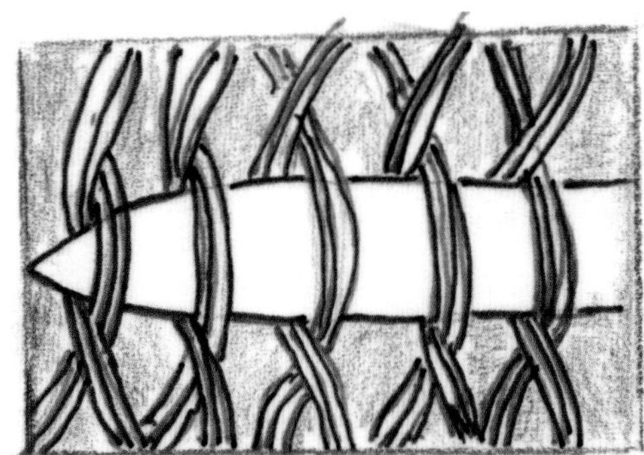

Figure 24
Illustration of loom tool use (after Brown 1998). Author's rendering.

188–91). The Neolithic cultures of the Longshan, Shimao, and Erlitou produced these artifacts (Rawson 2002: 188–91, 10:21, Figs 1–5). A variant of this curious type is called a "forked blade," and it occurs in great number at the Bronze Age site, Sanxingdui (Bagley 2001: 164–5, Plates 54, 55). Rather than having a concave scoop, this form has an end with a deep V-shaped notch. Though their lengths are sword-like, between 27 and 55 cm with widths between 5 and 9 cm (one example of exceptional length is 68 cm), their forms, in my view, do not signify weaponry.

The concave top edge of the first type suggests a pair of horns or hooks that might be used to reach up and snag something on the two projection points. Could that possibly be silkworm cocoons spun among tree branches? The concave jade edge might function well to scrape moth eggs off tree limbs without damage to the bark. The Sanxingdui forked blades would have been even a better tool for gathering cocoons and eggs. Possibly, these blades had a connection to gathering wild cocoons and eggs.

Jenny So discusses a Sanxingdui blade incised with human figures and images she interprets as hills or mountains. She also cites a freestanding bronze tree having the same hill motif on its base with kneeling figures presumed to hold blades. The coincidence of tree, hill, and blade images in these two artifacts suggests to her that they "refer to rituals that were performed in hilly terrain and that involved the forked blades so common at Sanxingdui" (Bagley 2001: 162; So 1993: Fig. 53, 119, Pl. 28). I realized her speculation about the images associated with ritual use of the blades has relevance to my own thoughts about a practical activity.

The forked bamboo batten, used by the Thai woman to assist in reeling silk from cocoons (Figure 14), caused me to associate the Sanxingdui V-notched blades with this batten. Her tool is positioned on top of the cocoons in the heated kettle, and she is unreeling silk threads through the split in the bamboo batten (Conway 1992: 67). The forked batten guides the unwinding threads through the hole in a cross bar above, similar to the bar in Figure 16b. The threads then pass over the conducting reel and onto the spool.

If a Sanxingdui "forked blade" were to be placed in like manner on the cocoons in a kettle, the V-shaped notch on its end might also serve the same purpose as the forked bamboo batten. Perhaps the blade had a dual purpose and might have been used to gather cocoons as well.

Though these propositions are highly speculative, they do not rely on the often questionable standby explanation, the "ceremonial" function.

Conclusions
Part One
Textile arts of the Neolithic period were preceded by twenty millennia of textile practices. The advanced state of textile arts in the early Neolithic should not be a surprise, although it does seem surprising that evidence for textile production in China has not yet been found earlier than 5000 BC. I have tried to show, however, that a body of visual evidence has survived that attests to Chinese cultures having had a budding silk textile industry during the early Neolithic. In part, the evidence hinges on the recognition that the *taotie* or "monster" images, consistently depicted on most Neolithic jades, do portray the silk worm-silk moth life cycle.

The Shang Dynasty's advances in sericulture seem to be reflected in their artifacts. Shang bronzes display beautiful decorative elements derived from the intricate patterns of silk fabrics. Silk moth eggs and silkworm larvae decorating jade and bronze artifacts indicate that domestic cultivation of the silkworm had already begun in the Shang Dynasty. The silkworm-moth icon grew increasingly stylized and ultimately lost its status as an iconic image. At the end of the Shang, the Chinese Dragon chimera emerged as the new symbol for China's dominance in sericulture and silk textile production. Isao Kishida's silkworm and moth images provide visual testimony that Dragon and Lion Dancer forms stem from the silk worm. In the ancient world, sericulture reached a peak during the Zhou Dynasties. So, it seems ironic that by the end of the Eastern Zhou Dynasty the silkworm chimera was no longer seen as the symbol of China's triumph in sericulture. During the late Zhou and Han Dynasties, the chimera acquired reptilian characteristics and new associations. The Dragon ultimately became China's national symbol whose Neolithic origins the Chinese now do not seem to recognize.

Part Two

Examined with an eye toward ancient China's flourishing textile trade, at least some jade artifacts are shown to have been actual textile tools fashioned in a material that has survived for millennia and is highly suitable for working with silk. The best example is the spindle and whorl that women invented to spin thread. It is the earliest expression we know of a

mechanical principle that is the basis for countless mechanical innovations that Chinese cultures of the Neolithic and Bronze Ages developed to great advantage.

Evidence that other artifacts were implements of the textile trade is suggestive rather than conclusive. The perspective of this article is to present a new viewpoint from which to consider the purpose and meaning of these ancient jade treasures.

Notes

1. Wearing a string skirt is said to be a signal of sexual maturity. The so-called Venus figurines may have been used ritually in sexual initiation of girls. The figures resemble male sex organs or a pregnant female, depending on the view of the object's orientation.

2. In correspondence, September 2, 2006, Dr Elizabeth Barber agreed the square-shaped image in the Yag Shao pottery bowl from Banpo could represent a ground loom, but questioned my spider identification of the other image. Dr Eleanor Guralnick who corresponded with me in October 2006, about this article, had the opposite opinion. I appreciate the time both took to review my ideas.

   The image I propose to be a back-strap loom is interpreted by others as a "fish," which is not supported by other Neolithic images of fish (for images see Rawson 2002: 23, Fig. 7; 24, Fig. 10; 47, Fig. 35; 204, Fig. 2; 215, Fig. 12:9; Shang images: 228–9).

3. China Page (2009): "Dragon occupies a very important position in Chinese mythology. It shows up in arts, literature, poetry … the origins of Chinese dragons is unknown, but certainly pre-dates the written history" (http://www.chinapage.com/dragon).

   Zhou (2006): "Throughout the centuries scientists came up with many explanations and theories about the dragon. It's beyond any doubt that it must have been in its earliest appearances a reptile, a snake or lizard" (http://www.cdot.org/history/dragon-articles.htm). Other websites that discuss theories of dragons having totem, reptilian or totally imaginative origins are: http://chineseculture.about.com/library/weekly/aa082998.htm and http://en.wilkipedia.org/wiki/chinese-dragon.

4. In Bagley (2001: 317) Xiwangmu is described as a "dispenser of good fortune … who has the sheng [weaving spool?] … in her hair."

5. In Palmer (1967: 16, 20-21), historic slurry mixtures and lapidary methods are described. An oval "collared" sandstone slab might resemble the grinder Palmer describes (see Bagley 2001: 175, Fig. 6.3). For more discussion of lapidary work, see Hansford (1967).

6. On September 27, 2006, I had a conference with Dr Deborah Valorma, instructor in the textile department at California College of the Arts, Oakland, regarding ideas I had about jade textile tools. The same day, Joyce Hulbert, Berkeley, textile restorer, also conferred with me. I thank them for their time and advice. Both were doubtful the jade combs would work well as beaters on a loom, that they would snag threads, nor was the tooth configuration suitable for this task. Neither did they think other blade forms I asked about, were tools for a loom.

   In regard to the holes drilled in these blades, Dr Barber's comment in correspondence September 2, 2006, was "function?? (not made just for fun)." I had to agree the holes had no function in a beater, but had a strong intuition the artifacts were used in textile work.

7. Rawson (2002: 141–2) says: "All such pronged plaques have complex holes … A large hole pierces the centre and there are two shallow holes, on either side. There are also complex holes for attachment at the upper ends. Here, small holes on the sides lead into slots that are open at the top of the fitting."

References

d'Argence, Rene-Yvon Lefebre (ed.). 1983. *Treasures from the Shanghai Museum : 6000 Years of Chinese Art*. Japan: Shanghai Museum and the Asian Art Museum of San Francisco.

Barber, E. J. W. 1991. *Prehistoric Textiles*. Princeton, NJ: Princeton University Press.

Barber, E. J. W. 1994. *Women's Work: The First 20,000 Years*. New York: W. W. Norton & Co.

Bagley, R. (ed.) 2001. *Ancient Sichuan: Treasures from a Lost Civilization*. Princeton, NJ: Seattle Art Museum with Princeton University Press.

Birrell, V. 1953. *The Textile Arts*. New York: Schobin Books, Harper & Row.

Brown, Rachael. 1998. *The Weaving, Spinning, and Dyeing Book*, 2nd edn. New York: Alfred A. Knopf.

Chang, K. C. 1989. "An Essay on Cong." *Orientations* June: 70.

Childs-Johnson, E. 1988. "Dragons, Masks, Axes and Blades: From Four Newly-documented Jade-working Cultures of Ancient China." *Orientations* April: 50, Figs 2, 3, 7.

China Page. 2009. "Dragons in Ancient China." http://www.chinapage.com/dragon, accessed 2006 and 2009.

Chung, Y. 2005. *Silken Threads: A History of Embroidery in China, Korea, Japan, and Vietnam*. China: Harry Abrams Inc.

Clunas, C. 1997. *Art in China: Oxford History of Art*. Oxford and New York: Oxford University Press.

Conway, S. 1992. *Thai Textiles*. London: The British Museum Press.

Corbis. 2004. *Stock Photography and Pictures*, #NL005836, N. Rabonowitz; #TS002792, T. Streshinsky; #VV11703, Underwood & Underwood; #U7247961NP, Bettmann; #AAEZ001112, French; #YMO12916, M. S. Yamashita. http://pro.corbis.com, accessed August 12, 2004.

Crockett, C. 1977. *The Complete Spinning Book*. New York: Watson-Guptill Publications.

Dinkum. 2004. Thailand Travel, Silkworms." Image of silkworm cultivation. http://www.dinkum.nl/travel/thailand/silkworms.jpg, accessed October 7, 2007.

Ebrey, P. B. 1999. *China: Cambridge Illustrated History*. Hong Kong: The Press Syndicate of the University of Cambridge.

Geijer, A. 1979[1972]. *A History of Textile Art*. Trans. R. Tanner. London: Southeby Parke Bernet.

Hajek, Lubor and Foreman, Werner. 1996. *A Book of Chinese Art: Four Thousand Years of Sculpture, Painting, Bronze, Jade, Lacquer and Porcelain*. London: Artia and Spring Books.

Hansford, S. Howard. 1967. *Chinese, Carved Jades*. London: Faber and Faber.

Hecht, Ann. 1989. *The Art of the Loom: Weaving, Spinning and Dyeing across the World*. New York: Rizzoli.

INetours. 2004. S*an Francisco Chinese New Year Pictures*, Lion Head. http://inetours.com/Pages/SFbrhds/Chinese-New-Year.html, accessed August 12, 2004.

Investigations and Studies in Jade. 1906. *Investigations and Studies in Jade: The Heber R. Bishop Collection*. New York: Private publisher.

James, J. M. 1991. "Images of Power: Masks of the Liangshu Culture." *Orientations* June: 101–10.

Jao, T.-I. 1988. "Some Notes on the Pig in Early Chinese Myths and Art." *Orientations* December: 62–3.

Johnson, Silvia and Isao Kishida.1982. *Silkworms: Lerner Natural Science Book*. Minneapolis, MN: Lerner Publications.

Lawton, T. and Merrill, L. 1993. *Freer: A Legacy of Art*. New York: Smithsonian Institution and Harry N. Abrams Inc.

Needham, J. 1965. *Science and Civilization in China*, Vol. IV: 2. Cambridge: Cambridge University Press.

Nelson Gallery–Atkins Museum Catalog. 1975. *The Chinese Exhibition: The Exhibition of Archaeological Finds of the People's Republic of China*. Kansas City, KS: Nelson Gallery Foundation.

Okladnikov, A. P. 1981. *Ancient Art of the Amur Region*, New York: Abrams.

Orientations. 1997. *Chinese Jade: Selected Articles from Orientations 1983–1996*. Hong Kong: Orientations Magazine.

Palmer, S. J. 1967. *Jade*. Prague: Spring Books.

Pearlstein, E. 1993. "Salmony's Catalogue of the Sonnenschein Jades in the Light of Recent Finds." *Orientations* June: 134, Fig. 16d.

Pope, J. n.d. *The Freer Gallery of Art: 1 China*, Tokyo: Kodansha and Freer Gallery of Art.

Rawson, J. 2002. *Chinese Jade: From the Neolithic to the Quing*. Chicago, IL: Art Media Resources.

Salviati, F. 1995. "The Dongxi Collection of Chinese Jades." *Orientations* November: 164, Fig. 1.

Sayer, Chloe. 2002. *Textiles from Mexico*. Seattle, WA: University of Washington Press.

Schoeser, Mary. 2007. *Silk.* New Haven, CT, and London: Yale University Press.

Shanghai Museum: Ancient Chinese Jade Gallery. n.d. Shanghai: Shanghai Museum.

Shanghai Museum: Ancient Chinese Bronze Gallery. 1995. Catalog. London: Scala Books.

So, J. 1993. "A Hongshan Jade Pendant in the Freer Gallery of Art." *Orientations* May: 124–9.

Soffer, O. and J. Adavasio. 1995. "Stone Age Fabric Leaves Swatch Marks." *Science News* May: 276.

Vainker, S. 2004. *Chinese Silk: A Cultural History.* New Brunswick: British Museum Press with Rutgers University.

Wen Fong (ed.). 1980. *The Great Bronze Age of China: An Exhibition from the People's Republic of China.* New York: The Metropolitan Museum of Art and Alfred A. Knopf Inc.

Wormspit. 2007. "Silk Reeling Lao Style." www.wormspit.com/laoreeling.htm accessed June 29, 2007.

Wu, Hung. 1985. "Bird Motifs in Eastern Yi Art." *Orientations* October: 21.

Yang, Boda. 1995. "Jade *Zhang* in the Collection of the Palace Museum, Beijing." *Orientations* February: 141–8.

Zhao, Q. 1989. "On Bi and Cong." *Orientations* May: 65–9.

Zhou, Guoxin. 2006. Crystal Dragon of Taiwan, "Myths, Theories and Explanations." http://www.cdot.org/history/dragon-articles.htm, accessed July 2006, 2009.

The ...etic Fun...tion of C... ...Drawi...s by Sha... ...elly

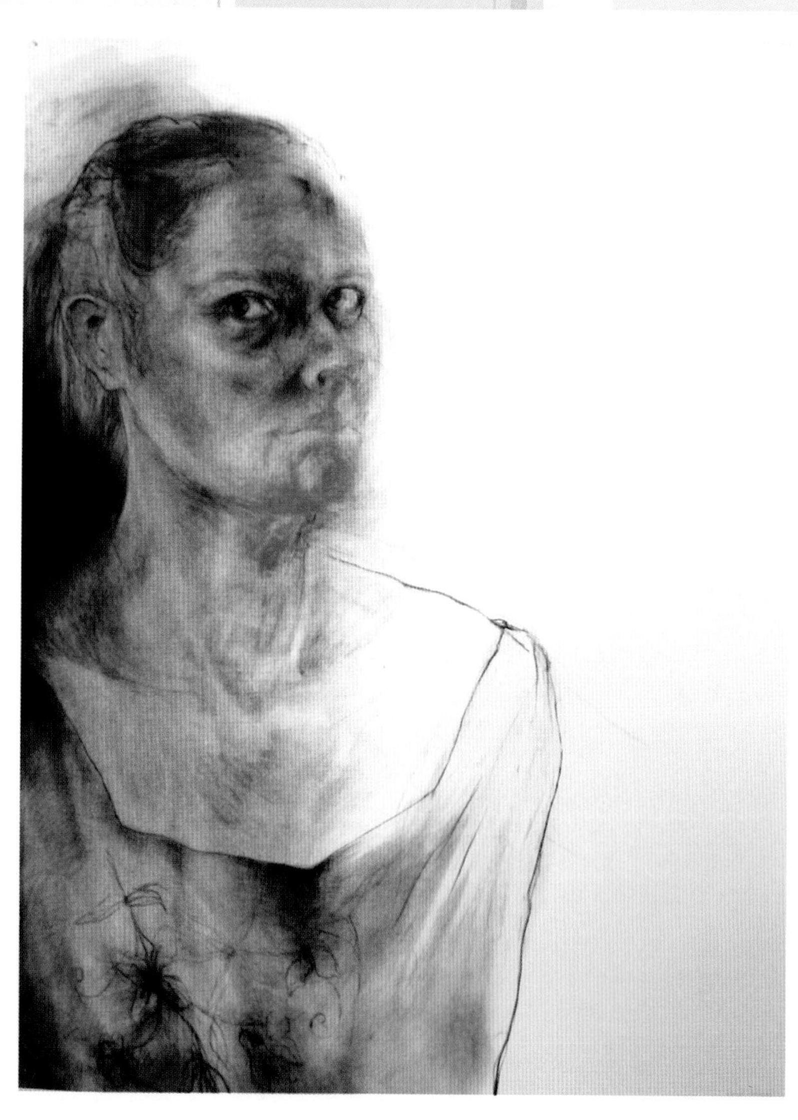

Abstract

Sharon Kelly focused her art practice on charcoal drawings, later adding several video pieces. Her use of cloth ranges from providing a ground for an image to becoming an image, to a trope of a particular state of mind. Pertinent to my inquiry are Wittgenstein's thoughts on use as the hinge for creativity, the use connects us to a complicated network of similarities, overlapping and crisscrossing (Wittgenstein 1953: 66). My proposition is that cloth and garments enter into a variety of relationships with and within the drawings. An active and visually sophisticated response of an artist to textiles brings forth the capacity of a cloth or a garment to convey any or several of the following: identity, expression, gender, age, mood, intent, attractiveness, social status, and even honesty. Applied outside the range of its normal use, the textile does no actual work at all, yet it is not an idle wheel or ornament. The cloth or a garment in Sharon Kelly's art is not subordinated to the art: there is no hierarchy. Rather, the aesthetic function isolates the object from the everyday use and fastens our attention powerfully to it. The fabric transforms itself into a gatekeeper of feeling.

Keywords: charcoal drawings, garments, emotion, memory, portrait

SLAVKA SVERAKOVA

Slavka Sverakova has higher degrees in aesthetics and art history and her research focused on art and architecture of the fifteenth (e.g. H. Bosch) and twentieth centuries (mostly Slovak and Irish artists). She has taught at undergraduate and postgraduate levels for forty-eight years in two different countries and five different universities.

Textile, Volume 7, Issue 2, pp. 204–215
DOI: 10.2752/175183509X460092
Reprints available directly from the Publishers.
Photocopying permitted by licence only.
© 2009 Berg. Printed in the United Kingdom.

The Aesthetic Function of Cloth in Drawings by Sharon Kelly

Preliminary Reflections

- Sharon Kelly, the middle child of Anne and Michael Kelly, was born in Wroughton, Wiltshire, in 1960. She planned to study Geography and German Language, when a series of evening art classes led her to apply to a Foundation Year at the college in Swindon. Having successfully passed the diagnostic year, she chose to study at the Ulster University in Belfast. There she graduated with BA(Hons) in Fine Art and in 1989 in with an MFA.

- Ever since tapestry became too expensive in the fifteenth-century Florence, it moved out of the limelight of art history, leaving the stage free for the fast-developing panel and wall painting. Nevertheless, tapestries not only survived, but achieved successful revival during the twentieth century, with addition of Art Protis as well as the erudite open fiber art, exhibited at the Biennales in Lausanne.

- The motif of textile in paintings or drawings assisted the transformation of an illusion into convincing truth, namely in portraits and biblical stories. Mathis Gotthardt Nithardt, known as Grunewald (1470–1528), mastered the metaphoric power of visual and tactile qualities of fabric to connect to human condition: the elegant polychrome attire of Madonna tells of her splendid role of the Queen of Heavens; the tattered white cloth, in which her baby rests, foretells his secular fate. The so-called Christmas Picture of the Isenheim Altar dated 1515 (Musee d'Unterlinden, Colmar, France) in that way responded to the society aspiring to spiritual and ethical norms. Grunewald's painting became an object of study by Sharon Kelly in her postgraduate year, 1989. The aristocratic attire and the pauper's rag connect to Christian ethics as if in support of Wittgenstein advice "not to look traditionally and dogmatically for one essential core meaning as in common use … but (to) travel with its use … " (Wittgenstein 1953: 66).

- A flag, for example, "travelled" from appearing as itself in the performances of Viennese Actionists, to becoming an illusion of itself in paintings of Jasper Johns (b. 1930). Modernism explored the identifying power of a garment as well as the cloth's malleability for associations with other parts of our culture, or other culture (e.g. installations by Una Walker, b. 1955). Alastair MacLennan (1943) chose a blackened

Union Jack in an installation reflecting on the political history of Northern Ireland.

The Concepts in Kelly's Art Practice

Textile appears to be particularly willing to connect with memory, to the things the mind already knows, and with care.

Joseph Beuys (1921–86) used felt, the fabric that predates weaving and knitting as a mode of protection. While the *Felt Suit*, 1970, simply replicates a useful object and turns it into a relief on the wall, the *Infiltration-homogen for Grand Piano*, 1966, opens the realm of similarities, overlapping and crisscrossing. A concert piano is wrapped in felt with a Red Cross sign on one side. Jonathan Jones (2005) perceives this work as an image of Germany: "The piano is German culture, the heritage of Beethoven, sealed now inside felt, with an ambulance sign … it is the sculptural equivalent of the sanatorium in Thomas Mann's The Magic Mountain." The thought that people neither should evade the past nor be destroyed by it presents wisdom renewed by Germany and Ireland in recent European history. Sharon Kelly translates this need into and over her personal experiences.

The high gloss of the piano surface is both hidden and protected. It is ready to be shipped from a place to place, crossing from one culture, that of the settled well-off household, to a nomadic mode, in some parallel to the story of Beuys being saved by Tartars, wrapping him in felt and fat after they found him in snow. Felt profoundly changes the piano's use. Several musical instruments have an element made of felt; in automotive industry, felt functions as dampener of vibration and barrier for dirt to enter some sensitive bearings. Consequently, the felt offers easy associations with protection and care. The piano wrapped in felt also triggers an association of a sound being trapped inside, akin to our past being trapped in our not so flawless memory. Salient points of similarity between Beuys and Kelly focus on the way a fabric conveys its capacity to protect, remember, heal, and conceal.

While Beuys's piano covered in felt conveys concerns with more than just a personal story, Jim Dine (b. 1935) produced self-portraits of a strange kind in *Bathrobe Series* (1964–2005). It is his bathrobe observed over many years from an almost identical viewpoint, printed or painted in yellow, blue, red, etc. The series of robes (as well as those of hearts, tools, and the Venus de Milo) confirm Dine's conviction that emotional content does not depend on a difference, but on intense observation and excitement with which he records what he observes. As if listening to Wittgenstein's "Don't think but look" (1953: 166), Dine elevated the immediacy of drawing, a paradigm shared by Sharon Kelly.

Evidence offered by the art of Beuys and Dine supports Wittgenstein's shift from concept of meaning as a representation to a view, which concentrates on *"use as the hinge of investigation"* (1953: 43). The capability of aesthetic function to facilitate different meanings for different contexts enhances those hinges of creativity. Jan Mukarovsky (1966[1934]: 26 ff.) proposed the concept of openness, transparency, and all-inclusiveness of aesthetic function as it can attach itself to any object or act in place of any original function that was lost. In practice, it secured the ground for aesthetic experience and aesthetic judgment encompassing intrinsic and instrumental values of art as complementary. The cloth in Kelly's drawings received the immediacy of living energy. In turn it offered back its power to protect, care, heal, reveal, and conceal.

Cloth as a Ground

The first use of cloth in Kelly's drawing is a kind of recycling. In *Confirmation and Denial*, 1989 (Figure 1), Kelly used men's shirts, torn and stretched, placed in front of wrapping or newsprint paper as a ground for charcoal drawings of a partially concealed nude figure. Although this large installation does not exist any more, its two characteristics permeate all subsequent drawings: awareness of fragility of life and deeply held trust in mimesis. Kelly recalled:

> I could not afford expensive materials and worked with quite basic palette (paper, canvas, remnants, wood, clothing, white paint, charcoal, etc). I hardly ever used colour, preferring the natural colour of the material to be evident. The inspiration for these pieces came from both within and from the world around me. Belfast in the late 1980s was a very different place to walk around and to live in. Destruction, decay, and waste were visible everyday. The fragility of life was very much in my mind. I thought about these things very much and about how being in the cocoon of the art college felt against the "outside world"—if you

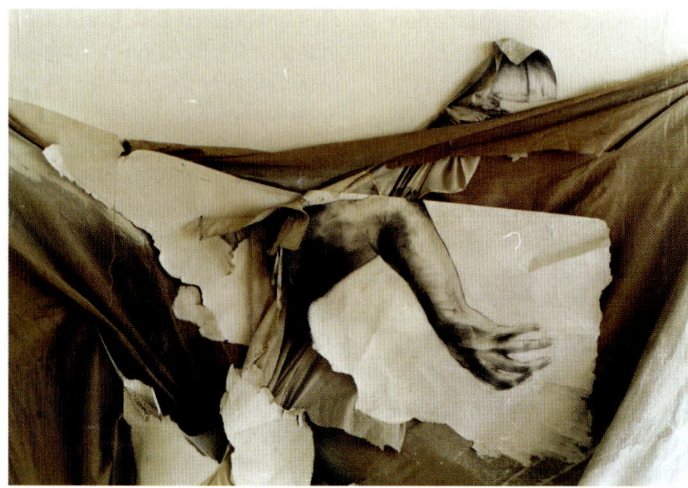

Figure 1
Confirmation and Denial, 1989, mixed media, 10 feet × 10 feet (detail).

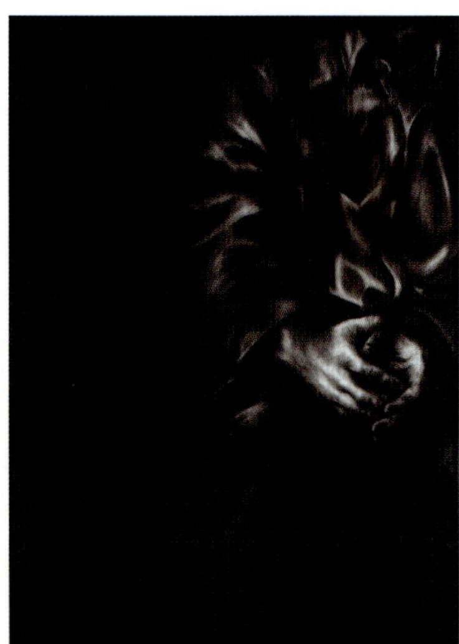

Figure 2
Borne, 1992, charcoal on paper, 143 × 108 cm.

looked out of those large college windows, another world faced you directly and yet some of the things that were being engaged with by some students and staff, during my life as art student made no connection with that world.

On another level, I was creating artwork, destroying its wholeness and fragmenting pieces, creating something else. The process was important. I also played with the idea of 2D and 3D space as these pieces existed on both levels, hovered over, or were torn between spaces. I felt like that myself privately with the life of mother and art student and at the tail end of a very destructive relationship. (Sverakova 2008)

Black Drawings on Black Ground
In 1992 Kelly exhibited eleven charcoal drawings—intentionally made to stay as private as her grief after the deaths of her three newborn children. She changed her mind after the maternity hospital where one of them was delivered had been demolished:

In regard to the later work, there is a strong continuity of subject matter—loss. There is the personal loss, which inspired the work, then there is the communal loss of a hospital and the end of era for the midwifery and other medical staff. I created images, which I hoped would forge a connection outside of my experience of the hospital, which was both positive and negative. I am interested in the layers of personal, universal, beginning, ending, creation, destruction, renewal; the nature of grief and existing. (Sverakova 2008)

Borne, 1992 (Figure 2) and *Woman 5,* 1992 (Figure 3) should be installed facing each other. A somewhat imagined continuity of a space between the two persons stands in a dynamic opposition to the motionless dark grounds.

Headless, faceless seated bodies are stunned by what they know. They muster energy only for a hesitant hand gesture: the palm of one hand supports the back of

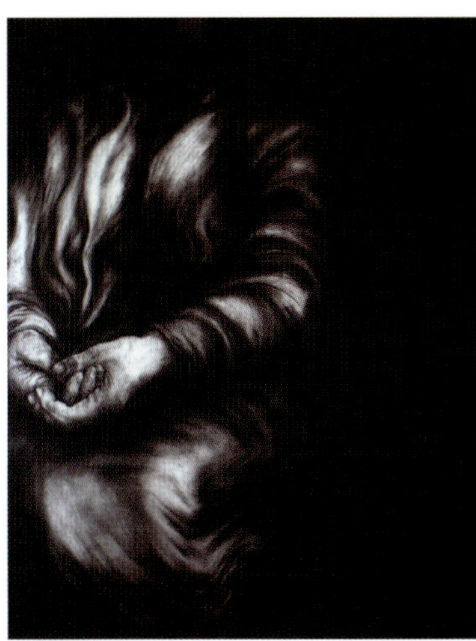

Figure 3
Woman 5, 1992, charcoal on paper,
143 × 108 cm.

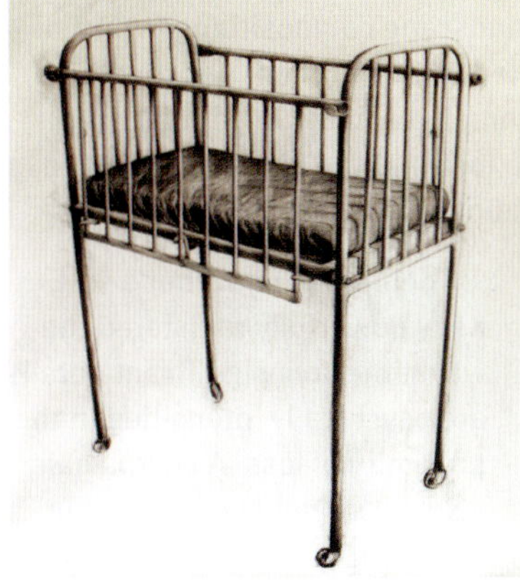

Figure 4
Cot, 2004, pencil on paper, 127 × 153 cm.

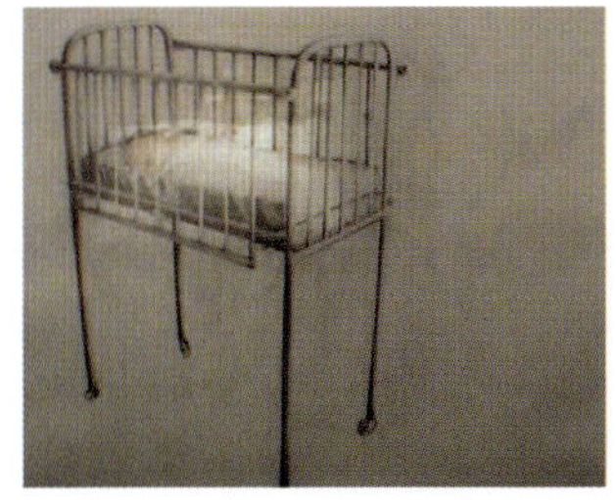

Figure 5
Life Drawing with Polaroid, 2004, still
from a video.

the other hand. Rarely appearing in art, it is a gesture of passive mourning, of the silent phase after the veiling. Both bodies follow a concave curve of a paralyzed empty embrace. Like Sophocles' Ajax, the man and the woman sit quietly without food, without drink, without a sound (Sophocles 324 f.). Their clothes contradict their silence with a visual riot of highlights over softly outlined volumes. The garments were given improbably deep folds next to white highlights to enable the clothes to carry the emotional charge of tragic death. Eloquent light and dark slivers mime the turmoil of a mind injured by the irretrievable loss of life, just touching the edge of madness. The garments are the carriers of screams that the man and the woman cannot make. The images are a direct expression of existential anguish; the drawings are immersed in the never-ending pain of losing an infant to death. The man and woman walk a tightrope between scream and silence.

Portrait and Self-portrait

Kelly made a video of the process of drawing the *Cot,* 2004 (Figure 4), and recorded the sounds of charcoal on paper. The video progresses gradually from a blank sheet of paper to the completed drawing and back to the blank sheet of paper. Once the drawing was completed a Polaroid of Kelly's son, who died soon after birth, was projected over the drawn sheet (Figure 5). The soft fabric accepts the lens-based image not only with grace but also with the force of an illusion. The light dissolves the charcoal drawing of

the fabric, which fuses with the baby's head in a persuasive mass of hope.

Intrinsic to the meaning of my expression is hope. In much of my work light emerges from darkness and sounds punctuates silence. (Kelly 1999)

Pablo Picasso predicted such art in 1934:

It would be very curious to record by means of photographs, not the stages of a picture, but its metamorphoses. Perhaps one would perceive the path taken by a mind in order to put its dream into a concrete form. (Friedenthal 1963: 256)

Kelly commented on her use of linen in *Portrait in Black Dress,* 2004 (Figure 6):

The integration of the body image and the dress that features in the series (and I guess this idea has resonance in connection with the clothing drawings, uniforms, etc.), has to do with memory, very personal—for instance that black linen dress, embroidered with colourful flowers, has been with me for almost 30 years.

I found it in a second-hand charity shop. I believe it was hand-made from a tablecloth, so it has a life history very rich before it was worn by me! Every year I wore the dress through the summer and it is now threadbare and fragile. I was recording it almost by every fibre, feeling it as it hung in my studio, as an act of both joy and defiance at its fading, but also acceptance of this as a law of

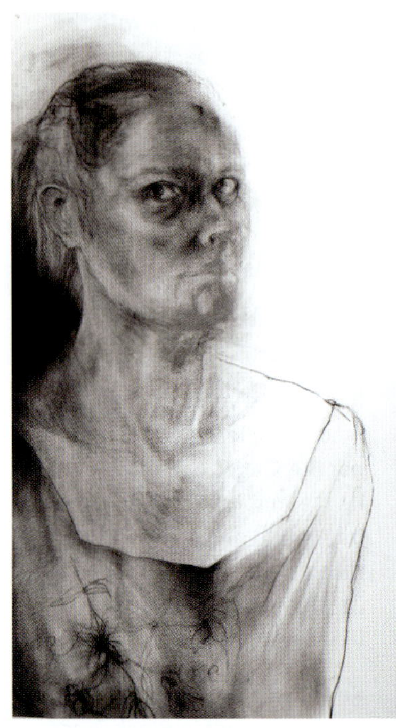

Figure 6
Portrait in black dress, 2004, charcoal
on paper, 76 × 56 cm.

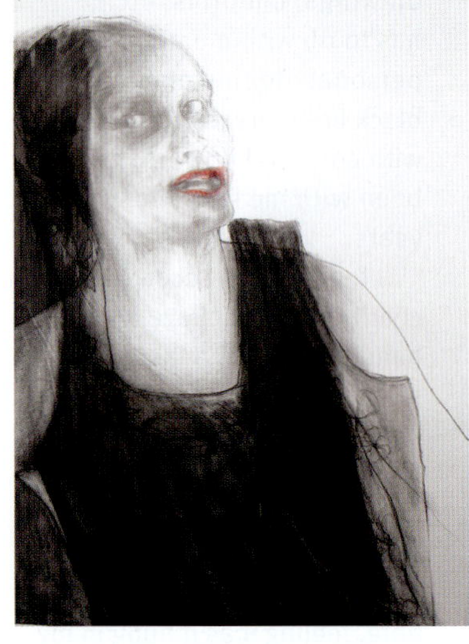

Figure 7
Portrait with red lips, 2004, charcoal on
paper, 76 × 56 cm.

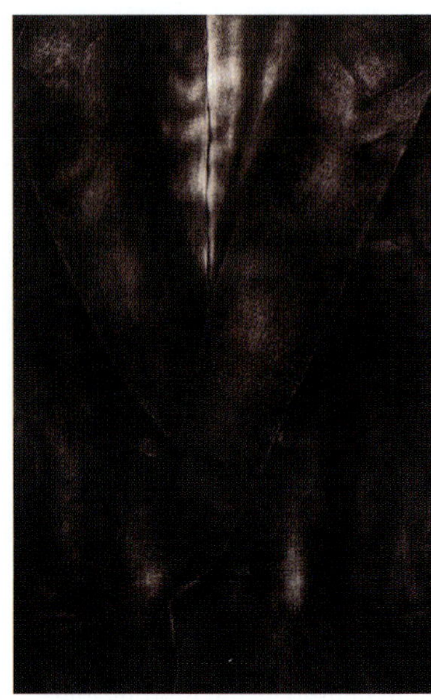

Figure 8
Best Suit, 2000, charcoal on paper,
58 × 36 cm.

life. For the process of drawing the suit and tools of my father after he died, the objects were, at the same time heavy with life/potent with *something* and yet completely inert an object. (Sverakova 2008)

The above contamination of ordinary use with feeling, memory, and reflection manifests the power of aesthetic function to attract and hold our attention. The dress realizes itself through it without contradiction or confusion. The everyday use and this new use coexist fluently, as they have done in all historical portraits. Kelly adds another quality, that of animation of different kind. The dress is the favorite intimate witness to her life story. And it is not narrating, it only announces that it is mute. The gossamer-like fabric works as a visual metaphor for incapacity, particularly in contrast to a black dense area in the *Portrait with red lips* (Figure 7).

The self-portraits integrate the body and the dress in memorable images of self-sufficiency: the artist is the maker, the model, and the observer of Self. The dress determines the gender, age, and mood with moving efficiency.

The Garments

Quite another case of constructing identity is represented by charcoal drawings Kelly made while on residency in Co. Mayo, in 2000. In a response to her father's death, she drew his tools and clothes in compositions akin to a laboratory observation and reminiscent of landscape compositions. A partial view of the garment fills the frame completely inducing our attention to lock into the image. Chris Agee (2004) observed:

> … depicting her father's suit, Kelly powerfully registered the way hitherto insignificant details are psychically intensified in the proximity of loss. A coat, a hair, a smell: somehow, something is there that holds something or someone who is not there, who is nothing. Somehow the not-there—as with mimesis itself—is there.

Best Suit, 2000 (Figure 8), recalls the composition of the torso in *Borne* and *Woman 5* without the volume. The flattened garment, nevertheless, somewhat remembers the body, evoking ambiguity about what is and what is not. Positioned as an insider of the experience in which her drawing is anchored, Kelly aims at a distance from it. The

Figure 9
Flat Sleeve, 2000, charcoal on paper, 28 × 38 cm.

Figure 10
Returning suit IV, 2000, mono/dry point, 28 × 38 cm.

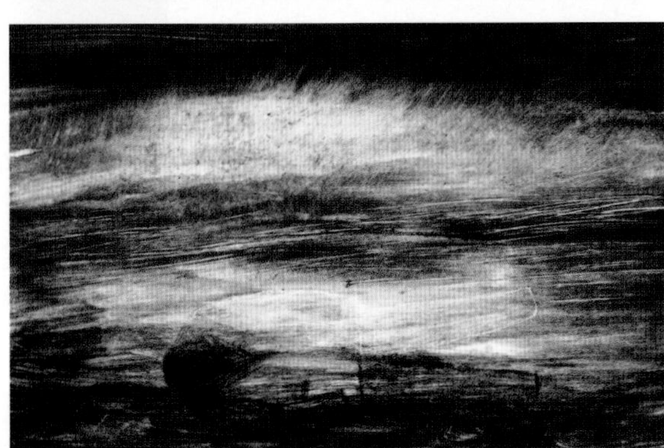

becoming rather than the being acts as a rigorous guardian of the threshold between the personal and universal. The images act as keepsakes, relics to be kept for the sake of the giver, who, often, is not present anymore. A combination of modesty and almost religious belief in the importance of the objects allows the garments, even if fragmented, to become receptacles for memory, love, and respect. Compositions become temporary places governed by restraint that facilitates asymmetries between the focus on and absence of the rest of the garment.

Kelly's residency in Ballycastle, Co. Mayo, sited her observation onto the ocean, the solitary trees,

and sky. In a psychological transfer, this is perceivable in her drawing *Flat sleeve,* 2000 (Figure 9).

The sleeve is composed as a horizon in a landscape, like for example, *Returning suit IV,* 2000 (Figure 10). The transforming power of the metaphor soars to its boundaries in *Long Trousers,* 2000 (Figure 11), the garment is placed where a landscape would have a high sky above a low ground.

After the atmospheric mood in the images of fragments of garments, Kelly developed two different strategies, one dense and focused on material, e.g. *Hood,* 2001 (Figure 12), the other reviving the earlier mode of construction by mimesis juxtaposed with

extreme abstraction. This strategy coincides with garments worn by women or children, e.g. *Bonnet,* 2003 (Figure 13). One part is fully drawn in a delightful illusion, the other is left empty, paraphrasing the dilemma of desire: all or nothing, e.g. *Uniform 1,* 2004 (Figure 14).

The drawings of her father's clothes respect the rough ground of daily use, the man's identity and lifestyle. Death removed the life energy from them grudgingly allowing the mind's desperate search for memories, sensual memories, like touch, smell, and all an eye can remember.

The drawings of garments worn by women and children appear

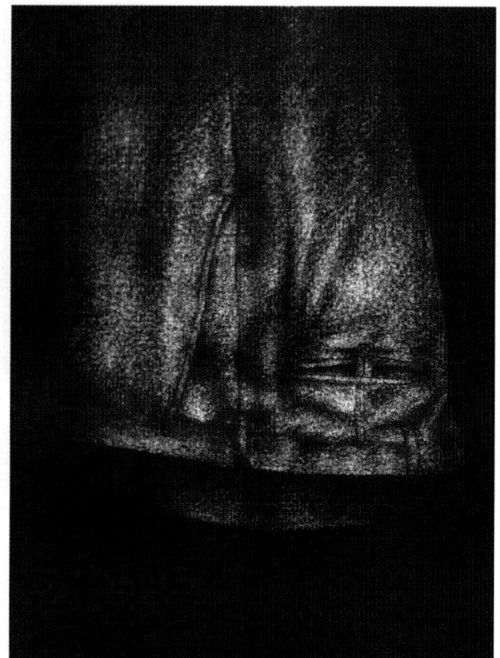

Figure 11
Long trousers, 2000, charcoal on paper,
23 × 16 cm.

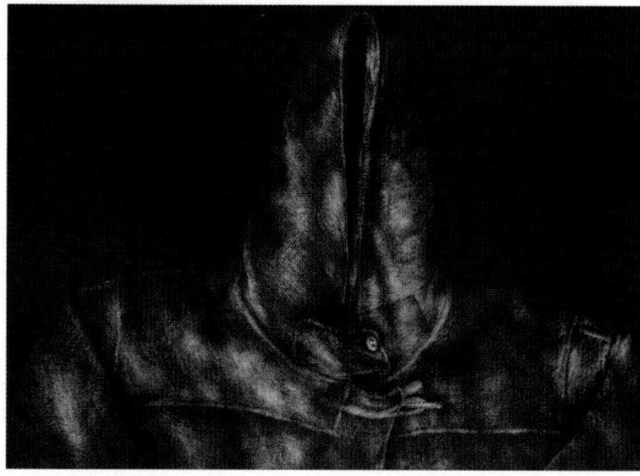

Figure 12
Hood, 2001, charcoal on paper, 56 × 76 cm.

also to suggest a history; however, one that is still pulsating, thus partly still a presence, rather than a remembered past. While a part of the garment is drawn in meticulous illusion, another part is not there at all, areas are empty, bar a whisper of an outline. Neither saved nor condemned, the absent parts actively collaborate with the mimesis as pointers to *memento mori.* As sound needs silence, the perceived and the imagined complement each other. Moreover, the dance-like animation in *Nightgown,* 2003 (Figure 15) tells of graceful reverie or reverts to a desperation of playful loss in *Lost Nightgown,* 2003 (Figure 16).

The garments act as conspirators hiding a body evoking protection and care. The ensuing

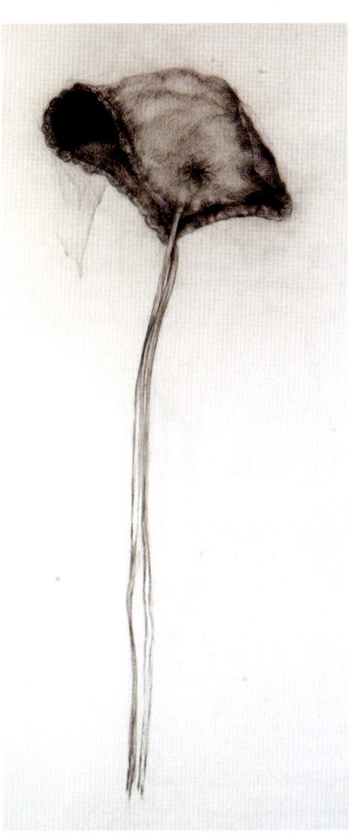

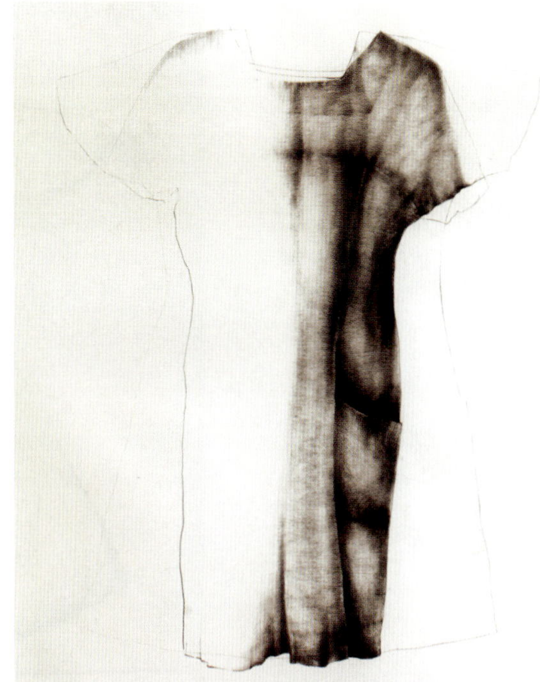

Figure 13
Bonnet, 2003, charcoal on paper,
76 × 56 cm.

Figure 14
Uniform 1, 2004, charcoal on paper, 200 × 95 cm.

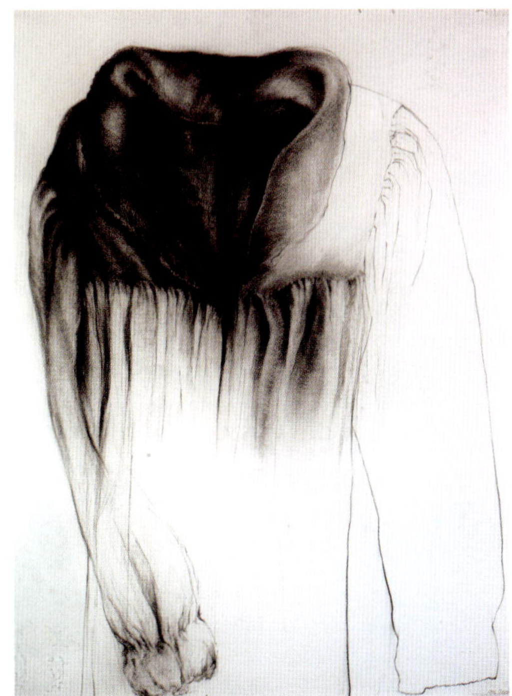

Figure 15
Nightgown, 2003, charcoal on paper,
76 × 56 cm.

Figure 16
Lost Nightgown, 2003, pencil on paper,
19 × 14 cm.

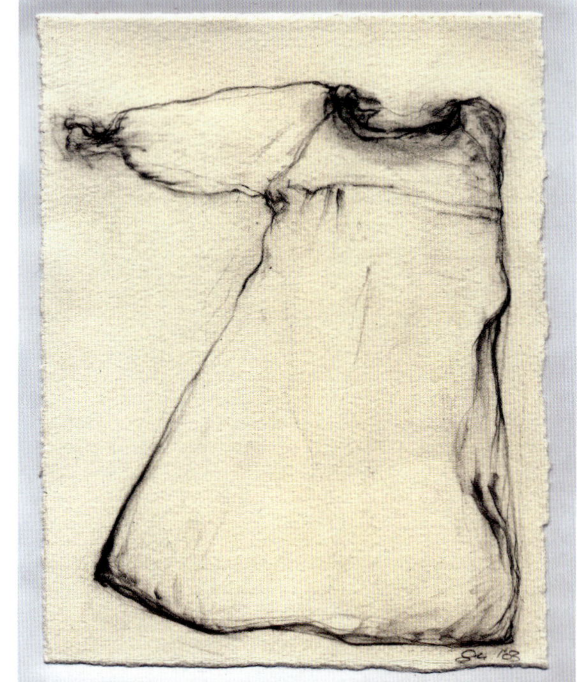

Figure 17
Earth Dress, 2002, charcoal on paper,
76 × 56 cm.

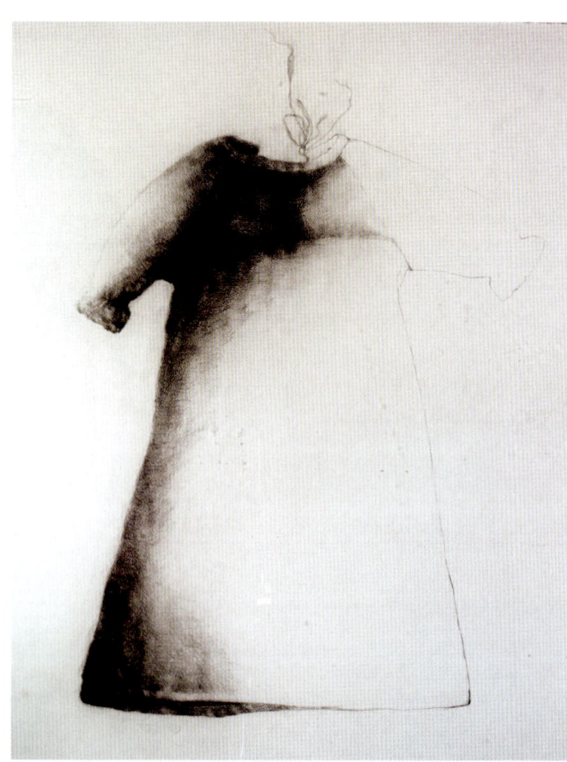

paradox invests both in mimesis and its subversion, the ground is revealed as a confident part of the image. The observer is offered the duty to settle the score between an illusion and reality, between observation and imagination, between a conviction and reverie, a kind of harmony between being and not being, e.g. *Earth Dress*, 2002 (Figure 17). Kelly's art either looks for a wearer while focusing on the garment, or deconstructs the garment to characterize a wearer. Her observation is given the task to present that power of clothes; her imagination turns them then into the gatekeepers for feelings on the path back to living, even living with pain. The becoming is then the threshold between the personal experience and human condition: a spiritual value.

References

Agee, Chris. 2004. "Drawing on Life." In Sharon Kelly, *The Tears of Things*, exhibition catalog. Belfast: Ormeau Baths Gallery.

Friedenthal, Richard. 1963. *Letters of the Great Artists, Vol 2:256*. New York: Random House.

Jones, Jonathan. 2005. "Wounds of History." *The Guardian*, January 29, *Features and Reviews*: 16.

Kelly, Sharon. 1999. In Lynda Joy Sperling (ed.) *Out of Belfast*, p. 38. Granville, OH: Denison University Art Gallery.

Mukarovsky, Jan, 1966[1934]. *Studie z estetiky*, Prague: Odeon. (Trans. M. E. Suino as *Aesthetic Function, Norm and Value as Social Facts*, Ann Arbor, MI: University of Michigan, 1970).

Sverakova, Slavka. 2008. "Slavka Sverakova interviews Sharon Kelly by email February–April 2008." www.recirca.com/articles/2008/sk.shtml, April 9, 2009.

Wittgenstein, Ludwig. 1953. *Philosophical Investigation*. Trans. G. E. M. Anscombe. Oxford: Basil Blackwell.

The Interpretation of Sartorial Boundaries, Systems and The Transmission in Clothing and Domestic Textiles, c.18[...]39

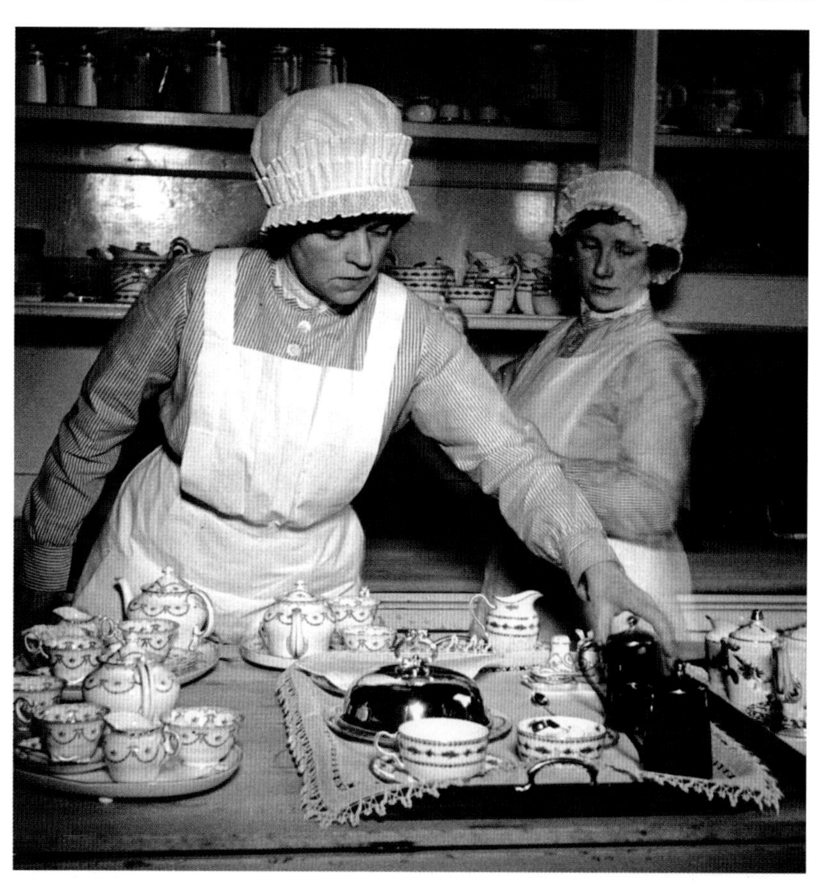

Abstract

This article examines the surface qualities of textile objects in the 1880 to 1939 period, analyzing representations and descriptions of both highly finished and maintained textile surfaces, and degraded and ill-maintained garments. It is argued that the finishing techniques applied in manufacture were carefully replicated in domestic processes, and that qualities of surface and finish in textiles were important both materially and symbolically in the stratified social systems of late nineteenth- and early twentieth-century Britain. Theoretical insights from Julia Kristeva and Mary Douglas are used to understand the meanings of textile objects in use and wear, in their relationship to the bodies that wore them, and in the processes of maintenance to which they were subjected.

Keywords: textiles, surface, finishing processes, boundaries, social history

VICTORIA KELLEY

Victoria Kelley studied at the Victoria and Albert Museum and Royal College of Art. She coordinates staff research and research degrees at the University for the Creative Arts in Rochester, UK. Her book *Soap and Water – Cleanliness, Dirt and the Working Classes in Victorian and Edwardian Britain* is forthcoming (I. B. Tauris, London, late 2009).

Textile, Volume 7, Issue 2, pp. 216–235
DOI: 10.2752/175183509X460100
Reprints available directly from the Publishers.
Photocopying permitted by licence only.
© 2009 Berg. Printed in the United Kingdom.

The Interpretation of Surface: Boundaries, Systems and Their Transgression in Clothing and Domestic Textiles, *c.*1880–1939

Introduction

> Historical reference in dress has never been about evolution, continuity ... In dress, surfaces float free of their histories ... Curating is like creating a new grammar, new patterns of time and reference ... Unlike language, but more like the multiple meanings of a pack of tarot cards, objects can be read back to front and side to side.
> (Clark 2004: Preface)

Thus writes Judith Clark, historian and curator of fashion. This statement is indicative of a way of thinking about fashion, its history, and its contemporary practice, that emphasizes bold leaps of imagination, recognizing the way that fashion as a principle raids the past for visual and conceptual inspiration, breaking history from chronology. The *Spectres* exhibition at the Victoria and Albert Museum (curated by Clark) used the image of a baffling system of turning cogs bringing old styles and modern reinventions and innovations into constantly changing alignments (Clark 2004), and Ulrich Lehmann has used the image of the *tigersprung*, the "tiger's leap" back into the past, as a symptom of fashion's relation to the past in the modern period (and, in the process, has claimed for fashion a role at the center of modernity) (Lehmann 2000). This image has also been taken up by Caroline Evans in *Fashion at the Edge*, her influential work on the complicated interaction between contemporary fashion and its many pasts (which formed the theoretical basis for the *Spectres* exhibition). Evans explores the ways in which, in recent fashion, "the distinction between past and present is almost imploded" (Evans 2003: 13).

I have no quarrel with any of the arguments presented by Clark, Lehmann, or Evans; quite the contrary. If we think of Clark's "histories" as historical genealogies, the transmission of influence in the stylistic or even conceptual form of garments, and their representation in the fashion image, then historical returns and references are indeed intricately complicated and convoluted, looped, and twisted. However, "histories" in fashion, dress or textiles, could also mean the *particular history of a particular garment in use and wear*. How has it been worn, and by who? How many times has it been dirtied and washed? Has it been ripped, torn, or frayed? Has it been mended, and what other maintenance techniques has it been subjected to? Looked at from this perspective, which concentrates more on use than on design, and on material qualities rather than representation, garments—fashionable or unfashionable—and indeed textile objects more generally, do have very particular and not at all free-floating histories. These histories are directly inscribed upon their *surfaces*, and determined by influences from without (the world around) and within (the body of the wearer).

As editorials and articles in various issues of this journal and others make clear, the fields of textiles, dress, and fashion (their histories and theories) are closely connected and intersecting in concerns and approaches (Barnet 2003; Honeyman and Godley 2003; Palmer 1997; Styles 1998). Variously influenced by business and economic history (emphasizing changes in production), by museology (stressing the *object* of study), and by cultural studies (concerned primarily with systems of representation) the three fields have nonetheless made many attempts to meet and communicate: an increasing attention to the material qualities of objects is common to all three. This article has commenced with reference to literature that is closely allied to fashion history and theory, because the concerns of all the authors cited has a clear relationship to the subject matter of this article; textile objects in their relationship to time and its effects. However, this study takes the subject into territory that fits comfortably into a wider

historiographical context, spanning approaches sympathetic to textiles, dress, and fashion. The main emphasis is on materiality (though it is recognized that sometimes materiality can only be approached through representation), materiality that is the result of both production techniques, and everyday techniques of maintenance. What are the social meanings of these techniques, and of worn and dirty, clean and pristine, textiles?

In 1903 novelist and journalist Jack London published a book called *The People of the Abyss*, based on an undercover investigation into poverty in the East End of London. The author describes his "descent" into the "abyss," a process commencing with the buying of a set of clothes from a second-hand dealer: "a pair of stout though well-worn trousers, a frayed jacket with one remaining button, a pair of brogans which had plainly seen service where coal was shovelled, a thin leather belt and a very dirty cloth cap" (London 1903: 9, 11). London notes the fact that these clothes had belonged previously to what he calls "other and unimaginable men" (London 1903: 11). The phrase evokes the fact that these second-, third- or fourth-hand garments had a (somewhat mysterious) history, its traces eloquently marked upon their surfaces in a pattern of dirt and decrepitude.

Just as eloquent is a photograph, taken in the 1930s by Bill Brandt (see Figure 1). The garments depicted here (the maid's cotton dress and apron and fine lawn cap) are as extreme in their material, surface qualities as those London describes (here these qualities are mediated through the lens and

the photographic print rather than written description). The *absence* of fraying, wear, dirt, and dust in this photograph are not merely incidental qualities of clothes that are newer than London's; rather, there is a deliberate strategy of surfaces operating here. The way that the sleeve of the woman's dress creases crisply at the elbow implies starch, the apron appears to have a sheen produced by glossing or glazing, and the cap, with its precise and stiff ruffles, would have taken starch, considerable skill with a goffering iron, and a significant investment of time, to achieve. The shine of the tea set and the silver dish-cover reinforce the impression that this image depicts a social system in which the highly finished surface was imbued with considerable significance. As Pennina Barnet has noted, in the very first issue of this journal, "the meaning and value attributed to qualities of surface can vary'" (Barnet 2003: 3); it is the material, surface qualities of textiles and textile objects, their production, the influences that degrade them, the attempts made to maintain them, and their socially variable meanings, that I intend to explore in this article.

In pursuing such a subject, I turn to a very literal everyday chronology of wear and tear and maintenance in fashion and textiles that may seem somewhat prosaic in comparison to the dizzying conceptual somersaults identified in the work of Clark, Evans, and Lehmann, with their turning cogs and tiger's leaps. However, I would counter any accusation that this research is too plodding and pedestrian by saying that the subject matter I will describe—the finishing and refinishing of surface qualities in response to damage

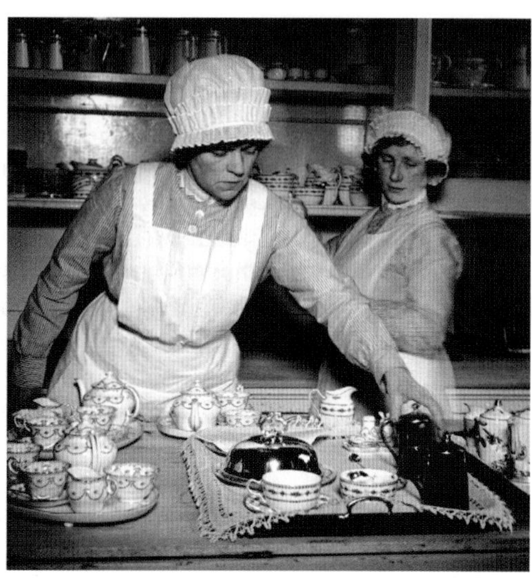

and dirt—also, like cogs and leaping tigers, brings the past and the present into interesting juxtapositions and confrontations. The decay that time and use visit upon textile objects is insistent and inexorable, while resistance to it in the work of cleanliness and maintenance is both heroic and ultimately futile, patterned by repetitions and cyclical procedures, and inevitably, at the period in which I am interested, associated with class status and difference, and with strictly gendered domestic labor. These issues are intimately connected to the body; clothing and domestic textiles such as bed linen or table linen are marked by their direct contact with the body and its functions; what might these marks, and the strenuous efforts made to remove them, mean? In Simone de Beauvoir's words, "washing, ironing, sweeping, ferreting out rolls of lint from under wardrobes—all this halting of decay is also a denial of life" (de Beauvoir 1993[1949]: 474). Might we say that it is equally a denial of *death*? "Reflection on dirt involves reflection on the relation

of order to disorder, being to non-being, form to formlessness, life to death," is the rather more open formulation of anthropologist Mary Douglas, a statement that suggests very strongly the ambivalence of everyday battles to maintain and keep clean textile objects (Douglas 1991[1966]: 5–6). The struggle could be characterized as either heroic denial *or* futile celebration of life *or* death, indicative of a resistance to embodiment, or alternatively of solicitous care for the sensual body.[1] It should be apparent by now that I am interested in the textile object not as a static museum piece, but as a material *possession* that is subject to *process*. Process, in terms of the effects of decay, has received a certain amount of attention in the study of material culture in recent years (see for instance deSilvey 2006). What I wish to examine here is process, or rather a set of processes, that involves decay but also its deliberate reversal, so that textile objects can slide rather dramatically back and forth between dirty/worn and clean/maintained states, at the volition of their owners, although the long-term tendency, however protracted, will always be towards disintegration. One of the virtues of this approach is that it allows a full consideration of agency in the relationship between people and things.

A brief note on methodology and sources: as my two initial examples (Jack London's written description and Bill Brandt's photograph) indicate, this article is fueled by the contrasts between the two extremes of this subject. On the one hand are dirt and dereliction, and on the other cleanliness and maintenance. The first is found in a literature on poverty, homelessness, and tramp life, and photographic representations of this subject matter, and the second in household advice literature, which sets out didactically the complex techniques and rituals involved in the domestic maintenance of textile and other surfaces, as well as analogous visual evidence. Although much of my material in this initial exploration is thus rather polarized, I would like these extremes to suggest also the many gray areas and gradations that lie in between. Yet the fact that extremes are prominent in historical evidence suggests a fascination, in the period under discussion, with both the pristine and the degraded surface that may have social, and perhaps psychological, significance. To explore this more fully, I will turn in later sections to the theoretical constructs of both Mary Douglas and Julia Kristeva.

Wear and Tear in Contemporary Textiles

Ever since Rei Kawakubo first sent a (carefully and deliberately) holed and frayed jumper down the catwalk in Commes des Garçons' first Paris catwalk show in 1981 (Kawamura 2004: 199–200), high fashion has been alert to the possibilities of decay and degradation as an aesthetic strategy. Arguably this high fashion approach was inspired by the punk subculture that arose in the second half of the previous decade, in which the ripped and torn garment became the badge of a crude (and some would say crudely playful) nihilism (Arnold 2001: 24). In the decades since, this strategy has reappeared in many different forms, from the 1980s street fashion for jeans worn through at the knee, to Hussein Chalayan, Martin Margiela, Alexander McQueen, and others' sophisticated explorations of the many ways in which the non-pristine surface can represent echoes of mortality, morbidity, and nostalgia. It has helped to fuel an ever-growing interest in vintage clothes, and the phenomenon of "new vintage," new clothes that look old (Cronberg 2006; de la Haye and Dingwall 1996; Evans 2003; Palmer and Clark 2004).[2]

This use of imperfect, worn, old or old-looking textiles has been associated with a wider strategy of "deconstruction" in fashion, gathering pace into the late 1980s and early 1990s (Arnold 2001: 25–6). As well as being subjected to artificial processes of wear and tear that break them down from a perfect "finished" state, garments have also been deliberately left unfinished, have had their usually hidden constructional elements turned to the outside and exposed, or have been created through the reassemblage of preexisting textiles or garments. The term deconstruction in fashion derives from a philosophical trend largely inspired by the work of Jacques Derrida, which in turn has been associated with a broad cultural climate of "postmodernism" (Gill 1998). Although today the coherence or validity of postmodernism as a generally applicable cultural critique is open to question (Norris 1993: 18, 145–52), the use of distressed textiles in a playful, ironic or knowing manner to imbue garments with layers of meaning and a sense of complex historical quotation still continues. Caroline Evans has labeled this practice "dereliction" and, as already mentioned, it informs her analysis of a fashion system in which the past always returns to haunt the present (Evans 2003).

This deployment of the worn textile surface as a form of historical quotation is not, however, what this article is about. The deliberate achievement of a torn, frayed, or distressed look through artificial and accelerated means is very different from the sort of wear and tear that happens as a consequence of everyday life and the duration of time. It might reference the body and its processes, but it is not a direct result of them—rather, a *simulation*. I will concentrate on a historical period when no designer or manufacturer of clothing would ever have dreamed of sending out a garment that was less than pristine in its surface qualities, and when the overwhelming social norm was the assiduous maintenance of surface in textiles.[3] In this context, the degraded surface usually represented just that; degradation, poverty, and destitution. In part, then, I have invoked the recent history of the "postmodern" deconstructed garment in order to clear it away from the space that this article intends to explore: we must forget the "shabby chic" of Margiela or Demeulemeester to understand the rather different, more desperate and more serious, meanings of frayed and torn garments of an earlier period. Yet the two territories are nevertheless related: I would argue that a historical analysis specifically focused on the period immediately preceding the late twentieth century contributes to an understanding of the playful postmodern deployment of dirt and imperfection in fashion, because it is this history that gives modern deconstruction whatever frisson and power it possesses. The *artificially* frayed or worn garment seems "edgy" and interesting, with just a hint of rebellion against social norms, because of the memory of a time when the *authentically* frayed or worn garment signaled poverty and abjection. Yet it is precisely because wear and tear, in our affluent society, no longer have such a meaning, but only a memory of it, that they are able to become aestheticized, sanitized, absorbed into the fashion system rather than posing a threat to it. This, however, is a subtext, in an article that is chiefly concerned with the historically specific meanings of textiles and their surfaces from 1880–1939, a period during which the frayed and worn, or the finely maintained, textile object carried particularly potent cultural meaning.

Wear and Tear, Starch and Polish in Social Context

Although many of the ideas explored in this article could be relevant to other historical periods, both before and after the particular period under analysis here, my declared intention is to produce a watertight analysis for just this one (albeit relatively long) moment in historical time, from the late nineteenth century through to the Second World War. Furthermore, my emphasis is specifically on *British* culture, material culture, and society of this period. What I will say about the importance of textile surfaces is set against the backdrop of a society deeply fissured by minute class distinctions, in which advances in material wealth were dramatic but very unevenly spread across the population, and in which the urban infrastructure was in the process of being renewed, yet only partially, by modernity.

According to many social historians, the late nineteenth century was the period when notions of class emerged in Britain in their modern form (Harris 1993: 6–11); despite structural changes into the twentieth century, and particularly the growth of the middle class, the existence of acute class stratification went largely unchallenged (McKibbin 1998). What it meant to belong to one class or another was increasingly expressed in material terms. This had long been the case for the upper reaches of society, but as living standards rose (albeit haltingly and patchily) for the working classes too from the late nineteenth century onwards (Boyer 2003), status was increasingly marked out in things owned, and, I would argue, the physical state (old or new, clean or dirty, well-maintained or battered) of these things. The 1880s and 1890s was the period when laundry soap, starch, and "blue" became branded, advertised, mass-market products, increasingly associated with social values (Kelley 2009). Perhaps not coincidentally, it was also the moment when mass-market fashions began to be available and accessible to a wider segment of the population, a trend that continued into the twentieth century (Wilson 2005[1985]: 79). Yet such developments emerged alongside the persistence of serious poverty and deprivation (Boyer 2003). And if small portable consumer goods like soap and fashionable clothes were becoming more common, this was often within a setting of squalid, overcrowded, and decayed housing, the legacy of almost a century of rapid urbanization and industrial growth (Daunton 2000: 31–2). Legislative reform had an impact on housing standards in the pre-1914 period (Daunton 2000: 7), and suburbanization gathered pace into the 1920s and 1930s (although this process was halted in many areas when economic depression brought severe stagnation to the erstwhile industrial heartlands of the country) (McKibbin 1998: 112; Pooley 2000: 436-8). This dirty and decrepit infrastructure, as well as the persistence and even resurgence of serious poverty, influenced the way people felt about the surfaces of their personal possessions. The many social observers and explorers who investigated and documented the material conditions and social mores of the time consistently emphasized the importance of cleanliness and dirt, efforts at maintenance, or the squalor produced by neglect, in their accounts of class structure.

For illustration we can turn to an autobiographical account written by Grace Foakes, a dock laborer's daughter born in London in an East End tenement in the first years of the twentieth century (Foakes 1972,

1975). Early in her account Grace recalls her mother buying a bundle of worn and used baby clothes when a new baby was about to be born (Foakes 1972: 15). By the late 1920s, Grace herself, when her own first child was born, was able to afford to dress her in fine white bonnets trimmed with swansdown. Yet she was distressed by the dirt and soot that stained these bonnets after just a few hours in the smoky atmosphere of her home amongst the Wapping docks (Foakes 1975: 36). A move to a new council estate in Dagenham in Essex brought freedom from the dirt and decay of the inner city (Foakes 1972: 81–2, 1975: 37), and Foakes was able to express her pride and status in the state of the garments she pegged on her line each washing day:

> Each house with its windows gleaming, its lawns neat and trim, its flowers and its trees. This was a clean new town and we were part of it. Our children could play in the garden while we women did our housework and washing, each taking pride as to who could make her whites look the whitest or her coloured clothes the most colourful.
> (Foakes 1975: 40–2)

Foakes and her family left their rented Dagenham home to take on a mortgage in nearby Hornchurch, yet their economic stability was threatened in the precarious economic conditions of the 1930s. Foakes's husband's wages were cut, and when he was injured in an industrial accident he found his earning power further reduced in a competitive labor market, and the family lost their home (Foakes

1975: 58–64). Foakes's experiences demonstrate the tension between material advance and the possibility of a return to poverty that form the particular background to social interpretations of the surface qualities of textiles at this period.

Surface Qualities and the Textile Object

The physical—visual, tactile—qualities of textiles are dependent upon a number of factors, the most important of which are fiber, yarn structure, weave structure, color (created by dyeing the yarn or finished cloth), and pattern (created at the weaving stage by the arrangement of different colored threads, or applied later through surface techniques of printing or other forms of embellishment). However other, less well-known, surface qualities are also important in giving different sorts of textiles their distinctive identities: I am thinking here of the contribution that various *finishing* techniques make to the texture, crispness or softness, body, luster or sheen of textiles. There are a number of evocative industry terms that conjure up the tactile qualities of textiles, examples being "handle" (in other words, what fabric feels like in the hand) and "loft" meaning lightness and fullness: these qualities are imparted by a combination of different factors amongst which surface finishing techniques are of vital importance.

Yet finishing techniques are not generally the subject of conscious scrutiny in the study of either textiles or fashion and clothing: textile historian Mary Schoeser identifies a list of surface treatments that includes "rubberizing, metallizing, waxing, oiling, plasticizing, hot 'de-fuzzing', [and] mercerization" that, she says, have been shown "little attention" (Schoeser 2003: 191–2). I would add to this list more basic and commonplace processes such as bleaching, glazing, fulling, and pressing that contribute a great deal to the characteristics of textiles and garments, but that are not extensively considered in the secondary literature on textiles, and even less so in analyses of historical fashion. As already discussed, where processes overtly concerned with the textile surface are taken note of, it is usually in consideration of particular types of deconstructive finishing in recent and contemporary fashion. Yet historical fashion too owes much of its character to its surfaces: a source from 1899 notes simply that "all classes of fabrics alter in appearance, handle, and firmness of texture in the finishing processes" (Beaumont 1899[1887]: 450). The techniques involved are specific to particular fibers, and immensely varied in their methods and their results (see Figure 2). There are various secondary technical sources on the characteristics of textiles that set out details of fiber, weave structure, etc. in contemporary and historical textiles, and that also deal with surface treatment.[4] There is also a relatively large trade literature dating from the period under discussion here that gives technical details of these processes. (Beaumont 1899[1887]; Edge 1911; Dyer and Calico Printer (the editors of) 1907) This is a large and complex subject and the comprehensive tabulation or description of all textile-finishing processes of the late nineteenth and early twentieth

centuries is well beyond the scope of this article. Here I introduce just a few relatively simple examples, which I hope will be sufficient to establish the importance of surface finish in consideration of textiles.

Both "woolen" and "worsted" fabrics are derived from sheep's wool (the two terms denote broad categories of wool fabric that share certain basic qualities; each group contains within it many subcategories of different sorts and grades of fabric, often denoted by specific names). Despite their common fiber, woolens and worsteds have very different qualities, differences that are heavily accentuated by the finishing processes to which they are subjected. Woolen fabric is soft and bulky, made from yarn quite loosely twisted from short-staple fibers and woven with a plain weave structure (Gioello 1982: 13). It thus contrasts with worsted, which is made from long-staple fibers, assiduously carded to align them along their length, spun with a tight twist and often woven with a twill structure (a weave structure incorporating filling yarns that produce a diagonal pattern), to give a close and hard, rather than soft and bulky, feel (Gioello 1982: 13). Finishing processes have long reinforced these contrasts: while worsteds are often steamed or singed to emphasize the crispness of their surface texture, woolens are "fulled." Fulling involves raising a nap and then shearing it back, a process that can be repeated several times, and results in a thickened, warmer cloth, given extra bulk, as well as softness and a porous quality that contrasts markedly with the tight, hard finish of worsteds (Crowfoot *et al.* 1992:

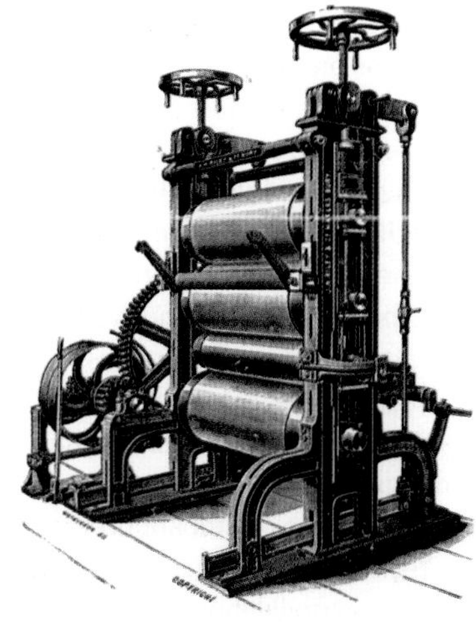

Figure 2
Four Bowl Soft Finish Calendar: "This gives the cloth a nice feel and smooth appearance, but less glaze than the heavier Calenders" (Dyer and Calico Printer (the editors of) 1907).

35–6). Fulling results in the warp and weft texture of the weave being heavily obscured by the nap raised over it: "as a woollen cloth is milled or fulled ... the thready surface which characterizes it on leaving the loom totally disappears ... causing the fabric to resemble a felted rather than a woven production" (Beaumont 1899[1887]: 450). Woolens, due to their softer surface, absorb dust and dirt more easily than worsteds, though worsteds *show* dirt more obviously on their tight surface. Woolens are less durable, becoming threadbare with time, though worsteds, while not actually wearing out so readily, can acquire a shiny look at stress points.

Cotton fabric was also heavily finished. A 1911 source identifies various substances added to the cloth in the final stages of manufacture, from softeners and conditioners (to "insure a smooth mellow feel, and add lustre and closeness of texture") to starches and fillings (able to impart "any particular handle or feel, that may be required") to antiseptics to prevent mildew, and "blue," a mild solution of blue dye that counteracted the yellowing caused by the bleaching the fabric had been subjected to earlier in the process of manufacture (Edge 1911: 20–39). The discriminating use of such finishing processes helped to distinguish different types of fabric, and in addition a range of mechanical processes was employed, often in conjunction with the substances above. These included "scutching," "stenting," "singeing," "beetling," and "calendering," as well as the use of mangles and drying machines (Edge 1911: 85–103). Calendaring was a process also applied to linen, the crisp texture and often lustrous surface of which has traditionally been imparted by the application of heat and weight, through a smooth metal or glass implement, to impart a very particular sheen (Crowfoot *et al.* 1992: 81).

Such finishing processes are intrinsic to the manufacture of textiles; when a garment is subsequently constructed from lengths of new cloth, further finishing processes, and in particular pressing, add again to the surface integrity of the finished object. Yet the qualities that result are very fragile, prone to breaking down or being worn away in everyday use. This fragility is accentuated by the particular use to which garments and household textiles are put, specifically their proximity to both the body and the spaces and places that it inhabits. If textiles are given character by surface, they are also in and of themselves a surface that intercedes between the human body and the world outside it. They absorb from within secreted wastes, and from without the many different sorts of dirt that the external environment produces (in the period of this study this could include many varieties of industrial pollution, mud from the streets, ever-settling dust, and the smoke, soot and smuts of domestic coal fires) (Kelley 2009). And as well as dirt, garments are also a surface vulnerable to being rubbed and worn. Collars are abraded by stubbly chins and necks, socks worn through by rough shoes and sharp toenails, trousers holed in the seat and the knee by the constant pressure of being caught between the body inside and the hard rough surfaces of the external environment.

Yet qualities of finish in textiles, although fragile, can also be replenished or reapproximated.

Each of the industrial processes described above had a domestic equivalent, so that textile objects were constantly subjected to both dirt and wear and to deliberate, strenuous, often highly routinized or even ritualized processes to clean them and refinish their surfaces (see Figure 3). The soft deep pile produced by fulling could be brought back by brushing (which also removed dirt and dust). This technique, used regularly on woolen garments, was advocated in etiquette and household advice manuals and recalled in autobiographies of the time (Ezard 1979: 18; Foster and Walkley 1978: 33). The body, smoothness, and whiteness of new cotton was reapplied by a complex process of starching, blueing, mangling, and/or ironing. Linen was subject to similar treatment, with an added emphasis on glossing or glazing, to bring back its surface luster (Browne 1877: 191–3; Jack 1898). The fact that these replenishments took place in the domestic environment means that in the period under discussion in this article, the performance and results of this work were tangled in complicated ways with issues concerning women's role in domestic labor, and with social position and status.

Textile objects are by their nature "soft," more mutable than many other designed objects, and more vulnerable (partly because of their nature and partly because of the uses to which they are put) to degradation and dereliction. It is necessary at this stage to make a small but important distinction—there are two sets of paired categories intrinsic to this subject matter that I have not up to this moment clearly disentangled. At one end of the scale (the end that could be identified as signaling either newness or strenuous efforts at upkeep) are both *cleanliness* and *maintenance*. Their opposites (being indicative of either age or neglect in textile objects) are *dirt* and *wear*. (For another recent treatment of cleanliness and dirt in the context of textiles, see Klepp 2007.)

While generally the two terms that cluster together at each end of the scale are closely associated, in some respects they operate differently, even contradicting each other, and particularly in the processes concerned with surface qualities. A dirtied cotton shirt, its whiteness spoiled by grime, is washed in order to reassert its pristine color—this is the work of cleanliness. After washing the shirt must also be ironed, to reassert its pristine texture—and this I would describe as the work of maintenance. In some circumstances the processes used to reestablish cleanliness might even interfere with the work of maintaining surface, putting the two principles into opposition. The cotton shirt, while made clean by being washed, will be even more crumpled as a result of the process than it was before, and wool fabric cannot usually be washed at all without running the risk of irreparable damage to its surface qualities. Even with fabrics that can be washed, this method of removing dirt can disrupt surface texture beyond just crumpling it. A series of Persil advertisements from the later 1930s makes this clear. Two young women wear identical checked blouses: "Judy's

blouse is new ... Jane's blouse has been washed dozens of times with Persil ... You can't tell the difference between a new blouse and a Persil-washed blouse ... so next time you're washing your silks and woollies use Persil, and see how soft and new looking it leaves them" (*Picture Post* December 17, 1938: 4). Making the distinction between the two related sets of principles— cleanliness/maintenance and dirt/ wear—makes clear the extent to which the care of textiles in general, but particularly in the period under discussion here, is a complex system. Straightforward functional hygiene (cleanliness pure and simple) is not the only factor that must be considered; the symbolic aesthetic qualities of surface also require attention.

Boundaries, Systems, Abjection, and the Textile Surface

I would like here to introduce some theoretical considerations, in an effort to construct an apparatus that will allow a fuller understanding of the significance of textile surfaces, both in general but specifically for the 1880–1939 period under consideration. Both Mary Douglas and Julia Kristeva have written on the subject of dirt: I will take what they say and apply it to the dirt (and therefore also the cleanliness) of this particular place and period, as well as attempting to think how their ideas might impact upon the closely related but distinct categories of maintenance and wear. The thinking of these two theorists is related; in *Powers of Horror*, the essay in which she established most fully her concept of abjection, Kristeva drew quite

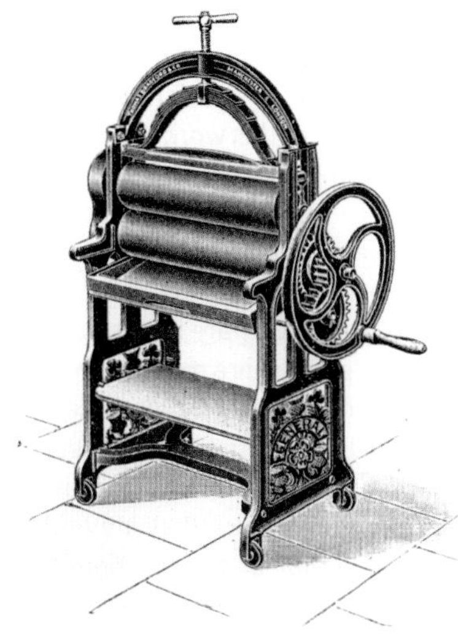

Figure 3
Domestic mangle (Marsh 1914).

heavily on Douglas's work (Douglas 1991[1966]; Kristeva 1982[1980]). However, in the end I will focus on the distinctions between their thought, in making a case for Douglas's approach (that stresses the social context) as being more relevant to this historical study than Kristeva's (that stresses individual or psychoanalytical motivation).

Mary Douglas's work in *Purity and Danger* gives a very useful foundation for understanding attitudes to the practices (and indeed the rituals) that are associated with cleanliness and dirt. The fact that *Purity and Danger* is still so widely cited some 40 odd years after it was first published is testimony to that usefulness. Douglas's intention in *Purity and Danger* (a work that blends anthropology with the comparative study of religion) was to explode what she saw as the myth that "primitive" religions frequently conflate the sacred and the unclean, introducing materials, actions or contacts that they see as unclean into their religious rituals. In the process, Douglas examines issues of purity and contagion, making a very strong case for them as an excellent way into understanding not just primitive religion, but also the "great" religions, and indeed many aspects of secular human society. At the heart of her argument is a consideration of the way that dirt can be defined as part of a *system*, and in turn helps to define that system: "I believe that ideas about separating, purifying, demarcating and punishing transgressions have as their main function to impose system on an inherently untidy experience" (Douglas 1991[1966]: 4). Thus dirt is essentially "matter out of place,"

the category of what is left over once the world has been systematically ordered. Its definition as such is a powerful tool in the construction of cosmologies—ideas about how the world should be. Douglas's emphasis on systems leads her to stress the importance of those boundaries and margins without which no system can function. She further asserts that "all margins are dangerous," as "any structure of ideas is vulnerable at its margins." And she notes the centrality of bodily margins in many of the rituals that build and support social structures in the case study material she considers. Bodily orifices represent the body's margins, and "matter issuing from them is marginal stuff of the most obvious kind" (Douglas 1991[1966]: 122).

Now, is it too obvious to say here that what issues from the body's margins (including that grandly marginal organ, the skin), is usually mopped up by clothing or a textile object of some sort? Joanne Entwistle has attempted, through the methodologies of sociology, to uncover the often neglected *bodily* nature of fashion and clothing, the study of which is frequently dominated by an emphasis on image and representation that de-emphasizes the real body. Entwistle asserts the role that garments play in mediating "the meeting place of the private and the public ... the intimate experience of the body and the public realm" (Entwistle 2000: 7). Clothing covers the body, represents it to the outside world, *and can even stand in for it*—skin and cloth are not infrequently conflated. An example of this is Georges Vigarello's analysis of how, in courtly society in seventeenth-century France, the

wearing of white linen under rich outer clothes represented the skin within, so that the ritualized changing of the linen as it became dirtied by the skin's excretions achieved, both literally and metaphorically, a gesture of cleanliness (Vigarello 1988[1985]: 228).

Julia Kristeva is also concerned with boundaries and margins in her category of the "abject": "it is ... not lack of cleanliness or health that causes abjection but what disturbs identity, system, order. What does not respect borders, positions, rules. The in-between, the ambiguous, the composite" (Kristeva 1982[1980]: 4). Kristeva's motivation is essentially a psychoanalytical one, and she is most concerned with maternity, and the threat to the discrete identity of subject and object posed in the processes of pregnancy and childbirth. Judith Butler characterizes Kristeva's idea of abjection thus:

> The "abject" designates that which has been expelled from the body, discharged as excrement, literally rendered "Other" ... The boundary of the body as well as the distinction between internal and external is established through the ejection and transvaluation of something originally part of identity in a defiling otherness. (Butler 1999[1990]: 170)

And this seems to tally quite clearly with the link already made above between the textile object and the body's dirt. Clothing and household textiles such as bed linen and table linen that also, like clothing, function in intimate contact with the body, are subject to dirt coming from the body within, and this sort of dirt might be said to be *abject* dirt, where what is within the body or of the body becomes without or separate, in which case it immediately seems anomalous and distasteful or even disquieting.

Douglas and Kristeva deal with dirt; they do not make overt reference to worn or torn or frayed garments. Yet I would argue that the ideas discussed above are applicable here too. Just as dirty garments are, to use Kristeva's term, "abject," so too are frayed garments. Clothing is positioned at that vulnerable margin between the world and the body. Qualities of finish preserve the integrity of garments, but once that finish begins to break down, even if dirt is removed, abjection still lingers. This is the case with crumpling and creasing, and even more so with fraying, that reveals the textile structure beneath the finish even as that structure of warp and weft begins to disintegrate. *Systems* are broken down and time is allowed in. Boundaries are damaged. This dissolution of system is made all the more obvious because textile objects are so systematic in their construction: "weaving can be described as a sort of soft-engineering, with its system of warp and weft comparable to the binary code of modern computer programming" (Robertson 2005: 299). It only takes one broken thread for the integrity of the whole object to be threatened in a process of unraveling. It has already been noted that recent and contemporary designers play with references to wear and frays. While the frays may be physically "real" (though artificially achieved), the dirt that often accompanies wear is more judiciously handled, and the

citation of human waste products, in particular, is avoided. The "abjection" of dirty garments still retains some of its ability to provoke disquiet.

Are Douglas and Kristeva's ideas a good basis for understanding the extreme attention to textile surfaces (distaste at the dirty and degraded, fanaticism in pursuit of the clean and pristine) that seems to be a characteristic of the 1880–1939 period? I would argue that, for all the psychological drama of Kristeva's approach, Douglas is the more useful in this context. She deplores the fact that many interpreters, when looking at religious ritual, have jumped from any ceremony that involves the body, to a concentration on the individual (taking "body" to mean "individual") and thus have turned to psychoanalytical rather than social explanations for what they observe. Douglas makes this point quite snippily ("public rituals enacted on the human body are taken to express personal and private concerns. There is no possible justification for this shift of interpretation just because the rituals work upon human flesh"; Douglas 1991[1966]: 116). Yet this does not seem to have deterred Kristeva from doing what Douglas warns against, using Douglas as one of the springboards for her psychoanalytical approach. For the period under discussion here, to follow Douglas into a consideration of the social meanings of the clean and dirty, maintained or worn textile surface does seem to match the evidence on offer better than Kristeva's thinking, despite the aptness of Kristeva's "abjection." I return here to Jack London, cited in the introduction: London describes his reaction to the rough, dirty clothes of his disguise in social terms, not personal ones. He is more interested in the way these clothes make others see him than in the way they make him feel, and particularly refers to the way his disguise allows him to move across class boundaries:

> No sooner was I out on the streets than I was impressed by the difference in status effected by my clothes. All servility vanished from the demeanour of the common people with whom I came in contact. Presto! in the twinkling of an eye, so to say, I had become one of them. My frayed and out-at-elbows jacket was the badge and advertisement of my class, which was their class. It made me of like kind, and in place of the fawning and too-respectful attention I had hitherto received, I now shared with them a comradeship. The man in corduroy and dirty neckerchief no longer addressed me as "sir" or "governor". It was "mate", now—and a fine and hearty word, with a tingle to it, and a warmth and gladness, which the other term does not possess. (London 1903: 12–13)

Writing 30 years later, George Orwell, in *Down and Out in Paris and London*, was remarkably consistent with this approach: the stated primary objective of both Jack London and Orwell in their adventures with poverty was to understand society, and not to investigate themselves (Ingle 2006: 47–8). Like London, Orwell, as part of his experiment in living amongst the lowest strata of society, swapped good clothes for worn and dirty ones at the shop of an old clothes dealer:

> The clothes were a coat, once dark brown, a pair of black dungaree trousers, a scarf and a cloth cap. I had kept my own shirt, socks and boots, and I had a comb and razor in my pocket. It gives one a very strange feeling to be wearing such clothes. I had worn bad enough things before, but nothing at all like these; they were not merely dirty and shapeless, they had—how is one to express it?—a gracelessness, a patina of antique filth, quite different from mere shabbiness. (Orwell 2003[1933]: 137)

Orwell's initial reaction was to record how these clothes, with their distasteful patina, provoked in him a sense of "shame," so that he felt "genuinely degraded" (Orwell 2003[1933]: 138). Yet, like London, he quickly linked this to the social perceptions of those around him, and he also, like London, described how ordinary men on the street now called him "mate" (Orwell 2003[1933]: 137).

Surfaces and Social Distinction

In the particular historical moment with which this article is concerned, a Britain characterized by economic and social inequality in which boundary maintenance and status were heavily emphasized, Douglas's ideas seem particularly applicable, and perhaps help to explain an emphasis not just on functional cleanliness in textile objects, but also a semi-ritualistic attachment to highly finished surfaces. This pursuit of the pristine surface demanded both time and labor, and was thus both directly and indirectly dependent on economic capital. Its reverse was the particular degradation and shame reported by or on behalf of those whose economic and social resources did not allow them to participate in the maintenance of surface.

The period with which I am concerned was thus a period when the surface was invested with enormous social and symbolic importance. To wear clothes whose surfaces were decrepit or neglected was an eloquent sign of poverty and despair. I have already cited George Orwell's *Down and Out in Paris and London*: throughout this account of poverty-stricken life in the 1930s, Orwell makes frequent reference to worn and dirty garments and textiles; worn collars, frayed trousers and out-at-elbow coats, holed socks, leaking shoes, and sheets gray and stinking from long use and lack of washing (Orwell 2003[1933]: 20, 26, 28, 32, 36, 51, 177, 198). Orwell also describes his friend Boris, an unemployed waiter in Paris. At the point at which we meet him, Boris is destitute and has recently been homeless. However, the chance of a job drives him to extraordinary efforts to disguise his ragged state, to the extent of inking in the flesh revealed by the holes in his socks, to give at least a surface impression of social and economic competence (Orwell 2003[1933]: 28).

At the opposite end of the cleanliness/maintenance and dirt/wear scale is F. L. Calder and E. E. Mann's school textbook, *Elementary Laundry Work*. This source demonstrates what might almost be described as fanaticism for the pristine surface, in, for instance, a section that outlines the complex processes necessary to the washing and finishing of table linen and "body linen" (undergarments and shirts). I briefly outlined this process earlier, but it is worth here revisiting its complexity, and the way in which it is didactically prescribed. The steps outlined include not just washing and drying but also meticulous finishing processes: cleanliness is important, but beyond this, actions are specified that are concerned with achieving a certain surface texture and integrity. The addition of "blue" to the final rinsing water to counteract the yellowing produced by the use of soap is demanded, as is starch to restore the crispness of the fabric, with a stronger or weaker solution recommended depending on the nature of the article and the effect required (Calder and Mann 1891). After drying and ironing, the final step these authors describe is an arduous glazing process, repeating at home a professional manufacturing technique:

> When plainly ironed lay the article on the table right side up, and rub over smoothly with a damp rag. Take a bright and well-heated polisher or glossing iron and rub over the surface to be polished, leaning heavily, and rubbing backwards and forwards over a small surface, till the desired brightness is obtained ... the finer the linen the more brilliant the gloss.
> (Calder and Mann 1891: 58)

And other advice books of the period recommend similarly labor-intensive processes in the washing and "'getting up" of cotton summer dresses, for instance (Calder and Mann 1891; Jack 1898). Women's linen or cotton "washing dresses," men's white shirts and their stiff detachable collars, maids' caps and aprons, babies' frocks, and girls' pinafores

from the late nineteenth or early twentieth centuries all demanded work and skill in the maintenance and replenishment of their surface qualities (Foster and Walkley 1978). And although in the latter part of this period changing fashions and the introduction of new synthetic fabrics were beginning to counter some of the stiffness of the Victorian and Edwardian aesthetic, in comparison to later periods an emphasis on hard-won finish remained predominant (Handley 1999: 30–50; Wilson 2005[1985]: 40–3). In the present day, we are habituated to easy-care fabrics, soft jerseys, and crease-resistant synthetic blends. Contemporary fashion embraces the soft, the unstructured, and the informal, borrows from work-wear, and has learned from deconstruction the aesthetic possibilities of wear and benign neglect. From this perspective, it is easy to overlook the labor involved in the maintenance of textiles to a more exacting standard of perfection.

The importance attached to such perfection is reinforced when we examine the ways in which representations of clean or dirty, maintained or worn garments are woven into the moral discourses surrounding poverty and wealth. Orwell (and Jack London) described, in reasonably dispassionate terms, worn and dirty clothing as a material sign of poverty and despair. Yet the contrast between ragged, dirty poverty and sleek, clean prosperity had already been used many times before this as a consciously manufactured cliché in stories of redemption from destitution. A well-known example is cited by photographic

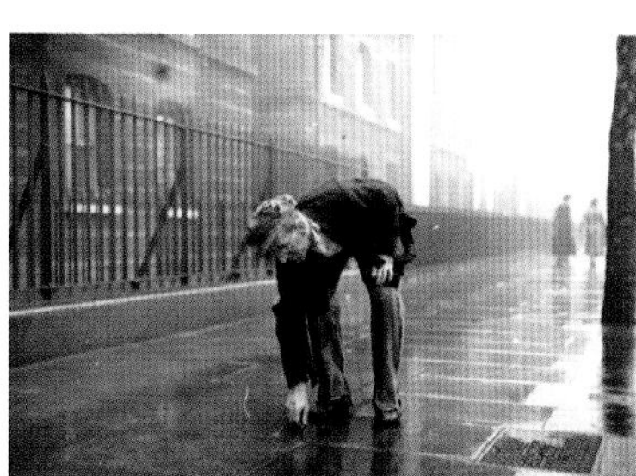

Figure 4
Photographer unknown, "The Salvation Army" (*Picture Post* December 10, 1938). © Getty Images.

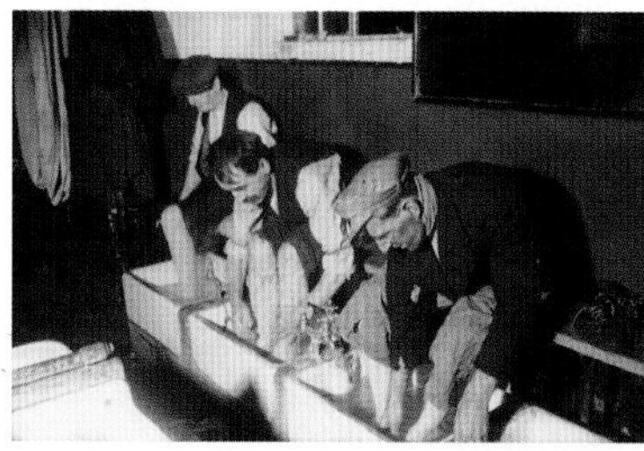

Figure 5
Photographer unknown, "The Salvation Army." Bill Smith is the figure on the right: the caption explains how "the first thing a man does on entering a Salvation Army hostel is to have a thorough wash with hot water and soap" (*Picture Post* December 10, 1938). © Getty Images.

historian John Tagg: in the 1870s Thomas Barnardo used faked before-and-after photographs of homeless children given shelter in his children's homes, deliberately exaggerating their transformation from dirt-smeared, ragged urchins into neat and cared-for objects of Victorian philanthropy (Tagg 1993: 83–5). Continuing in this long tradition is a photo-story from *Picture Post* magazine from 1938. An article about the Salvation Army is illustrated with the story of one Bill Smith, staged as a narrative of redemption in 14 frames, and looking suspiciously as though it has been posed from start to finish (see Figures 4 and 5).

Smith is shown initially as a homeless, jobless derelict dressed in ragged clothes. He is pictured as he is taken into a Salvation Army hostel, shaved, bathed, and given new clothes, food, and a bed with clean sheets. He joins in evening prayers, and "after a week or two … the brigadier succeeds in finding him a job." Frame 14 shows Smith, wearing a new suit, walking away from the hostel down the street: "and now, built up in health, decently dressed, and with confidence restored, Bill Smith goes out to his new job—one of more than 100,000 men for whom the Salvation Army finds work in a year" (*Picture Post* December 10, 1938: 25–32).

These last two examples are photographic representations: using photographic evidence compounds and complicates the issue of surfaces in some potentially interesting ways, because photographs are themselves a surface, and one that can be consciously manipulated. I cited Bill Brandt's photograph of servants at the outset: many other photographs by Brandt suggest strongly that he was interested in surface qualities (textile and other) and their implication in the social contrasts and peculiarities he depicted as an émigré photographer in Britain in the 1930s. Raymond Mortimer, in his introduction to Brandt's 1936 book of photographs, *The English At Home*, described Brandt as both an artist, with "the artist's faculty for being surprised and excited by things other people would not notice," and an anthropologist, who "seems to have wandered about England with the detached curiosity of a man investigating the customs of some remote and unfamiliar tribe" (Mortimer 1936: 4). Photographs such as Figure 1 indicate a complex engagement with the interactions between the material and the social worlds (although Brandt was by no means interested in a simplistic or polemical portrayal of the contrasts between wealth and poverty) (Lifson 1989: 264–5). Yet the "descriptions" of surfaces that Brandt's photographs contain have qualities that are dependent as much upon darkroom processes as upon the material objects that Brandt photographed. Despite the clarity and precise detail of Figure 1, Brandt preferred many of his prints to be "dark and muddy," and many of his photographs of this period, especially as they appeared printed quite cheaply in periodicals such as *Picture Post*, have a grimy quality about them (Warburton 1999: 319). The fact that not all of his photographs portray surface detail so deliberately would seem to suggest that in Figure 1, Brandt deployed polish and shine consciously, almost rhetorically, as socially expressive material qualities.

The written description and visual manipulation or exaggeration of raggedness and dirt confirm the social power of the textile surface: social distinctions were marked out by the quality, age, state of cleanliness, and state of maintenance of garments and textiles, in a system of values that had great normative power.

Concluding Speculation: Surface, Romanticism, and Modernity

Mary Douglas, as has already been noted, identifies margins and boundaries as the points at which any system is at its weakest. Yet Douglas also asserts the creative power that can accrue to margins. In the final chapter of *Purity and Danger*, "The System Shattered and Renewed," she uses the wonderful phrase "composting religion" to describe those faiths that incorporate pollution or broken taboos into their religious rituals, symbolically recycling anomalous or transgressive objects, substances or actions. (Douglas 1991[1966]: 164). This acknowledgment of the possibility of a challenge to the social system ultimately reaffirms that system's power.

Up to this point I have cited literature or photographic representations that describe the dirty ragged garments associated with poverty, destitution and dereliction as evidence of a social system that valued the pristine textile surface. However, might it be possible to identify, functioning alongside these values, a countervailing tendency to be fascinated by or even take delight in dereliction, as an example of Douglas's "system shattered and renewed," and here specifically symptomatic of a reaction to modernity, rather than the postmodernity that is the context to dereliction in late twentieth- and early twenty-first-century fashion? There is some evidence of a minority tendency for the deployment of dirty and worn clothing as a conscious strategy, almost a rebellion, or a refusal. Elizabeth Wilson, in her work on Bohemians (artistic and literary alternative subcultures), notes that:

> … if the bohemian artist looked unkempt, it was not just that he was wearing his oil and paint-stained clothes, or even just that he was penniless: he was telling the world of his defiance, of his dissent from bourgeois values and of his poverty therefore as a moral rather than an economic condition. (Wilson 2000: 162)

George Orwell and Jack London's well-known and politically outspoken attempts to draw attention to poverty and its indignities were not the only empathetic accounts of destitute life produced in the period under discussion here:[5] "there is also a more general literature on the tramp and the gypsy that dates back to the mid-nineteenth century, and that had a resurgence in the early years of the twentieth" (Nord 2006). One of the best known of these accounts is WH Davies's 1908 *The Autobiography of a Super-Tramp*, a book that describes, critiques, but also to an extent celebrates the freedoms of tramp life (Davies 1908). Davies is probably best remembered today as a poet, and specifically as the author of the popular verse "Leisure": "What is this life if, full of care, We have no time to stand and stare" (Davies 1985: 51). The poem consciously embodies nostalgia for a time before modernity had made the pace of modern life fast and furious. In *The Autobiography of a Super-Tramp*, Davies describes a fellow tramp who took his disdain for the domestic norms and rituals associated with the maintenance of the textile object to an almost perverse extreme, rejecting not cleanliness and maintenance *per se*, but the *work* taken to achieve them (and preferring instead systematic begging):

> Rather than wash a good handkerchief he would beg an old one that was clean, and he would without compunction discard a good shirt altogether rather than sew a button on—thus keeping up the dignity of his profession to the extreme. (Davies 1908: 24)

The following is a description of another of Davies's companions on the road:

> an apparently tall man and large in proportion, who was dressed in seedy looking clothes, which were torn and patched in a good many places. In fact, something seemed to have been gnawing night after night at the bottom of his trousers, taking advantage of him in his sleep, for these hung in tatters and rags just below the calves of his legs. (Davies 1908: 197)

Much other tramp literature (as indeed the gypsy literature of the nineteenth century) consciously identified the vagrant life with the romantic tradition and a resistance to modernity. Stephen Graham's *A Tramp's Sketches* (1912) is the record of a journey around the shores of the Black Sea, through Russia, to Jerusalem: his final chapter asserts that "the great fact of the human world to-day is the tremendous commercial machine that is grinding out at a marvelous acceleration the smaller and meaner sort of man," and his journey is described as a conscious, somewhat mystical, attempt to find an alternative to life in such a world (Graham 1912: 330). Deborah Epstein Nord, in her history of the gypsies, has noted that literature on the houseless life "could remind modern men and women of a time before the corruptions of modernity corroded their souls" (Nord 2006: 9).

Mary Douglas notes that, "though it is only specific individuals on specified occasions who can break the rules, it is still important to ask why these dangerous contacts are often required in rituals" (Douglas 1991[1966]: 161). Could it be that the presence of dirty and decrepit clothing, and even a romantic indulgence of it in the figure of the tramp, ultimately served as a powerful reaffirmation of the norm of the clean and maintained textile object, and also of modernity? This was not a "playful" phenomenon, and nor was it directly embedded in the fashion system that has embraced the citation of artificial wear and tear in recent years. Rather it stood to one side, as a negative affirmation of deadly serious social values, expressed in material terms. Full exploration of this concluding speculation is beyond the scope of this article, but I offer it as an indication of territory yet to explore in the understanding of textiles and their surfaces.

Notes

1. This ambivalence is reflected in historical attitudes to the domestic work of cleanliness traditionally carried out by women: such work is often seen as a mark of virtue, its neglect the sign of a bad wife or uncaring mother. Yet women have also been under considerable pressure to keep this work, if not its results, invisible. Too conspicuous a concern with cleanliness is interpreted as a sign of sterility or frigidity, a refusal of the larger concerns of life in favour of trivial domestic minutiae (see Kelley 2009).

2. Although unfortunately unpublished, Cronberg's dissertation is, in my opinion, the best work on "new vintage."

3. Rebecca Arnold has noted Schiaparelli's Tear Dress as an example of "imperfection" from a much earlier period. However, what is notable about that dress, from the point of view of this article, is that, although it has tears depicted on its surface, it is *not actually torn* (Arnold 2001: 24).

4. See for instance Emery (1980[1966]), the primary aim of which is to establish consistent technical classifications of textiles for museum curators and conservators. Gioello (1982) is a useful technical overview intended more for contemporary textile designers and manufacturers, as well as designers and technicians working with finished textiles. See also Schick (1975/1977).

5. For a round up of other, earlier accounts, see Freeman (2001, 2003). For a taste of some of these accounts, see Keating (1976).

References

Arnold, Rebecca. 2001. *Fashion, Desire and Anxiety: Image and Morality in the Twentieth Century*. London: I. B. Tauris.

Barnet, Pennina. 2003. "Letter from the Editors." *Textile* 1(1): 1–7.

Beaumont, Roberts. 1899[1887]. *Woollen and Worsted Cloth Manufacture: being a practical treatise for the used of all persons employed in the manipulation of textile fabrics*, 3rd edn. London: George Bell and Sons.

de Beauvoir, Simone. 1993[1949]. *The Second Sex*. Trans. H. M. Parshley. London: Everyman's Library.

Boyer, George R. 2003. "Living Standards." In Roderick Floud and Paul Johnson (eds) *The Cambridge Economic History of Britain, Volume II: economic maturity, 1860–1939*, pp. 280–311. Cambridge: Cambridge University Press.

Browne, Phillis. 1877. *Common-sense Housekeeping*. London, Paris, and New York: Cassell, Petter and Galpin.

Butler, Judith. 1999[1990]. *Gender Trouble: Feminism and the Subversion of Identity*. New York and London: Routledge.

Calder, Fanny L. and E. E. Mann. 1891. *A Teachers' Manual of Elementary Laundry Work*. London: Longmans, Green and Co.

Clark, Judith. 2004. *Spectres: When Fashion Turns Back*. London: Victoria and Albert Museum.

Cronberg, Anja. 2006. "Second-Hand Clothing and Vintage Style, 1960–Today: Authenticity, Distinction and Material Memories." Unpublished MA dissertation, V&A/RCA History of Design MA.

Crowfoot, Elisabeth, Frances Pritchard and Kay Staniland. 1992. *Textiles and Clothing c.1150–1450*. London: Museum of London/HMSO.

Daunton, Martin. 2000. "Introduction." In Martin Daunton (ed.) *The Cambridge Urban History of Britain, volume III, 1840–1950*. pp. 1–58. Cambridge: Cambridge University Press.

Davies, W. H. 1908. *The Autobiography of a Super-Tramp*. London: A.C. Fifield.

Davies, W. H. 1985. *Selected Poems*. Oxford: Oxford University Press.

DeSilvey, Caitlin. 2006. "Observed Decay: Telling Stories with Mutable Things." *Journal of Material Culture* 11(3): 318–38.

Douglas, Mary. 1991[1966]. *Purity and Danger: An Analysis of the Concepts of Purity and Taboo*. London: Routledge.

Dyer and Calico Printer (the editors of). 1907. *Cotton Finishing*. London: Heywood.

Edge, J. Harold. 1911. *Practical Cotton Finishing*. London: The Trades Papers Publishing Co.

Emery, Irene. 1980[1966]. *The Primary Structures of Fabrics*. London: Thames & Hudson.

Entwistle, Joanne. 2000. *The Fashioned Body: Fashion, Dress, and Modern Social Theory*. Cambridge: Polity Press.

Ezard, Edward. 1979. *Battersea Boy*. London: William Kimber.

Evans, Caroline. 2003. *Fashion at the Edge: Spectacle, Modernity and Deathliness*. New Haven, CT, and London: Yale University Press.

Foakes, Grace. 1972. *Between High Walls: A London Childhood*. London: Shepheard-Walwyn.

Foakes, Grace. 1975. *My Life with Reuben*. London: Shepheard-Walwyn.

Foster, Wanda and Christine Walkley. 1978. *Crinolines and Crimping Irons: Victorian Clothes—How They Were Worn and Cared For*. London: Peter Owen.

Freeman, Mark. 2001. "'Journeys into Poverty Kingdom': Complete Participation and the British Vagrant 1866–1914." *History Workshop Journal* 52: 99–121.

Freeman, Mark. 2003. *Social Investigation and Rural England 1870–1914*. Woodbridge: Royal Historical Society/ Boydell Press.

Gill, Alison. 1998. "Deconstruction Fashion: The Making of Unfinished, Decomposing and Re-assembled Clothes." *Fashion Theory* 2(1): 25–49.

Gioello, Debbie Ann. 1982. *Understanding Fabrics: From Fiber to Finished Cloth*. New York: Fairchild Publications.

Graham, Stephen. 1912. *A Tramp's Sketches*. London: Macmillan.

Handley, Susannah. 1999. *Nylon: The Manmade Fashion Revolution*. London: Bloomsbury.

Harris, Jose. 1993. *Private Lives, Public Spirit: A Social History of Britain 1870–1914*, Oxford: Oxford University Press.

de la Haye, Amy and Cathie Dingwall. 1996. *Surfers, Soulies, Skinheads and Skaters: Subculltural Style from the Forties to the Nineties*. London: Victoria and Albert Museum.

Honeyman, Katrina and Andrew Godley. 2003. "Introduction: Doing Business with Fashion." *Textile History* 34(2): 101–6.

Ingle, Stephen. 2006. *The Social and Political Thought of George Orwell: A Reassessment*. Abingdon and New York: Routledge.

Jack, Florence B. 1898. *The Art of Laundry Work*. Edinburgh: T. C. and E. C. Jack and London: Whittaker and Co.

Kawamura, Yuniya. 2004. "The Japanese Revolution in Paris Fashion." *Fashion Theory* 8(2): 199–200.

Keating, Peter (ed.). 1976. *Into Unknown England: Selections from the Social Explorers 1866–1913*. London: Fontana.

Kelley, Victoria. 2009. *Soap and Water: Cleanliness, Dirt and the Working Classes in Victorian and Edwardian Britain*. London: I. B. Tauris (forthcoming).

Klepp, Ingun Grimstad. 2007. "Patched, Louse-ridden, Tattered: Clean and Dirty Clothes." *Textile* 5(3): 254–75.

Kristeva, Julia. 1982[1980]. *Powers of Horror: An Essay on Abjection*. Trans. Leon S. Roudiez. New York: Columbia University Press.

Lehmann, Ulrich. 2000. *Tigersprung: Fashion in Modernity*. Boston, MA: MIT Press.

Lifson, Ben. 1989. "European Documentary Styles." In Mike Weaver (ed.). *The Art of Photography 1839–1989*, pp. 264–5. New Haven, CT, and London: Yale University Press.

London, Jack. 1903. *The People of the Abyss*. London: Isbister.

Marsh, F. L. 1914. *Laundry Work in Theory and Practice*. London: Longmans Green.

McKibbin, Ross. 1998. *Classes and Cultures: England 1918–1951*. Oxford: Oxford University Press.

Mortimer, Raymond. 1936. "Introduction." In Bill Brandt *The English at Home*. London: B. T. Batsford.

Nord, Deborah Epstein. 2006. *Gypsies and the British Imagination 1807–1930*. New York: Columbia University Press.

Norris, Christopher. 1993. *The Truth about Postmodernism*. Oxford and Cambridge, MA: Blackwell.

Orwell, George. 2003[1933]. *Down and Out in Paris and London*. London: Penguin.

Palmer, Alexandra. 1997. "New Directions: Fashion History Studies and Research in North America and England." *Fashion Theory* 1(3): 297–312.

Palmer, Alexandra and Hazel Clark. 2004. *Old Clothes, New Looks: Second-Hand Fashion*. Oxford: Berg.

Pooley, Colin G. 2000. "Patterns on the Ground: Urban Form, Residential Structure and the Social Construction of Space." In Martin Daunton (ed.). *The Cambridge Urban History of Britain, Volume III, 1840–1950* pp. 429–66. Cambridge: Cambridge University Press.

Robertson, Kirsty. 2005. "Resistance and Submission, Warp and Weft: Unravelling the Life of Ethel Mairet." *Textile* 3(3): 292–317.

Schick, M. 1975/1977. *Surface Characteristics of Fibers and Textiles* (parts 1/2). New York: Marcel Dekker.

Schoeser, Mary. 2003. *World Textiles: A Concise History*. London. Thames & Hudson.

Styles, John. 1998. "Dress in history: Reflections on a Contested Terrain." *Fashion Theory* 2(4): 383–9.

Tagg, John. 1993. *The Burden of Representation: Essays on Photographies and Histories*. Minneapolis, MN: University of Minnesota Press.

Vigarello, Georges. 1988[1985]. *Concepts of Cleanliness: Changing Attitudes in France since the Middle Ages*. Trans. Jean Birrell. Cambridge: Cambridge University Press.

Warburton, Nigel. 1999. "Brandt's Printing Styles." In Bill Jay and Nigel Warburton (eds) *The Photography of Bill Brandt*. London: Thames & Hudson.

Wilson, Elizabeth. 2000. *Bohemians: The Glamorous Outcasts*. London: I. B. Tauris.

Wilson, Elizabeth. 2005[1985]. *Adorned in Dreams: Fashion and Modernity*, revised edn. London: I. B. Tauris.

Disturb... s: Spaces of Memory in Varda

Getzow

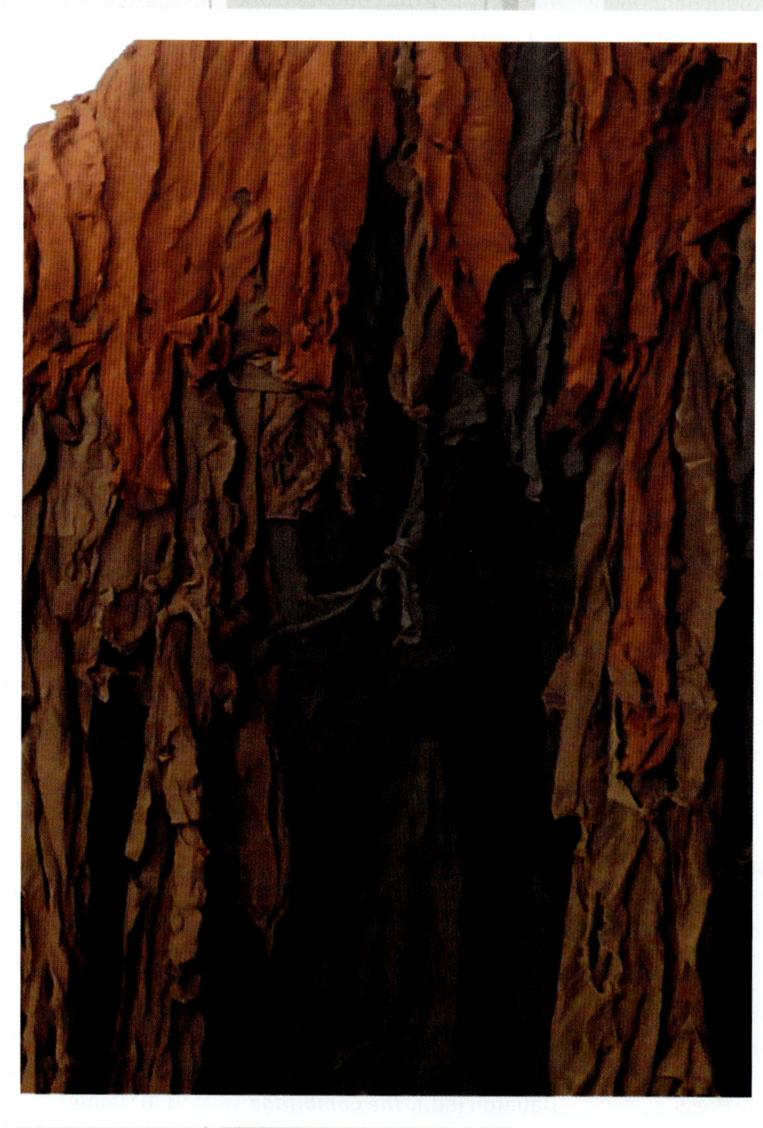

Review

Disturbing Beauties: Spaces of Memory in Varda Getzow's Work

A woman's high-heel shoe, the toe covered in cement as if frozen or enveloped in wax; drippings of passing time, of events and matter that cover the past and bury it, but do not allow it to fade. Or perhaps not—barely visible or not yet covered up is part of a sneaker that alludes to a wearer and it cannot be that long ago, just recently so to speak.

The plates that cannot be eaten off—because for example a shoe has been cemented to them—refer to those who cannot move on, cannot get away. These people's existence is made manifest through things. "Manifestness" that transcends materiality is sought here in vain; an unmistakable person, clearly defined corporeality is not shown. The pieces illustrate "being human" as a term that can only be concretized as attached to an object, rather than a subject. The eras the work is situated in merge or are displaced by these objects; as pieces of the present they find themselves in simultaneity with the past.

Absent Being

In Varda Getzow's work, attempts are made to store fragments of memory and to make past processes solidify into matter, tangible or perceptible; as if a preterit, an action or event of yesterday could at the same time be in the present, or refuse to leave the now. In "Midron" (Hebrew—slope) the artist places her installation, made up of thousands of shreds—ripped stockings—in the middle of an open plane. She evokes a contradiction to the harmlessness of a place that quasi-pledges its own innocence.[1] These works are charged with politics and history by a public that wants to engage with Jews who are no longer there—an intention that time and again leads to interpretations balanced awkwardly between conjuring up the supposedly glorious and unharmed German–Jewish symbiosis before the Holocaust, National Socialist crimes without perpetrators, and the so-called Zero Hour, after which Jews who again lived in Germany once

REVIEWED BY ESTHER DISCHEREIT
TRANSLATED BY LAURA RADOSH
Esther Dischereit, writer, lives in Berlin. Representative of so-called "young" contemporary German-Jewish literature, she writes fiction, poems, essays, and audio and stage dramas. From 2000 to 2006, she also worked as a curator in Berlin. The latest of her own installations is a memorial of speech and sound marks in honor of Jewish citizens, opened in December 2008 in Dülmen, Germany.

Textile, Volume 7, Issue 2, pp. 236–243
DOI: 10.2752/175183509X460119
Reprints available directly from the Publishers.
Photocopying permitted by licence only.
© 2009 Berg. Printed in the United Kingdom.

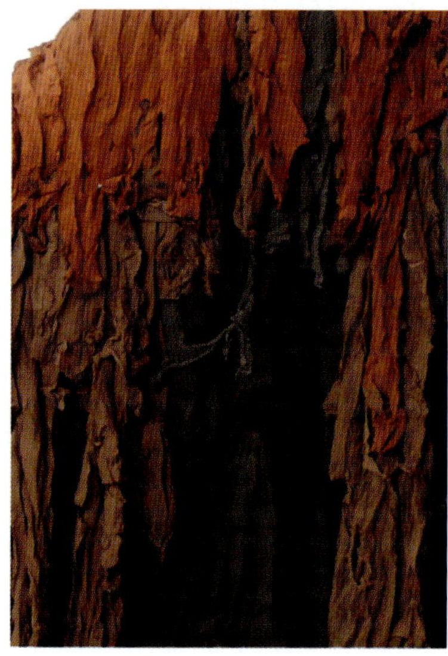

Figure 1
Varda Getzow, "Mapal" (detail), 2008.
Haus am Kleistpark, Berlin.

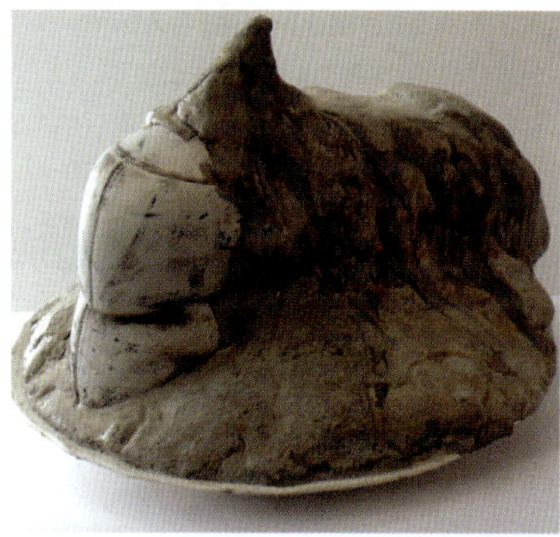

Figure 2
Varda Getzow, No title, 2007. Porcelain,
concrete, and shoes, radius 24 cm.
Haberent Collection, Berlin.

more became invisible and were, so to speak, incorporated into the state of Israel. Varda Getzow's work "Mapal" has also been reinterpreted in this way: Waterfall or rock debris—both meanings are possible in Hebrew—here Mapal is an installation in Berlin, 2008.[2]

This waterfall or rock debris of sculptural textile was juxtaposed with a 3 × 4 m digital print: Petra in Jordan, one of the Wonders of the World, a rider, a horse, invincible walls. Getzow alludes here to the myth of the red rocks. Although everyone knew of its indescribable, legendary beauty, for people in Israel Petra remained forbidden enemy territory; for decades very close, but inaccessible. Nevertheless, in the 1950s time and again it proved an irresistible attraction for young men. They went there as people follow a dream or an inner voice. It may have been romantic ideas of their own strength or invincibility that made them go. These young men were civilians, not soldiers. Those that went over were not following orders, but were ignoring an explicit prohibition. Varda Getzow herself did not see Petra until 2006; that ancient city, hewn from red cliffs, can only be entered through a single, narrow ravine. This ravine is dangerous in springtime as rain can cause sudden floods to rush through, taking with them any who happen to be passing, and it is dangerous because there is no escape for the victims of an attack. The steep rock cliffs of the ravine provide no way out. The young men had gone out to become heroes in enemy land and never came back. Their bodies were never found. When Getzow displays (as a photo)

the cliffs across from the temple—towering, terracotta red—she is referencing not only the silent exalted beauty but also the dead from a once secreted past.

Accumulated amorphous rock debris made of 2,000 shreds—again pieces of torn stockings—illustrates the material destruction. The red of the saddlebags is mirrored by the red mounds of the installation's material, here again a shift of time planes. A band between contemporary memory and what has long since been; present in the room, without us being able to personify or identify the carrier of this memory (Dischereit 2008).[3]

Varda Getzow's interventions in unwritten projected space work with shreds, with torn material; their uniform mass is as amorphous as rock and stone. These are not found objects, nothing has been thrown away and put back together. With these deliberately torn clothes, which seem to still retain bodily heat, Getzow creates sculptural landscapes and mountains that remind us of people and do not want to fit into their surroundings; they are disturbances.

This is true not only of "Midron" and "Mapal," but also of the installation she created for the Representatives' Hall in the New Synagogue Centrum Judaicum, Berlin, in 2001. In this work, white and gray towels refer to the present, to utilitarian objects that are also objects of intimate utility. They suggest daily usage and turn this idea around through an unasked-for suffusion with the presence of the absent. The stockings—and also the towels in the Centrum Judaicum installation—are like factory wares without any individual ascription to the person who carried the towel or owned the stockings. These wares do not breathe a sense of the personal or of individuality—they

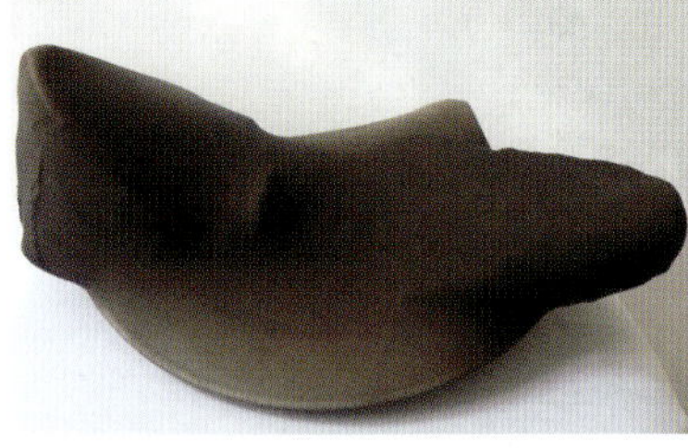

Figure 3
Varda Getzow, No title, 2007. Porcelain, nylon stockings, and a shoe, radius 32 cm. Courtesy of the artist.

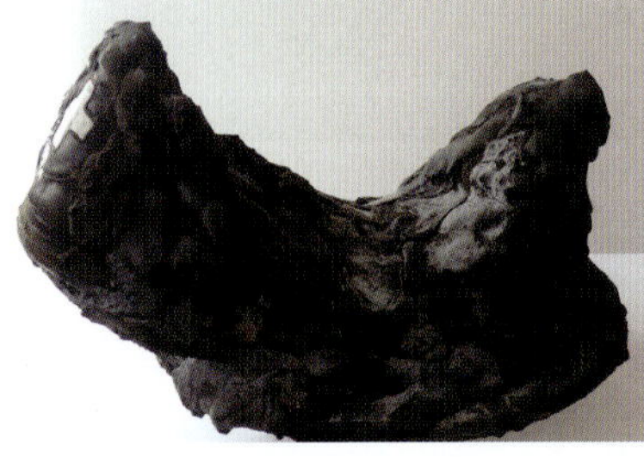

Figure 4
Varda Getzow, No title, 2008. Porcelain, concrete, and a shoe, radius 29 cm. Courtesy of the artist.

themselves are mass-produced. The commonplace way these threads are displayed is reminiscent of the movement of a person who puts on stockings or takes them off, who is washing him or herself, or is about to do the dishes and dry them. This proximity is strange and estranging, as if we were entering an Ingmar Bergmann room in which furniture hung with sheets emits a presentiment of inhabitants who will not be able to return; on the other hand it could also be a monstrous, almost indecent invitation to touch these pieces and put them aside. Placed in a rebuilt room that reminds us that thousands of members of a congregation once gathered here to pray, Getzow's everyday towels become charged with silence, a citation of the tallis that Jewish men put on to pray (New Synagogue Centrum Judaicum Representatives' Hall, Berlin, 2001); meant for religious acts. Instead, in its place, there is a serial towel, "unwritten," and unmarked, like a hotel or hospital towel. Who knows whether this object is or was meant to be used or just presents itself as if frozen, so that it could have been used, but never will

be used again. It breathes a trace of "has-been-there," like that of a stranger who is sure she or he came as a stranger and left as one. The room can no longer be used as it was before these unbidden mass-produced pieces replete with memory arrived. To touch the towel, to check the stockings for runs—such an immediacy of movement makes no sense. The threads of memory run through the stockings' stitches.

The Second Generation of the Shoah and the Visibility of the Small Ego

These pieces can be looked at in the context of the works of, among others, Tanya Ury or Arnold Dreyblatt.[4] Whereas Tanya Ury portrays the over-dimensional corporeality of the daughter provocatively almost screaming[5]— a daughter unable to desire and provoke the father, because he was murdered by the Nazis. Ury assumes a father who—one can almost say—must be the object of the daughter's sexual desire. Her provocation, offering the body of the daughter, falls into nothingness; cannot be answered, cannot be punished. All that remains is the

Figure 5
Varda Getzow, "Midron," 2008. Kunsthalle Luckenwalde. Nylon stockings and furniture, 160 × 910 × 200 cm.

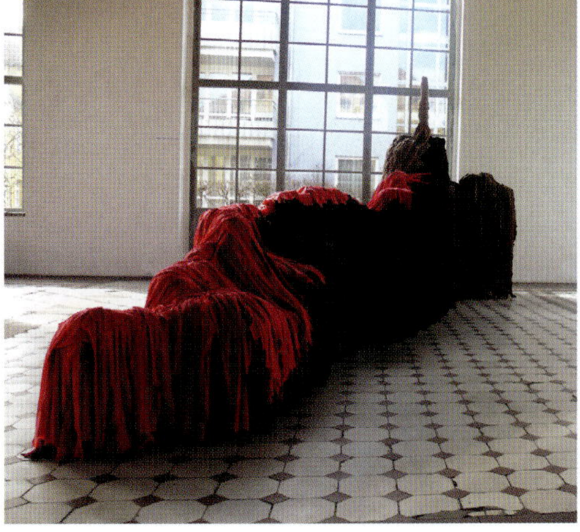

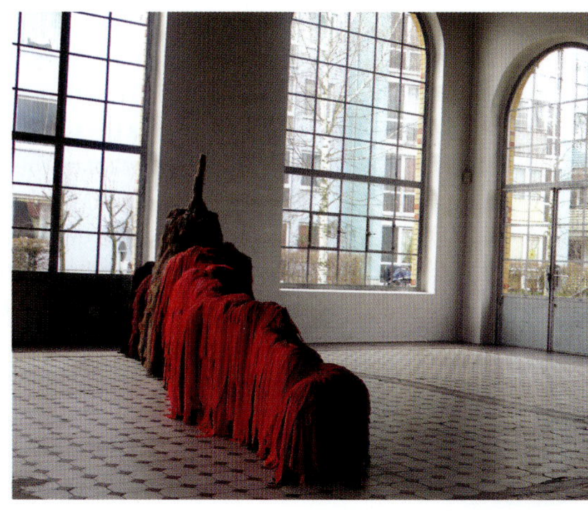

Figure 6
Varda Getzow, "Midron," 2008.
Kunsthalle Luckenwalde. Nylon
stockings and furniture, 160 × 910 ×
200 cm.

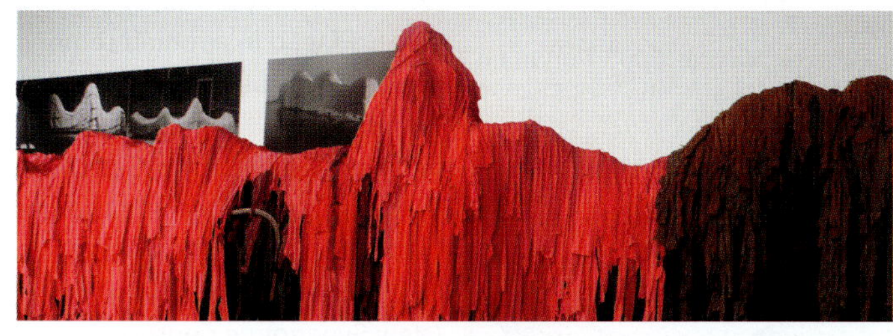

Figure 7
Varda Getzow, "Mapal," 2008.
Haus am Kleistpark, Berlin. Nylon
stockings, furniture and digital prints,
120 × 800 × 330 cm.

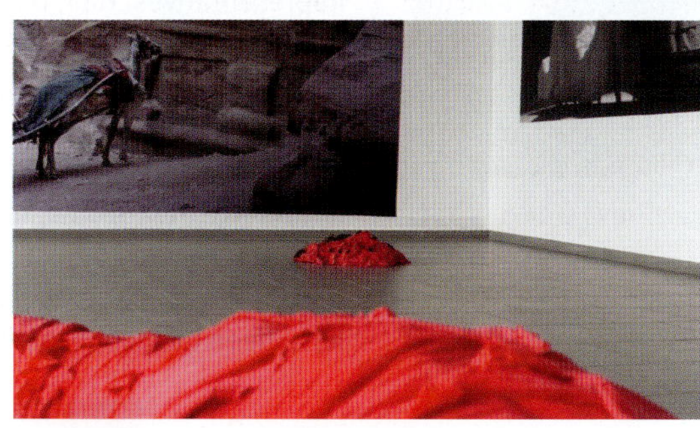

Figure 8
Varda Getzow, "Mapal," 2008. Haus am
Kleistpark, Berlin. Nylon stockings and
furniture, 120 × 800 × 330 cm.

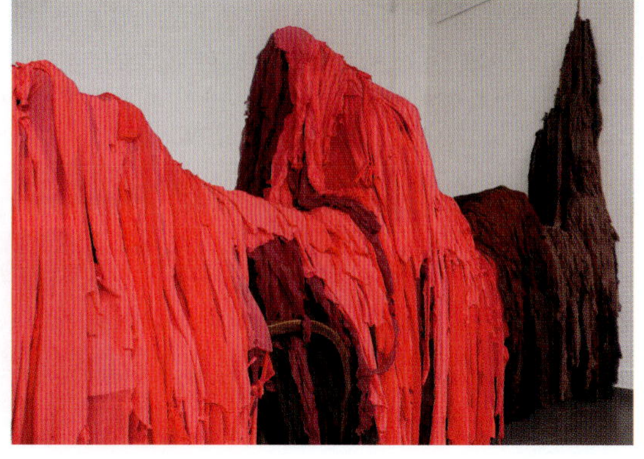

Figure 9
Varda Getzow, "Mapal," 2008. Haus am
Kleistpark, Berlin. Nylon stockings,
furniture, and digital prints.

daughter's aggressive, unanswered, sexual corporeality, an over-abundant presence. Getzow's and Dreyblatt's works are rather dominated by the disappearance of bodies and things in the process of time. They are about fading and evading, about how events become obscured by a strange moving transience of order and orderliness, which takes over behind the protagonists' backs; configurations in which the ego can only be seen indirectly, only as it clings to matter. Arnold Dreyblatt thematizes what has long since been, for example, by exhibiting emptiness itself: cupboards, which contain hardly anything; a classroom, which no longer is functional still contains the smell of those who were there, but nothing else. The spectator instinctively attempts to imagine what is missing—here, too, the trace of those, who have been, is in the material; traces that "cling" to the present—the intervention is hardly discernible, almost minimalist ("7d/1961—The Disappeared Classroom"). "The Reading Room," too, presents the past in its ordered inconspicuous objecthood out of which the history of individual Jewish citizens is extricated for a moment before it is placed back into obscure materiality, into the file.

Varda Getzow, too, starts from found materiality, cites it, cultivates it, and transforms its original meaning into loaded abstractions.

Varda Getzow, the child of Jewish-German and Jewish-Dutch parents, is a member of the so-called second generation of the Shoah and was born in Jaffa, Israel. A look at this literary scene shows that here too the children who long were silent have begun to speak:

"My writing is the result of the silence between my parents and myself," says Savyon Liebrecht.[6]

Literary scholar Mona Körte coined the term "literature of the small ego" (Körte 2008: 592) for the work of second generation of the Shoah writing in German, subsuming under this term such vastly diverse works as those by Gila Lustiger, Viola Roggenkamp, Eva Menasse, and Esther Dischereit. As different as the family novels Körte studied were,[7] the ego remained nameless, absent, or only an appendix to the stories of the survivors' generation: weak, sometimes completely passive as the literary scholar Eva Lezzi (1996: 117–48) also said.

These second-generation works are created in a political situation in which for the first time children of survivors in Israel are making their voices heard in public and daring to express their own needs. In contrast to the attention given to the Holocaust in Israel in its function as founding myth, in the society of "pioneers," the survivors themselves were empathetically ignored. How do their children talk about living with the nightmares of their parents?[8]

Ego and Matter

Getzow's works seem to be sated, satiated with history; there is not a small ego which cannot be seen here, but in its place rather matter under which the existence of an ego can only be guessed at. In "Baby Bonnet," a print of the people that once were is marked in matter, almost fleetingly, only a citation in cement on the wall of a house, no more; placed in the Ghetto di Roma on Giornata della Memoria, January 27, 2006. For Varda Getzow, objects appear as identification or proof of human "nature"; relicts which have become nature, landscapes branded by what has happened, that cannot be placed as belonging here or there without a doubt. Are they "landscapes" or "humanity?" How did it happen that these conditions are intertwined and dealt with archeologically? The work of the artist would then be to free the individual "layers."

In Jewish Space

These works are contextualized in the growing opening of a social space which the historian Diana Pinto has named the "Jewish space" (2006: 179–86) and which is not unknown to Ashkenazi Israelis—since they are often not only the descendants of their parents or grandparents who once came from various places in Europe; no small number of them live themselves in transnational "spaces" between Israel, the USA, and Europe. Pinto dates the new creation of this "Jewish space" in Europe at the beginning of the 1980s, when a series of memorial events were initiated at the political and cultural level; especially in 1995, the remembrance ceremonies for the liberation of Auschwitz and the end of World War II. This space has divorced itself from its immediate historical countries of descent—in particular Spain, Germany, and Poland—and now has little to do with how rich Jewish life once was here. When in European countries today people reflect on the past and the fate of the Jews, it provides a background against which a contemporary national discourse can arise on democracy, identity, pluralism, and respect.

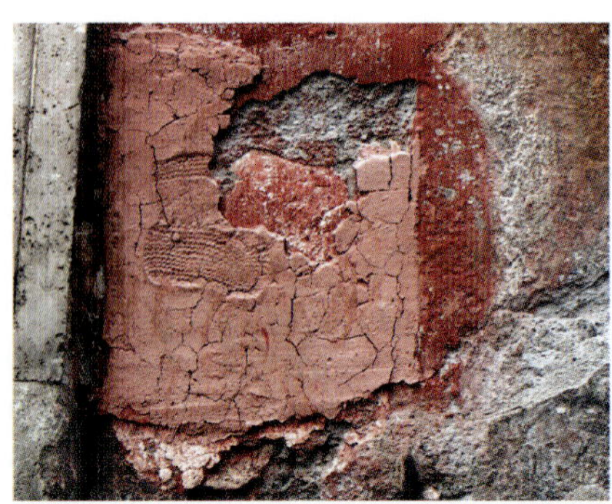

Figure 10
Varda Getzow, "Baby Shoe," 2006.
Ghetto di Roma (Giornata della
Memoria). Gypsum relief, 13 × 16 cm.

The discourse on remembering the victims of the Shoah created the point of reference for this Jewish space and led to a discussion on the reference points of democratic societies in general, their inherent polyphony and diversity. In this sense, we can claim that artistic works such as Varda Getzow's interpret "in more universal terms that very Jewish past" (Pinto 2006: 183). Varda Getzow is influenced by this past, from which her works move continuously away. Signs of this movement are generated and as they are created added to the past, so that the act of leaving behind itself is written on the object. She finds a means of expression which belongs to the universal discourse of cultures, of others and non-others: the results of her manipulations of shreds or particles are piled-up, foreign, no longer belonging, weird manifestations of memories as left-behind "landscapes."

Varda Getzow
Solo exhibitions
2008 Midron, Luckenwalde, Germany; 2006 Al Hanof/Galon Gallery, Tel Aviv; 2004 Beuys hosts Getzow in Apex, Edinburgh; 2003 Rosenthal, Achshav—now contemporary art, Berlin; 2001 New Synagogue Centrum Judaicum, Berlin; 1999 Orchideus/Room 906/ Sheraton Hotel, Tel Aviv; 1997 Museum of Israeli Art, Ramat Gan; 1996 Galerie Springer, Berlin; 1995 Goethe Institute, London; 1995 Room 506/Averard Hotel, London; 1995 Whitechapel Art Gallery, London; 1992 Korkinet/ Buchprojekt, Berlin; 1992 Galerie Pommersfelde, Berlin; 1992 Museum of Modern Art, Haifa; 1991 Head/The Israel Museum, Jerusalem.

Public collections
The Israel Museum, Jerusalem; Kupferstichkabinett, Berlin; Staatsgalerie, Stuttgart; The Museum of Modern Art, Haifa; The British Museum, London; New Synagogue Centrum Judaicum, Berlin.

Notes
1. "Midron," special exhibition of the Brandenburgisches Lituraturbüro during the reading series "1948–2008 60th Anniversary, Israel," "Israeli Authors in the State of Brandenburg," Luckenwalde, Germany, 2008.
2. Varda Getzow and Liane Birnberg. *Schichtung*. HAUS am KLEISTPARK, Berlin, 2008, www.hausamkleistpark-berlin. de, April 6–May 18, 2008.

3. See also www.hagalil.com/01/de/index.pho?itemid=2062, accessed April 4, 2008.

4. Arnold Dreyblatt, "The Reading Room, Biennale Bern, 2001"; see also "7d/1961—Die verschwundene Klasse," 2004, a multi-participant project led by Arnold Dreyblatt, Kastanienallee, Berlin, Germany.

5. Tanya Ury. "Triptych for a Jewish Princess Second Generation." In Dischereit *et al.* (1999).

6. Savyon Liebrecht, Israeli author born 1948 in Munich, the daughter of Polish-Jewish Shoah survivors, cited in Dischereit (2002: 38–9). Further works, among others: Lizzie Doron, (b. 1952 in Israel) (2007); earlier, Nava Semel, not only in "Gläserne Facetten" (2000), but also in her other, children's, books. She also binds the past on articles of clothing such as a pair of shoes which have been kept. This kind of clutching at objects is the subject of literary critics Mona Körte and Toby Axelrod, who ask about the meaning of objects that are the last remembrances of their parents kept by children sent on the Kindertransport in Körte and Axelrod (2004: 109–20). See also Körte (2007).

7. For Esther Dischereit's *Joëmis Tisch* the term "text with pieces that are or could be connected to family" would be more correct (Dischereit 1988; translated into English in "'Joëmi's Table' A Jewish Story in Contemporary Jewish Writing," in Morris and Remmler (2002). See also excerpts in Lappin (1994, 102–12), Bukiet. (2002, 263–73). See also Hall (2007).

8. Around 4 to 5 percent of the estimated 400,000 children of survivors are themselves acutely in need of therapy. An appeal for help for this group was made to the government of the Federal Republic of Germany in 2007, and turned down.

References

Bukiet, Melvin (ed.). 2002. *Nothing Makes You Free: Writings by the Descendants of Jewish Holocaust Survivors*. New York: W. W. Norton and Co.

Dischereit, Esther. 1988. *Joëmis Tisch*. Frankfurt am Main: Suhrkamp Verlag.

Dischereit, Esther. 2002. "Mama, darf ich das Deutschlandlied singen?" *Ambivalenzen, Die Frau in der jüdischen Kultur in Deutschland heute.* [Conference documentation] pp. 38–9. Bonn: Frauenmuseum.

Dischereit, Esther. 2008. "Fetzen der Erinnerung." *Tageszeitung taz*, April 4. www.taz.de/regional/berlin/tazplan-kultur/, April 4, 2008.

Dischereit, Esther *et al.* 1999. *DAVKA. Jüdische Visionen in Berlin.* Berlin: AvivA Verlag.

Doron, Lizzie, 2007. *Der Anfang von etwas Schönem*. Trans. Mirjam Pressler, Frankfurt am Main: Suhrkamp Verlag.

Hall, Katharina (ed.). 2007. *Esther Dischereit (Contemporary German Writers)*. Cardiff: University of Wales Press.

Körte, Mona. 2007. "Wiederkehr einer Reise." *Tagesspiegel* August 15: 3.

Körte, Mona. 2008. "'Die Toten am Tisch.' Deutsch-jüdische Familienromane nach dem Holocaust." *Zeitschrift für Deutsche Philologie Heft* 4: 573–94.

Körte, Mona and Toby Axelrod. 2004. "Bracelet, Hand Towel, Pocket Watch: Objects of the Last Moment in Memory and Narration. Shofar." *An Interdisciplinary Journal of Jewish Studies* 23(1): 109–20.

Lappin, Elena (ed.). 1994. *Jewish Voices German Words: Growing up Jewish in Postwar Germany and Austria. An Anthology.* North Haven, CT: Catbird Press.

Lezzi, Eva. 1996. "Geschichtserinnerung und Weiblichkeitskonzeption bei Esther Dischereit und Anne Duden." *Aschkenas. Zeitschrift für Geschichte und Kultur der Juden* 6: 117–48.

Morris, Leslie and Karen Remmler (eds). 2002. *Contemporary Jewish Writing in Germany: An Anthology.* Lincoln, NE, and London: University of Nebraska Press.

Pinto, Diana. 2006. "The Jewish Space in Europe." In Sandra Lustig and Ian Leveson (eds) *Turning the Kaleidoscope Perspectives on European Jewry*, pp. 179–186. New York, Oxford: Berghahn Books.

Semel, Nava. 2000. *"Gläserne Facetten": Ten Stories.* Trans. Mirjam Pressler. Frankfurt am Main: Dr Orgler Verlag.

Exhibition Review
Front of House

Marcos Corrales, Ângela Ferreira, Narelle Jubelin and Andrew Renton, with the UK premiere of *Maison Tropicale* by Manthia Diawara

Parasol Unit, London, April 16–May 28, 2008

Front of House brings together works built out of a set of "prior correspondences" between architect Marcos Corrales, artists Ângela Ferreira and Narelle Jubelin, and curator Andrew Renton, all of whom have worked with each other in different configurations over a number of years (*Front of House* 2008: 24). The personal histories of the artists (Ferreira was born in colonial Mozambique and grew up in South Africa and Jubelin is Australian but now lives in Spain) have in common what is described as a "postcolonial experience." Both artists have over the years consistently been concerned with the way in which they themselves are situated subjects, implicated in complex ways with histories of colonial domination and violence. Their works often track the multiple translations of modernism into different geographical and political contexts outside the Western canon, and have embodied migratory flows that stem from imperialism and the itinerant passages of the contemporary art world. Both have interrogated the circulation of art objects, aesthetics forms, and ideas through the uneven global routes, always drawing attention to the "unacknowledged debt the centre owes to the periphery" (Grace 2006).

What grounds *Front of House* is a set of ongoing dialogs and shifting relationships that find a temporary resting place for critical reflection in the transient space of the gallery. The inversions,

REVIEWED BY ROS GRAY

Ros Gray is a Lecturer in Critical Studies in the Department of Art, Goldsmiths College, University of London, and a visiting tutor in the MPhil/ PhD program Curating Contemporary Art at the Royal College of Art, London. Her PhD thesis *Ambitions of Cinema: Revolution, Event, Screen* investigated the cinema screen as a site of radical gathering and the circulations of filmmakers, films, and filmmaking practices through various revolutionary situations in Africa and Europe from the late 1960s to the early 1980s. She has written on contemporary art, world cinema, notions of textuality, and the metaphorics of textile in various art journals.

Textile, Volume 7, Issue 2, pp. 244–251
DOI: 10.2752/175183509X460128
Reprints available directly from the Publishers.
Photocopying permitted by licence only.
© 2009 Berg. Printed in the United Kingdom.

overlooked connections, echoes, and conversations (both real and imagined) that the works refer to thus provide a different kind of platform for art to the *tabula rasa* of the modernist gesture—one that is self-conscious about the entangled and compromised roots of all postcolonial cultural production. A "ground for participation" in a critical dialogue is constructed out of a series of overlapping stories that circulate through and cross-contaminate the histories and geographies of colonial and postcolonial modernity, out of which these new works have emerged as singular coalescences of multiple strands of origin (Deleuze 2001: 62). *Front of House* thus rightly claims for itself a "dialogic" approach for the exhibition, one concerned with reading into cultural forms "the forces at work in the culture system[s] from which they spring" (Bakhtin 1981: 425–6).

The title *Front of House* refers to "those areas in theatres and concert halls to which the public has access, excluding the stage and backstage areas." Its aim is to "bring those private, unarticulated spaces and narratives from the backstage into the foreground, within sight of the Front of House" (*Front of House* 2008: 9). The works themselves operate through various aesthetic strategies of pared down minimalist structures, historically loaded projected images and the intricate technique of Jubelin's petit-point embroidery that, combined, require a certain kind of dedicated close reading before the spaces and narratives they refer to can be recognized and understood.

A recurrent theme of the exhibition is the disjointed process by which ideas and aesthetic forms are translated between artists and architects and modified as they are transplanted into very different times and places. The first work to be encountered in the exhibition, Ferreira's *Die Vlermuis Huis* (*The Bat House*) (2006), is a wooden sculpture based on an actual house in Cape Town designed by South African architect Gabriël Fagan (Figure 1). Ferreira strips the design

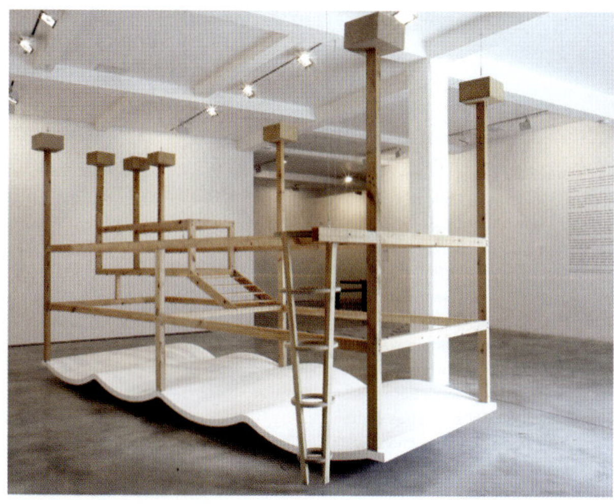

Figure 1
Ângela Ferreira, *Die Vlermuis Huis* [*The Bat House*], 2006. Courtesy the artists and Parasol Unit Foundation for Contemporary Art, London. Photo: Stephen White.

down to its structural elements and inverts it, so that the house hangs, bat-like, from the ceiling of the gallery. The work thus refers to the transposition of Modernism from northern to southern hemisphere in Fagan's design, but Ferreira also incorporates in her sculpture two features of the house that are a departure from Modernist architecture's utilitarian, rectilinear norms. A conical chimney (the architect's favorite part of the building), is included by Ferreira to represent "the dialogue between artist and architect which has informed the piece," while an undulating roof, a decorative feature designed to reflect the location of the house on the South African coastline, floats like a wave above the gallery floor (*Front of House* 2008: 16).

The next work, Narelle Jubelin's *A Few More Papers of Unknown Content.2* (2006–8), is formed out of 240 copies of the book published to accompany the exhibition *Walter Benjamin's Briefcase*, curated by Andrew Renton in Oporto in 1993, which was never distributed. The briefcase of the title was carried by the German Jewish philosopher as he attempted to escape Nazi persecution in 1940. Rumored to hold within it the manuscript of Benjamin's last book, the briefcase was lost after his tragic suicide when he was held up on the Spanish border. The books lie in a low pile on the floor in tribute to Carl Andre's seminal work of Minimalist sculpture *Untitled VIII*, a pile of bricks that was shown controversially at the Tate in 1966. Notes to this piece inform us, through a series of conversations reconstructed from memory, that

a "bricks" book was prepared that argued for the importance of the sculpture. It was never published, however, as the then director of the Tate thought "such a publication would fan the flames of the controversy" surrounding public funds being used to pay for such a work (*Front of House* 2008). Behind *A Few More Papers of Unknown Content.2* there is thus a tangle of stories about books that have never reached the public domain, either unpublished, lost or censored as a result of political persecution or institutional timidity in the face of populist backlash. The global flows of commodities, aesthetics, and ideas that construct art's histories are revealed to be pocketed with blockages and gaps.

Around a partitioning wall is the work *Crossing the Line* (1999–2008), a collaborative work between Ferreira and Jubelin that draws on just one fragment of the myriad personal trajectories through which mass experiences of colonial migration were lived out in microcosm. A 30-second color video loop of a young woman moving her head from side to side and sticking out her tongue is projected onto the wall. Accompanying this in a small white frame is a petit-point embroidery of the photograph on which the video image is based: a black and white photograph of the Ferreira family crossing the Equator in a cruise liner on their journey from Europe to Africa in 1964. Although Jubelin has spoken in the past of the labor she puts into to rendering in the tiny stitches of petit point "as photographic an image as possible," in this translation to petit point the detail that the girl is sticking her tongue

out is lost.[1] This is the eighth public display of "Crossing the Line," each of which has required that the work be transported across the equator to reach the exhibition venue—Barcelona, Cape Town, Maputo, Sydney, and Lisbon being amongst the places connected by the overlapping migrations of the two artists and their work across borders and routes drawn by different contemporary configurations of power.

Ferreira's *Double-sided (Parasol)* (1996–2008) continues the theme of cross-continental transposition through two large photographic prints that branch out to another set of parallels, this time those Ferreira identifies between two artists, one celebrated as a major figure of twentieth-century Minimalism, the other working on the periphery of the international art circuit. To the right is an interior shot of the Chinati Foundation in Marfa, TX, USA, the home and workplace of Donald Judd, where Ferreira built an installation based on the house of reclusive South African outsider artist Helen Martins in 1996. To the left is an interior shot of Martins' home and studio Nieu Bethesda in South Africa, where a year later Ferreira constructed an installation based on Judd's architectural office.

The final sculptural work encountered on the ground floor, Jubelin and Corrales' *Owner-Builder of Modern California House.2* (2001–8), interrogates the translations and circulations of Modernist domestic architecture through a more elaborate structural device that recalls Minimalist sculpture while also bringing together multiple elements whose interconnections are at once personal and art historical. Four wooden surfaces fold down from one of the gallery pillars, upon which are placed a series of petit-point embroideries, some books and two projectors. The petit-point embroideries form a visual essay that depicts the Sydney suburban house built by Jubelin's parents in the early 1960s (Figure 2). In a previous version, the work was contextualized within the frame of the Southern Californian "Case Study" houses.[2] The Californian origins of the design are not erased from the title, but stand as a reminder of the appropriation of a Modernist aesthetic onto a new terrain in Australia. The work speaks of the expression through domestic design of personal aspirations to be "modern" and partake in a certain cultural cosmopolitanism associated with Modernism. The implementation of generic Modernist forms by white settlers in Australia and elsewhere on the imperialist map has clearly involved processes of cultural imposition onto indigenous landscapes. But they have also tended to produce an amnesiac erasure of the complex histories through which the early Modernist "International Style" developed both through an engagement with African vernacular forms, and through commissions that where part of colonialist projects to regulate and control foreign territories (Overy 2005).

Again, rendered in exquisite petit point, the images demand a certain lingering attention as the images are extremely hard to read. What are these structural forms that seem strangely familiar? What is this indistinct landscape? Who is the figure? This duration of attention recalls the time invested in their labor, highlighting the tension between processes of making associated with the monumental forms of minimalist sculpture referenced by the framing device (which typically incorporates elements mass-produced or made by specialist craftsmen rather than the named artist), and the tradition of

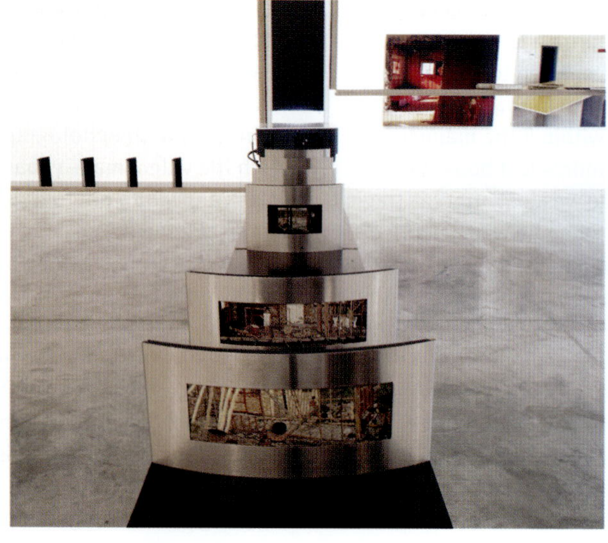

Figure 2
Narelle Jubelin and Marcos Corrales, *Owner-Builder of Modern California House.2*, 2001–8. Courtesy the artists and Parasol Unit Foundation for Contemporary Art, London. Photo: Stephen White.

domestic craft from which petit point descends, one usually excluded from the canon of modernist art. Other elements further complicate this intricate mapping, as the projections of slides taken by Jubelin's father during the construction of the house are interspersed with foreign archive material from the period of its inhabitation from 1964 to 2008. Quotations from Walter Benjamin pay homage to a way of doing history that attends to the multiple foldings and traversals of space and time through which our most banal and familiar surroundings take their form, the aesthetic strategies of the work rendering these intersections oblique, frustrating and intriguing yet again.

The works on the first floor of the exhibition echo, mirror, and extrapolate upon those at ground level (Figure 3). The first, *Crossing the Floor (Shadow Version)*, is a pared down variation on *Crossing the Line*, while the other works make yet more complex interconnections or set off on new trajectories. Jubelin and Corrales' *Ungrammatical Landscape.2* (2003–8) recalls *Owner-Builder of Modern California House.2* as a series of Jubelin's

petit-point embroideries are supported by a minimalist sculptural structure (Figure 4). The petit points form an essay of words and images that rework Ferreira's *Double-Sided Parts I & II* (depicted in the photographs on the ground floor); it also includes renderings of an anti-war poster designed by Judd; fragments of recent Spanish and Australian political graffiti; an image of the rural location where, following the 2004 train bombings, right-wing politicians claimed that ETA terrorists met with Islamic extremists; a photograph of Robert Smithson's *Overturned Rock* (1969). The embroidered images show different sites of political protest and/or artistic significance in South Africa, Texas, and Spain and are themselves double-sided—the sentence "A LANDSCAPE IS NOT SOMETHING YOU LOOK AT BUT SOMETHING YOU LOOK THROUGH" is amalgamated from individual words on the back of each image. Meanings spring from the connotations of each site, and how these are linked to one another through a series of personal trajectories and imagined connections, though these require

some dedicated research and speculative leaps to navigate.

Amid the denseness of these obscure intersections, Ferreira's *For Mozambique (Model No.2 for a screen-orator-kiosk celebrating the post-independence utopia)* (2008) is a work that is uplifting in both content and structure. Like previous works such as *Two Houses* (2001), *For Mozambique* reconstructs a design that has particular geographical and historical resonances with moments of modernist revolutionary social aspiration.[3] The work comprises a wooden structure that is a reconstruction of a multipurpose agitprop kiosk designed by Latvian–Russian Constructivist artist Gustav Klucis in 1922, at a time of radical artistic experimentation and mass political mobilization in the early years of the Russian Revolution before the onset of Stalinism. One of the many functions of the kiosk was to provide a screen for film projections, and Ferreira projects two films, one on either side of the surface, that "capture the celebratory spirit of post-independence Mozambique."

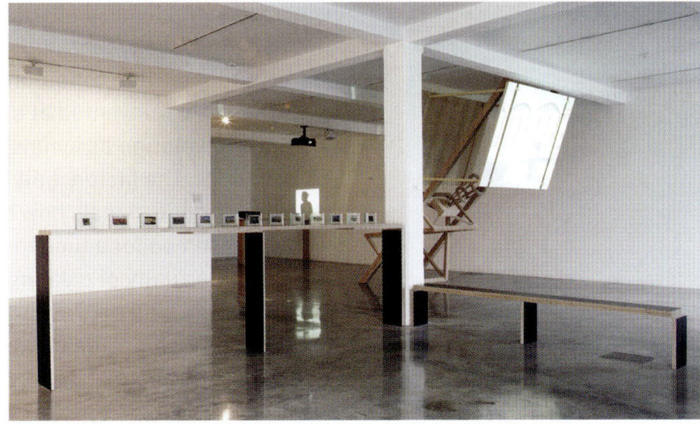

Figure 3
Narelle Jubelin and Marcos Corrales, *Ungrammatical Landscape.2*, 2003–8; Ângela Ferreira, *For Mozambique (Model No. 2 for a screen-orator-kiosk celebrating the post-independence utopia)*, 2008. Courtesy the artists and Parasol Unit Foundation for Contemporary Art, London. Photo: Stephen White.

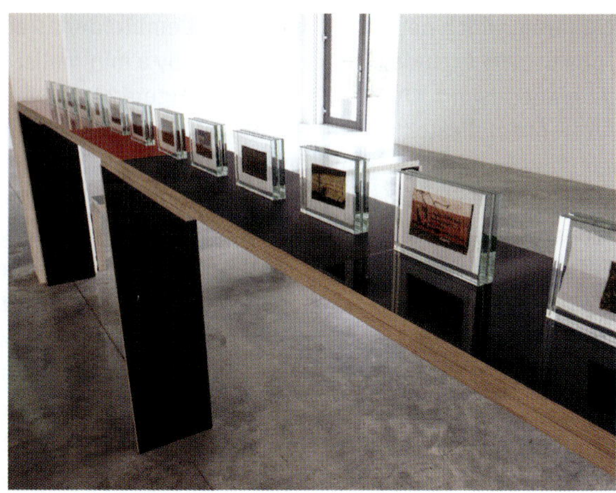

Figure 4
Narelle Jubelin and Marcos Corrales,
Ungrammatical Landscape.2, 2003–8.
Courtesy the artists and Parasol Unit
Foundation for Contemporary Art,
London. Photo: Stephen White.

Mozambique became independent from Portugal after years of armed struggle in 1975, and the immediate years following were a period of immense optimism, not only for Mozambicans but for the many foreign political activists and filmmakers who traveled there to participate in the process of decolonization, and to harness cinema's capacity to enable the collective imagining of a better future (Gray 2006). On one side of the screen is projected the short film *Makwayela* (1977) by French ethnographic filmmakers Jean Rouch and Jacques d'Arthuys. It shows factory workers singing and dancing outside a factory in Maputo, songs of protest that developed in the mines in South Africa where so many Mozambicans labored under terrible conditions, songs that were reinvented at the moment of revolution as hymns to independence. The factory building in the background signals how the revolution seemed for a time to offer the opportunity of creating a new liberated kind of African modernity. The other side of the screen shows footage of Bob Dylan in concert in 1976, singing the song

"Mozambique," in which the singer imagines himself sharing a wild atmosphere of freedom with the newly liberated people.

The inclusion of Manthia Diawara's film *Maison Tropicale* (2008) in the exhibition has something of the feel of a supplement to the show, as Diawara has not been party to the conversations and collaborations that have developed over the years between Corrales, Ferreira, Jubelin, and Renton. But it is a supplement that, in a Derridian twist, proves to be pivotal to the question the exhibition raises about point of view and the always partial positions from which art's histories are constructed. Diawara accompanies Ferreira as she undertakes the research for her commission for the Portuguese Pavillion of the 52nd edition of the Venice Biennale in 2007, but the artist's journey is framed by the diaspora filmmaker's own search to re-establish modernism's historical presence in Africa. The film investigates the sites in Niamey and Brazzaville where versions of Jean Prouvé's "Maison Tropicale" once stood. The houses were shorn of their domestic function, stripped of their context, and shipped back to Europe to be publicly displayed as seminal examples of modernist design. Interviews with former neighbors and residents record local responses to the alien form of the Maison Tropicale. These range from bewilderment or indifference to affection and pride, tinged with a sense of understated outrage that Niamey and Brazzaville have both had their significance as sites of modernist architecture stripped from them by the centripetal force of a Western art market that consigns other locations to the periphery. The film thus raises a number of important questions: who gets to tell the stories of Modernism's manifestations in Africa, and who decides upon their significance? Jubelin and Ferreira's bodies of work are highly self-aware and critical of the fact that their "postcolonial experience" derives from positions of privilege in situations of colonial and postcolonial white dominance. The film reminds us once again that there are other voices to be heard.

It is both the surprising points of intersection and those of dislocation that are the zones of intensity in *Front of House*. At certain moments these achieve a shift in how received histories of modernism, its aesthetics and epistemologies can be understood. Current postcolonial criticality involves an acute awareness of how cultural forms, once divided according to a Eurocentric logic of center and periphery, are and have always been entangled, and also awareness of the multiple positions from which these forms can be understood.[4] If such concerns are

driving some of the most pressing critical questions of the postcolonial present, then *Front of House* is an exhibition of this moment.

Notes

1. Narelle Jubelin, Constance Howard Memorial Lecture, Goldsmiths College, University of London, November 2001.
2. The "Case Study" house program commissioned thirty-six designs for domestic residences from architects including Charles and Ray Eames, Pierre Koenig, and Craig Ellwood. The brief was to design low-cost modern houses for actual clients. Running from 1945 to 1966, the buoyant years of America's postwar building boom, the program produced some of the period's most important works of residential architecture. Architects were short-listed by John Entenza, editor of avant-garde magazine *Arts & Architecture*.
3. *Two Houses* was shown as part of the group exhibition *[squatters]* at the Witte de With Center for Contemporary Art in Rotterdam in 2001, and was an installation based on two housing schemes for low-income groups, one designed by J. J. P. Oud in Rotterdam from 1925 to 1930, the other by Portuguese architect Alvaro Siza Vieira in Porto in 1974–7, the design of which celebrated the communal values of the 1974 Carnation Revolution (see *[squatters]* 2001: 30–4).
4. "Postcoloniality, in its demand for full inclusion within the

global system and by contesting existing epistemological structures, shatters the narrow focus of Western global optics and fixes its gaze on the wider sphere of the new political, social and cultural relations that emerged after World War II. The postcolonial today is a world of proximities. It is a world of nearness, not an elsewhere" (Enwezor 2001: 44).

References

Bakhtin, Mikhail. 1981 *The Dialogic Imagination*. Austin, TX: University of Texas.

Deleuze, Gilles. 2001. *Difference and Repetition*. London: Continuum.

Enwezor, Okwui. 2001. "The Black Box." In Okwui Enwezor (ed.) *Documenta11 Platform_5*, exhibition catalog. Ostfildern: Hatje Cantz.

Front of House. 2008. *Front of House: Marcos Corrales, Ângela Ferreira, Narelle Jubelin, Andrew Renton*, exhibition catalog. London: Parasol Unit.

Grace, Helen. 2006. "The Presence of Black: Narelle Jubelin and Reconciliation." http://coso6.kuva.fi/jubelin.pdf, accessed August 4, 2008.

Gray, Rosalind L. 2006. "Ambitions of Cinema: Revolution, Event, Screen." PhD thesis, University of London.

Overy, Paul. 2005. "White Walls, White Skins: Cosmopolitanism and Colonialism in Inter-war Modernist Architecture." In Kobener Mercer (ed.) *Cosmopolitan Modernisms*. London: InIVA, pp. 50–67.

[squatters]. 2001. *[squatters]*, exhibition catalog. Rotterdam: Witte de With Center for Contemporary Art.

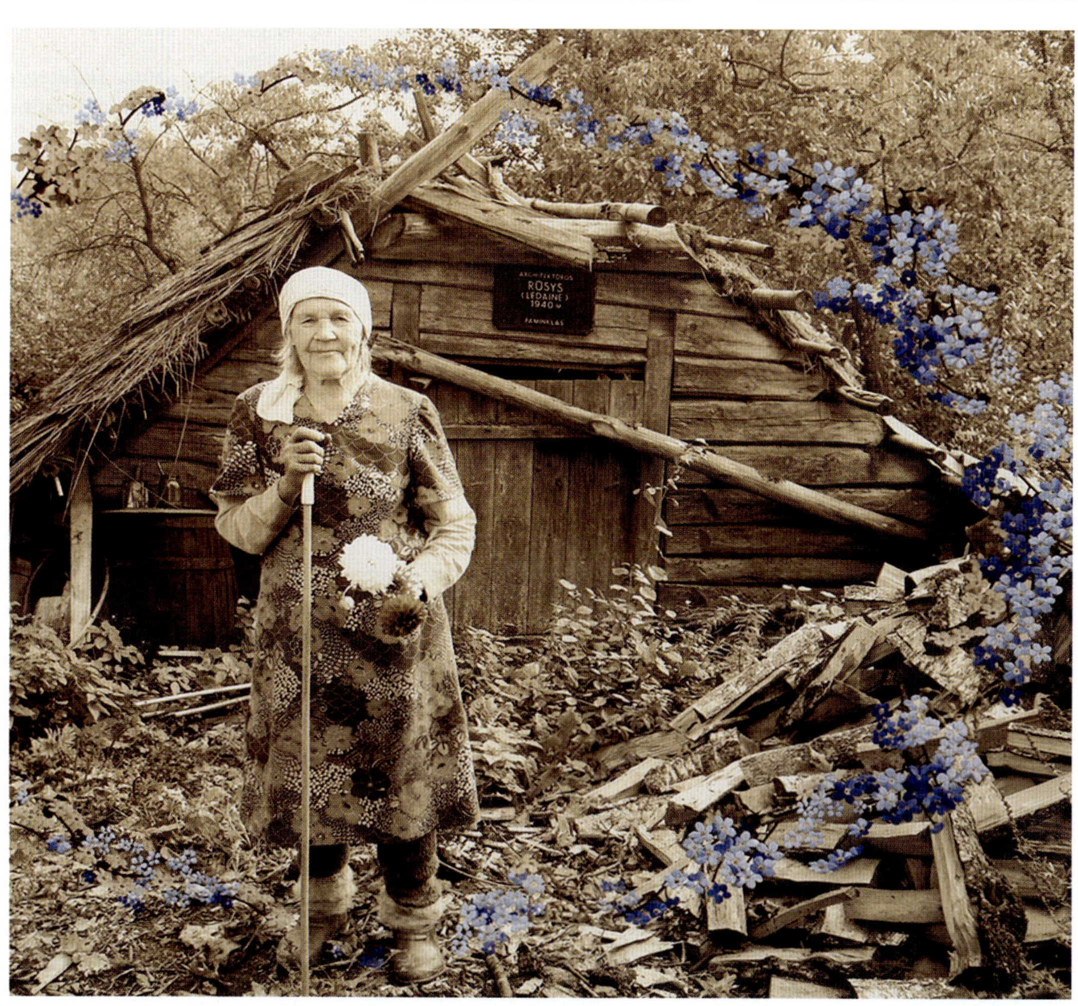

Exhibition Review
Cloth and Culture Now

The Sainsbury Centre for the Visual Arts, University of East Anglia, Norwich, January 29–June 1, 2008

The Whitworth Art Gallery, University of Manchester, September 17–December 14, 2008

The Sainsbury Centre with its mixed collection of ethnographic artifacts and modernist art is the perfect venue for a show of international textile work that crosses boundaries and disciplines. *Cloth and Culture Now* introduces previously unseen work from Estonia, Finland, Latvia, Lithuania, Japan, and the UK. Curated by Lesley Millar, it follows in the wake of two previous shows, *Textural Space* and *Through the Surface*, but broadens the range of exhibiting nations to rather diluted effect.

Overall the impression is of a miscellaneous collection of artifacts; the heterogeneity of forms and materials together with the intermingling of works from different countries, tends to diminish cultural references and give rise to some confusion as to the thrust of the show. Most of the individual works are not given sufficient breathing space for the audience to encounter them without impact by their neighbors, interaction or conversation between the pieces is minimal, contributing to a discordant effect. This is no criticism of the artists or their work.

The naming of a show leads the audience to have certain expectations; accordingly *Cloth and Culture Now* begs the question as to what is meant by "cloth" and equally "culture," and what relationship is intended by marrying the two concepts. "Cloth," for me, implies fabric put to practical, pragmatic, functional use; the *Oxford English Dictionary* (*OED*) would appear to agree as it mentions canvas as sail and cloth for costume. Many of the exhibits in the show fall well outside the dictionary definition as not being cloth at all—buttons are not cloth nor are fiber optic lights—although both easily fall within contemporary concepts of textile.

Thus the title seems a misnomer from the outset, with the notion of "culture" equally problematic. To refer again to the

REVIEWED BY
CHRISTINE ELLIOTT GREY
Christine Elliott Grey is a textile artist and writer. Her current practice focuses on aligning fiber with the written and the drawn through the medium of woven tapestry, and in so doing opening a door to interpretation of textile language. She has recently exhibited at New Hall, Cambridge.

Textile, Volume 7, Issue 2, pp. 252–255
DOI: 10.2752/175183509X460137
Reprints available directly from the Publishers.
Photocopying permitted by licence only.
© 2009 Berg. Printed in the United Kingdom.

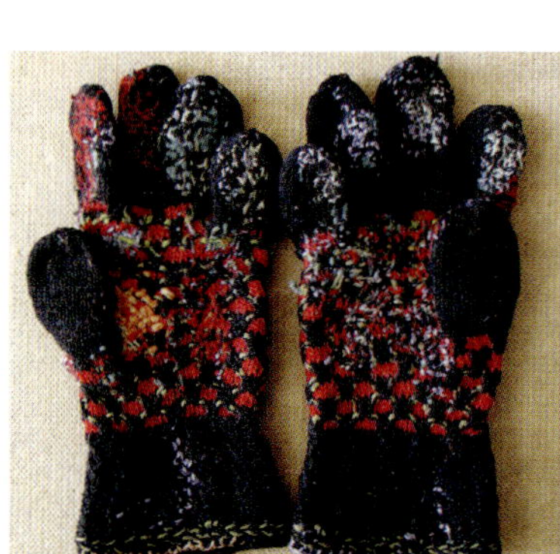

Figure 1
Peteris Sidaris's "Peteris in Courland."

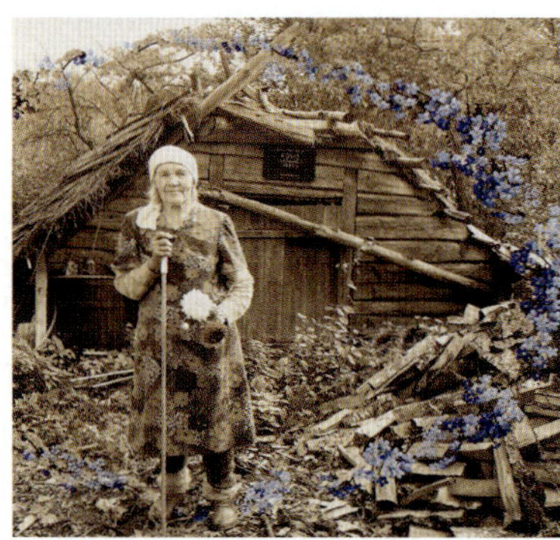

Figure 2
Lina Jonike's "Architectural Monument."

OED, "culture" etymologically derives from "*cultus*" to worship; other later meanings include to cultivate in both the agrarian sense and intellectual, and latterly the "artificial development of microscopic organisms." No mention is made of nationhood or nationality although there is a generally accepted usage in which national cultures are spoken of. What then is meant by culture in the context of this exhibition? Is there a relationship between the countries chosen? There seems to be no particular historical or geographical integrity to the selection of Estonia, Finland, Japan, Latvia, Lithuania, and the UK. Or is the term "culture" meant as in opposition to "nature?"

Despite these caveats there are some significant and moving individual pieces that gracefully embody the notions of cloth and culture most notably Peteris Sidaris's "Peteris in Courland" (Figure 1). This pair of worn, darned gloves speaks of handiwork, of the hands which made them, the hands which used them until they were threadbare, the hands that repaired them. They talk of making and making do, handicraft and history. The checkered stitch pattern is universal, the embossing of it and the cabled cuffs less so. The darning to the fingers and cuffs reference underlying holes, time, use, conjure a personal narrative of work as well as an embellishment, the joyous multitude of colors conjuring the vision (and work of cultivation) of a garden. The gloves encapsulate the themes of cloth and culture; they may also be interpreted as emblematic of the state of crafts in the twenty-first century.

In contrast Lina Jonike's "Architectural Monument" (Figure 2) is a large sepia photograph printed on such smooth canvas that the grain of the weave is lost; however, the image is of an intricate patchwork of textures. An elderly woman stands in a floral dress amidst a detritus of dead leaves, plants growing through a woodpile, a bare wooden ice house with grassy thatched roof, the flowers in her hand rhyming with the pattern of her frock, her woolly socks are topped with fur, the boarded shack shrouded by clouds of leaf, only a small patch of the image remains blank, the sky is clear space. A scattering of blue forget-me-knots is embroidered framing the woman and the shack, the oval stitching of the floral motif evoking hand-made tablecloths familiar from the postwar era, is very much of a certain time if not place. But the image itself crammed with a collage of textures, fragile and ephemeral, illustrates inspiration and source for textile artists as well as being product/result, is a demonstration of the ability of textiles to mediate between nature and culture.

Zane Berzina's "Membrane IV" also serves as bridge between the two concepts, makes a direct connection in the translation of skin patterns into fabric form. She interprets "culture" in the scientific sense and has produced a series of sample pieces each presented to be viewed through a magnifying glass as if cultured in a Petri dish. The equation of skin/textile is also pursued by Laima Orzekauskiene whose "The Optimal Position I, II" (Figure 3) magically and with tremendous craft skill, weaves

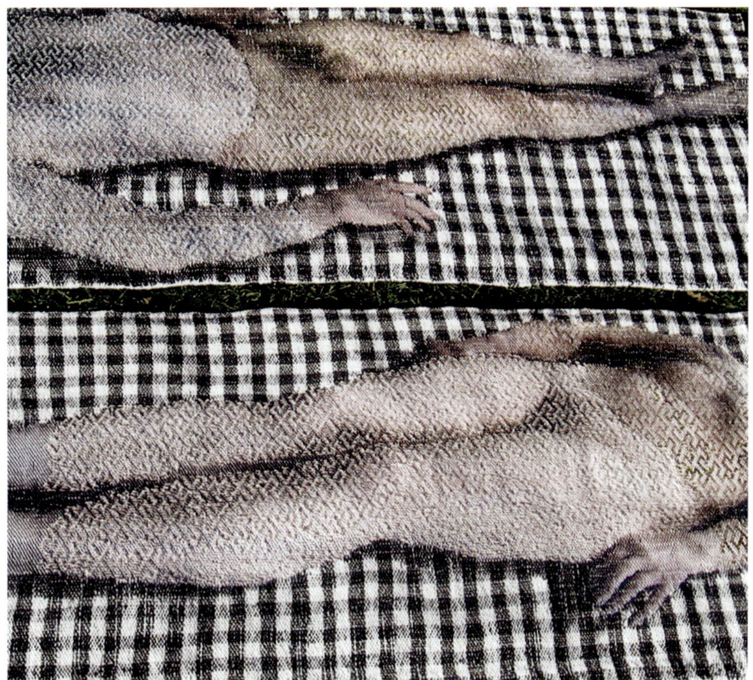

Figure 3
Laima Orzekauskiene's "The Optimal Position I, II."

traditional Lithuanian patterns to inscribe, tattoo a body lying on a blanket; national patterns become integral to the person, nationality as interwoven, the textile is the person, equally to be human is to be textile.

Sue Lawty's "Call and Response: Lead, Linen, Stone, Shadow," four large wall-hung pieces, describe the artist's journey from tapestry weaving to working with video and light, traces her progress from the material to the immaterial, from rocks as source for weave, to process as source for the insubstantial. The work sketches the arc, the narrative of contemporary textile art and as such it is well placed at the opening of the show.

While traditional skills are employed in several pieces—Shelly Goldsmith's tapestry woven dress "Robbing Peter," the shibori of Masae Bamba's "Flame" to name but two—many of the pieces introduce innovative techniques developed by the individual artist for specific projects. Some are whimsical—Severija Incirauskaite Kriauneviciene's "Autumn Collection" of cross-stitched rusty buckets, watering can, and other implements is aesthetically successful and diverting whilst Jun Mitsuhashi's whimsy, as illustrated in "Murmur of the Rain," arises more in the delightful parallels he imagines between fishing and sewing. Ieva Krumina's screen-printing of garbage bags in

"Nobody" is intriguing but the work shown in the catalog, butterflies with maps for markings, looks stronger. In many ways the catalog is as interesting as the show. It illustrates the range of the artists' work and it offers insights into working processes and how, as was said in the Sixties "attitudes become form."

The range of work in the show is broad, encompassing performance and video, patchwork, quilting, carpets, felt, wood, paper, wash, dyeing, and more, and more. Without any compass provided by title it becomes difficult to access; however, Lesley Millar must be congratulated on her continued efforts to energize cross-cultural engagement between textile artists, and to provoke debate.

Exhibition Review

A Summer Pavilion by Frank Gehry at the Serpentine

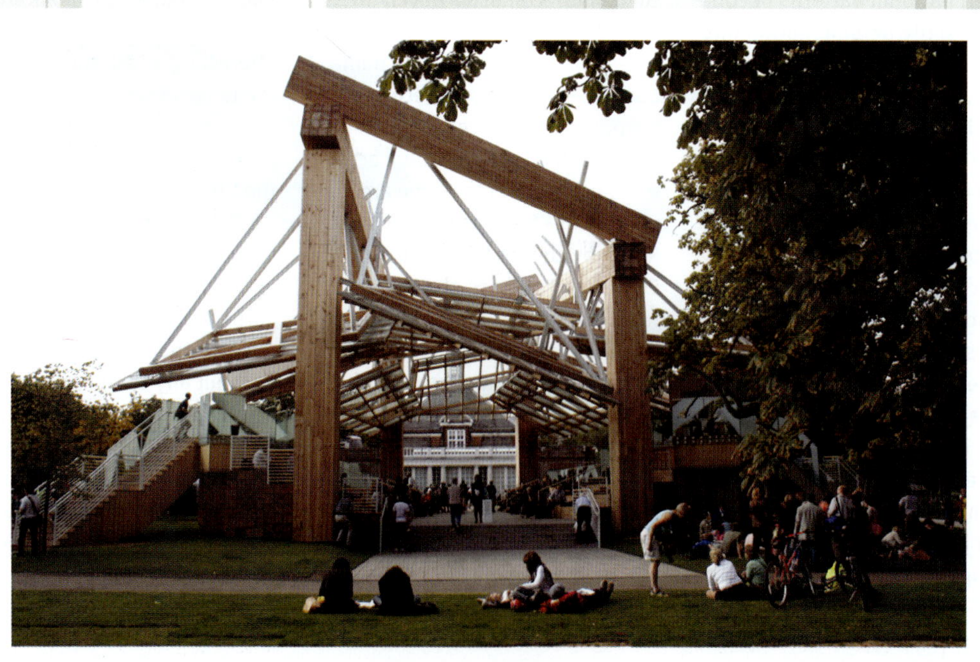

Exhibition Review
A Summer Pavilion: Frank Gehry at the Serpentine

Serpentine Gallery, London, July 20–October 18, 2008

The Pavilion at the Serpentine this summer was something of a surprise to those of us who are familiar with Frank Gehry's fluid organic forms. Approached through the park it was visible through and above the trees, a solid grounded structure with strong wooden beams forming a robust and somewhat awkward main framework, an air of permanence yet strangely alien to the classical 1934 tea pavilion building of the Serpentine Gallery behind.

The Summer Pavilion series, the concept of Julia Peyton-Jones, director of the Serpentine Gallery, provides the opportunity for "starchitects," who have not built in England before, to work on a relatively small impermanent structure with minimal functional design requirements, with the freedom to try out new ideas without too many constraints. So following on from architects such as Rem Koolhaus (2006), Toyo Ito (2002), and Zaha Hadid (2000), this is the eighth Pavilion in the series. As with each commission it has been completed within six months of the commission being awarded, and if Frank Gehry has been true to his previous form, it was also on budget.

Designed and engineered in collaboration with Arup, the Gehry Pavilion is said to be inspired by the Leonardo Da Vinci catapult drawings and the desire to "make an interesting timber structure with a bit of energy under the trees in Kensington Gardens" (Glancey 2008). The pavilion stands as high as the Serpentine Gallery, which is immediately behind, and is orientated on the same axis as the Gallery's cupola. The structure is 16 meters high, with a footprint of 526 square meters and is dominated by the huge wooden beams that create the main frame.

Nine glass panels are suspended at multiple angles

REVIEWED BY
SALLY FRESHWATER
Sally Freshwater is an artist and lecturer. Her current practice focuses on the use of textiles and pliable materials in the creation of tensile forms. She is Programme Leader for the MA Art & Design, University of Hertfordshire.

Textile, Volume 7, Issue 2, pp. 256–261
DOI: 10.2752/175183509X460146
Reprints available directly from the Publishers.
Photocopying permitted by licence only.

within this framework, described by Gehry as "stylised butterfly wings," bringing in the element of implied movement that is important to the design of all of his buildings. These "wings" create an overlapping roof canopy, which shades, if not protects, the long street-like performance area below that, with tiered seating on either-side, leads from the Gallery into the Park. With the complex multiple angles of the glazing panels it was a logistical nightmare to construct with little room for error, but the impression from inside the completed pavilion on one of the rare sunny afternoons this summer, was quiet calm, with an audience enjoying the carefully orchestrated space with its skilful nuances of light and volume on both an architectural and social level. Throughout the summer the pavilion was used for a series of performances, both during the day and at night, and it has provided an invaluable opportunity to experience a Gehry building in real space and time.

Gehry buildings have in the past been criticized for not withstanding close inspection, for poor attention to detail, working most effectively at some distance, and there are problems with this construction when it is examined more closely. The café and the lift sit outside of the careful central composition of overlapping planes and linear elements, and are not fully integrated into the rhythm of the space. The huge timbers are not the meter-square solid forms they appear to be from a distance but timber-clad steel, which was clumsily put together in places. The shading on the glass panels of the roof structure has a logic and geometry that works to emphasize the direction and angle of the panels but the etched patterning on the glass barriers to the back of the tiers rather goes against Gehry's modernist aesthetic for structures devoid of decoration. The roof panels are supported by numerous white steels, which are largely visible from an external viewpoint, adding another layer of apparently random linear elements whose precise positions are probably dictated by the complex angles of the glass. And this Pavilion, as with others before, is not watertight:

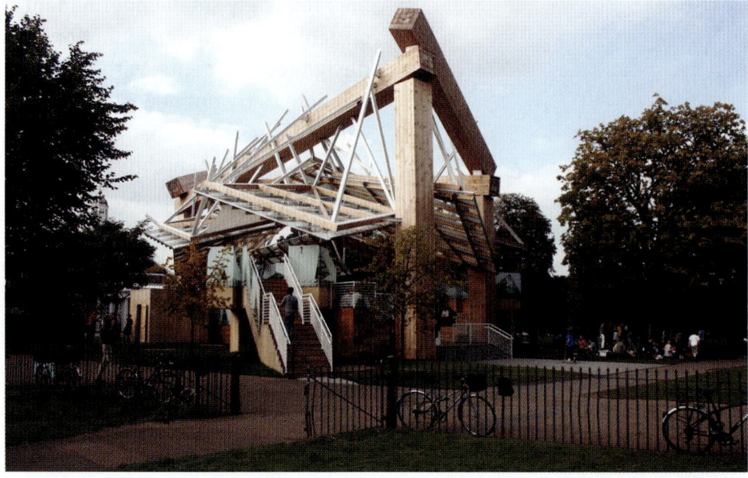

Figure 1
Photograph by Remi Young.

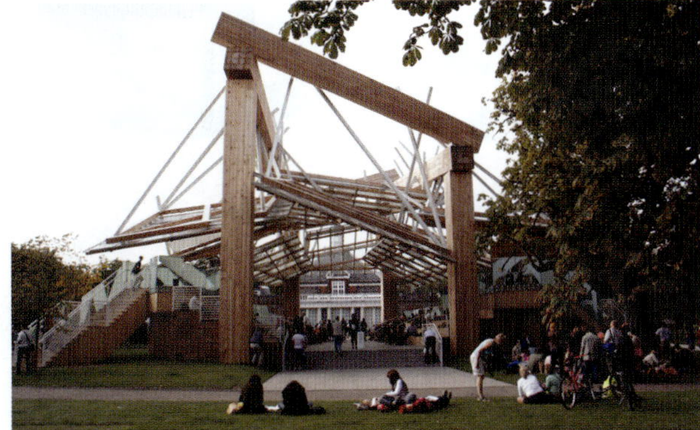

Figure 2
Photograph by Remi Young.

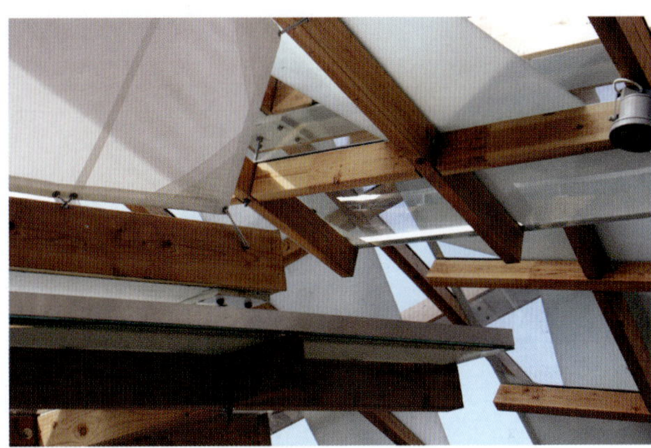

Figure 3
Photograph by Remi Young.

fabric canopies that were part of the original design were cut for budgetary reasons, while some small cosmetic sails remain interlinking some of the glass planes.

Though not as beautiful as some of his large-scale titanium buildings, the Pavilion is visually closer to the impression created by Gehry's own house in Santa Monica, originally built in the late 1970s, with its multi-layering of angles and use of conventional building materials to explode and reconfigure an existing house, playing with shapes and textures. This house marked the beginning of the evolution of his style, when after discussion with a client who asked why he was so expressive in his own house and so conservative in his other design work, Gehry decided to take his practice in a new direction. "It was like jumping off a cliff, an amazing feeling."[1]

While the outcome is more rigid and less sensual in the Summer Pavilion than in his more fluid metal forms, the process of creation follows much the same formula. From original concept drawings Gehry, who takes pride in the fact that he is computer-illiterate, uses a very direct hands-on method of model building to explore the development of shape and form. Models of the building are made on several scales so the model itself "doesn't become the object of desire."[2] A collaborative method of ideas generation is employed in the Gehry studio with models being built and revised with contributions from a creative team. The inspiration for the butterfly wings has been credited to Frank Gehry's son, Samuel, who at twenty-eight, has recently begun working with his father.

With all of his buildings, his obsession with movement and making the materials expressive is explored through endless paper models, exploring curves and interlocking shapes, with no initial concern for the structural

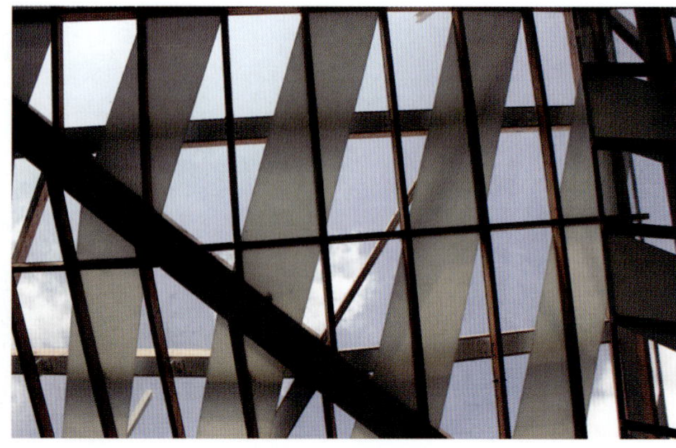

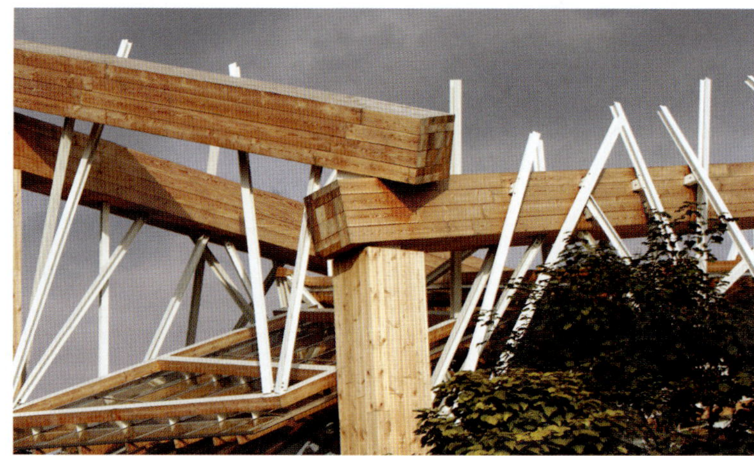

conundrums they create. The resolution of these less-linear buildings has been solved by the development of sensitive computer systems, which allow the architects to scan and digitize the models, transforming them into accurate three-dimensional (3D) computer visualizations,[3] the primary set of instructions, which contain all the information and data necessary for creating component parts for manufacture and construction.

Gehry gained worldwide recognition as recently as 1997 with his inspirational design for the Guggenheim Museum in Bilbao, which has become an iconic landmark for the city, with its reflective titanium curving surfaces that reflect the incredible colors of the Spanish sky and the surrounding water.

Having trained originally as an artist before switching to architecture, Gehry's early architectural designs were puzzling to other architects. In a television interview,[4] he describes his designs as toxic to architecture colleagues, but he found his ideas and concepts appreciated by artists: this validation of his ideas and the security of a like-minded group of creative people was important to his self-esteem. His early architecture

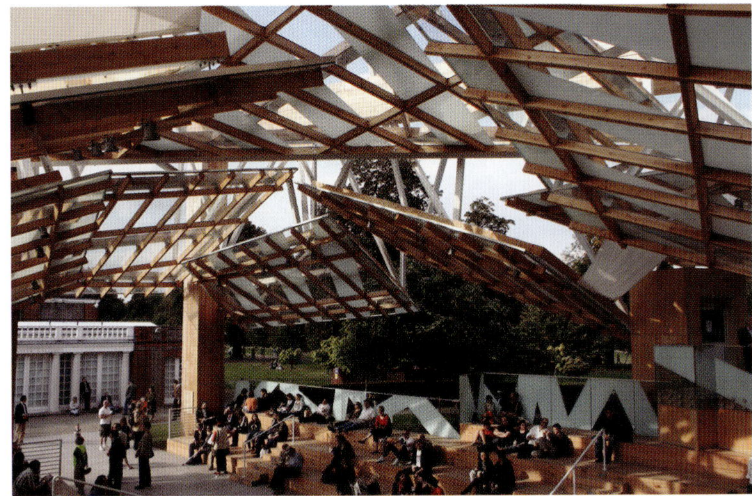

Figure 6
Photograph by Remi Young.

was routed within the modernist traditions of Neutra,[5] Eames,[6] and Schindler,[7] but he was working towards musical, lyrical buildings where the movement is expressed through the essential form of the structure rather than in decoration.

His use of sensual curved forms has become the recognizable style of the Gehry architectural practice, repeated in numerous large-scale buildings such as the Disney Concert Hall, Los Angeles,[8] and echoed in the more subtle and disturbingly elegant design for the 75-story Beckman Tower, his first Manhattan tower due for completion in 2010. This building, housing an elementary school at ground level and accommodation for the New York Downtown Hospital as well as nearly 1,000 luxury apartments, it is a curious fusion of public and private space encased in soft irregular steel folds.

At seventy-nine, Gehry is skeptical as to whether he will ever build anything permanent in England as he considers the critical response to his work to be very negative (Glancey 2008). His only building to date in Great Britain is Maggie's Centre, in Dundee, UK, completed in 2003. Inspired by the simple Highland dwellings known as Brochs, he has created a white curved walled center with a folded metal roof that houses a series of functional spaces. The design work, carried out *pro bono* for his friend, Maggie Keswick, has resulted in a restful retreat where the ambiance of the space relates closely to the healing process, allowing people with cancer to "see illness in a context that is bigger than themselves."[9] Now that the summer pavilion is gone, perhaps here in Britain, we will have to satisfy ourselves with this one small, beautifully formed example of his work.

Notes

1. Frank Gehry, *Sketches of Frank Gehry*, dir. Sydney Pollack, 2005.
2. Frank Gehry, *Sketches of Frank Gehry*, dir. Sydney Pollack, 2005.
3. The firm uses Digital Project, a sophisticated 3D modeling program developed by the aerospace industry.
4. Charlie Rose interviews Frank Gehry, July 2001.
5. Richard Joseph Neutra (1892–1970).
6. Charles Ormond Eames, Jr (1907–78).
7. Rudolph Michael Schindler (1887–1953).
8. Designed 1987, not completed until 2003 due to funding problems.
9. Charles Jencks, *Sketches of Frank Gehry*, dir. Sydney Pollack, 2005.

Reference

Glancey, Jonathan. 2008. "Let's Twist Again: Jonathan Glancey Interviews Frank Gehry." *Guardian*, July 1.

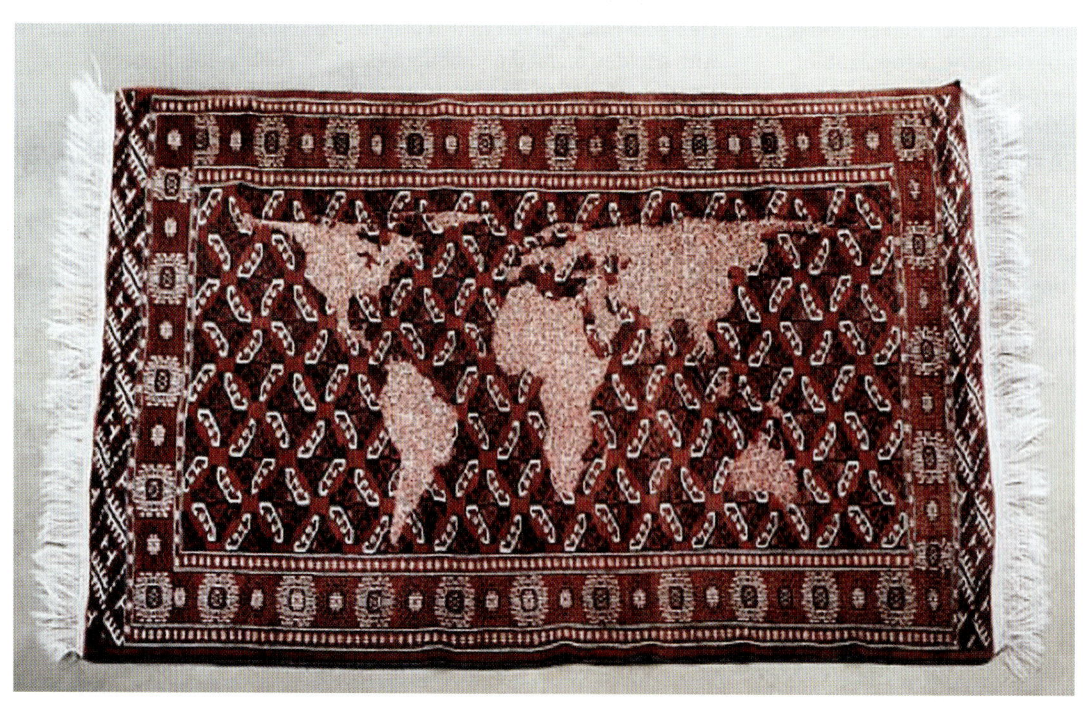

Exhibition Review
A Search for Belonging in the Exile's World: Mona Hatoum Exhibition at Parasol Unit

The Parasol Unit, London, June 13–August 8, 2008

A pertinent question when considering Mona Hatoum's diverse body of work is surely "where to begin?" especially when taking into account an oeuvre that has incorporated, amongst others, sculpture, performance, video, and installation art. Pertinent also is the recent twelve-year retrospective, *Present Tense*, which ran at the Parasol Unit,[1] and plainly illustrates the importance of themes such as travel and movement as sources of inspiration. Hatoum has long been established on the international art scene and many of the works on display illustrate this, being made in countries as diverse as Israel, Stockholm, France, and North America.

Movement across borders and enforced migration has also played a fundamental role in Hatoum's private life and so not surprisingly is seen as a recurrent theme in her work. Born in Beirut in 1952, Hatoum was already aware of a household in which displacement was no stranger. Before her birth, Hatoum's Palestinian family were forced to flee their home in Nablus, Israel, in 1948, to settle in Lebanon and on a visit to London in 1975, Hatoum experienced another displacement. Being unable to return home to Lebanon due to the outbreak of civil war, she found herself exiled, a foreigner twice over and so remained in Britain, where she enrolled in art school and began her journey as an artist.

The title of this retrospective, *Present Tense*, offers an insight into the complexity of the works on display. Shuttling between no past and no future, Hatoum

REVIEWED BY
KASHIF NADIM CHAUDRY
Nadim Chaudry is a freelance artist, whose textile-based practice explores issues around religious belief and secular identities. He has exhibited in various group shows and is currently working towards his first solo exhibition in Nottingham.

Textile, Volume 7, Issue 2, pp. 262–267
DOI: 10.2752/175183509X460155
Reprints available directly from the Publishers.
Photocopying permitted by licence only.
© 2009 Berg. Printed in the United Kingdom.

delivers a vision of the state of exile, of an identity of uncertainty and non-fixity. It would be difficult to pinpoint a home on Hatoum's sculpture "Globe" of 2007, for example (see Figure 1); confronted with this celestial map we are all foreigners. As the title of this piece would suggest the elegant construction of this geometric form veils a terrifying reading of a world in which the body of the earth is eaten away. There are no distinctions made between landmasses or seascapes, all topographic difference has been expunged, and arguably as a tool for navigation, this globe has lost all agency. What remains is a precision-made, prison-like cage, a skeletal corpse of engorged steel—the fixed markers of longitude and latitude that make up the margins of this sphere. We are left with a hollowed shell, powerfully conspicuous through its materiality and as a vision of a planetary prison, a view

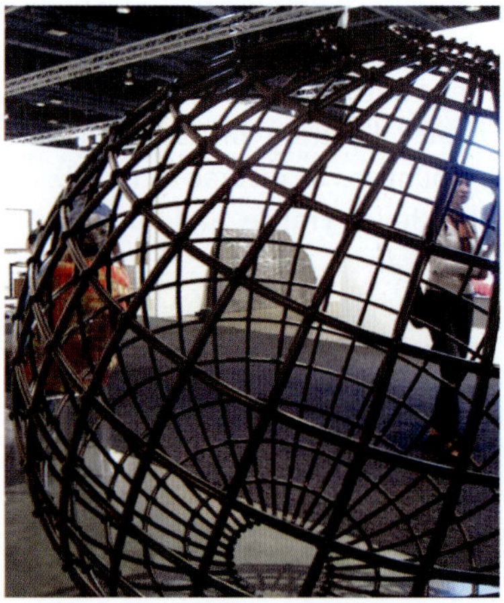

Figure 1
"Globe," 2007. Mild steel. Diameter: 66¹⁵⁄₁₆ in. (diam. 170 cm). Source: http://openmagazinepictures.wordpress.com/2008/06/16/mona-hatoum-at-parasol-unit/

of the exiles world, in which an identity of enforced uncertainty and irredeemable loss has spectacularly spread out over the entire planet, consuming all in its way.

The language of cartography with its stylized complexities of color, symbol, and sign has been adopted by Hatoum in many of her pieces and can be seen in her textile piece "Bukhara" of 2008 (see Figure 2). A map's primary function as "a tool for emplacement, of clarity and illumination" (Rogoff 2000: 74) is surely rendered dysfunctional in the wake of enforced dislocation, for what maps would serve the needs of the exile, who lives and has experienced an identity of displaced origins. Hatoum references this condition of imposed homelessness with "Bukhara"; however, in this instance the traditional aesthetic of the map is used in a more domestic context. Positioned on the floor, just beyond the threshold as you move from one space to another, we are humbly invited to gaze down at this mat, its placement within the gallery succinctly acknowledging its function, referencing similar rugs we may have at home. However, any association with the familiar are made instantly problematic; for here the everyday wear and tear of this carpet has rubbed away the pile to reveal a bare warp and weft, fashioned into an unfamiliar map of the world. Unfamiliar partly because Hatoum has used the Peters Projection, a representation of the world's landmasses which uses true proportions as opposed to the conventional Western-centric view of the world. But unfamiliar also when considering why such erosion has taken place. It could

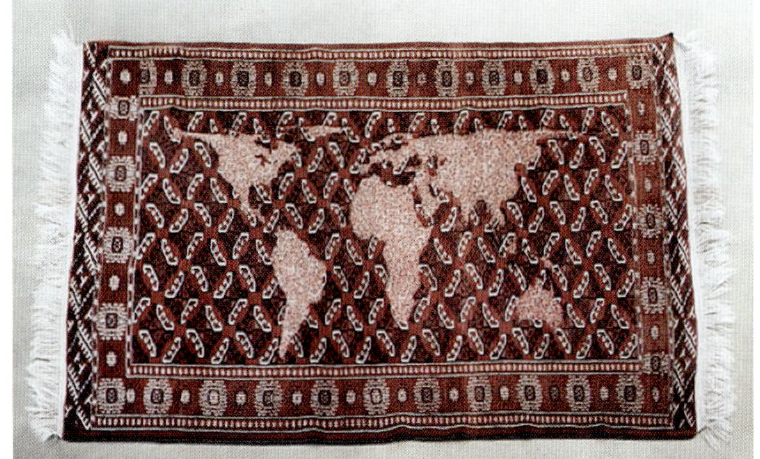

Figure 2
"Bukhara," 2008. Wool. H 143 × w 225 cm. Source: http://www.artnet.com/artwork/425644366/114501/bukhara-red-and-white.html.

be suggested that Hatoum makes reference to the physical reality of exile and other forced migrations, of an endless Diaspora, arranging and rearranging the material body of the earth in its search for belonging. Poetically rendered in this humble piece: for how many feet would it take to rub away a world? The material distress of this woven carpet bears witness to a world stripped away, a universal state of alienation in which there is no homeland, no borders to cross, and where we are cast into a world emptied of all difference. "Bukhara" is one of many rugs that Hatoum has made in her career, the symbol of this unassuming carpet, in the form of welcome mats and prayer rugs, has been spectacularly transformed by the use of such diverse materials as nails and cast intestines. With "Bukhara" the ascetic act of unpicking and hence the labor of the artist, mirrors not only the textile process of weaving but also makes manifest the very material body of this piece, an important element of Hatoum's practice, as she asserts:

I want the work in the first instance to have a strong formal presence, and through the physical experience to activate a psychological and emotional response. (Cited in Hatoum 2000: 28)

The title piece of this retrospective, "Present Tense" made in 1996 (see Figure 3) during Hatoum's first visit to Jerusalem, would no doubt have drawn out an immediate physical response from its audience. Made from over two thousand blocks of pure olive oil soap, the olfactory assault from this seam of fat would have been instantly recognizable to the local inhabitants. Pressed into the surface of this sensuous carpet are red glass beads (see Figure 4) which make up the outline of a map, drawn up in 1993, at the Oslo Peace Agreement, of lands to be returned to the Palestinians.

What immediately strikes is the apparent randomness of these demarcated areas, intensified by the sheer number of soap blocks, which could no doubt, be rearranged *ad infinitum* to produce just as confusing an arrangement. The sheer scale of this map also confounds, for here we are presented with a substrate, a literal land mass, exhibited at our feet. However, Hatoum's political awareness and sharp wit comes immediately into play, for there is no sure footedness to be found on this slippery ground, echoing the real life uncertainty of these disputed territories. Furthermore, Hatoum's choice of red beads and the flesh tones of this soap, combined with the organic pattern of these beads, bring to mind the aftermath of some horrifically violent situation, which has left a trail of bloody droplets. Once again, Hatoum illustrates how the familiar, once decontextualized, can offer a new potency. This everyday material, which has been in production relatively unchanged for centuries by the Palestinian people, has been transformed into a visual metaphor for place and belonging. The personal nature of its use, next to the body to cleanse and purify,

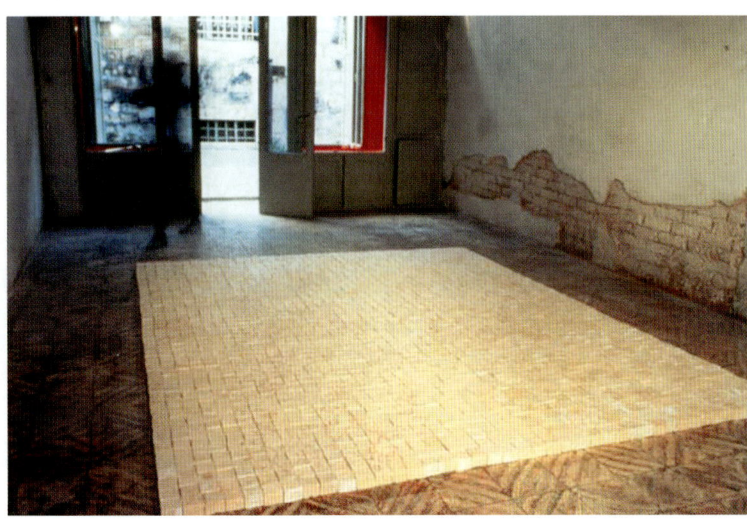

Figure 3
"Present Tense," 1996. Soap and glass beads. 4.5 × 229 × 241 cm. Source: http://universes-in-universe. org/eng/nafas/articles/2005/ al_ma_mal_foundation/photos/ mona_hatoum.

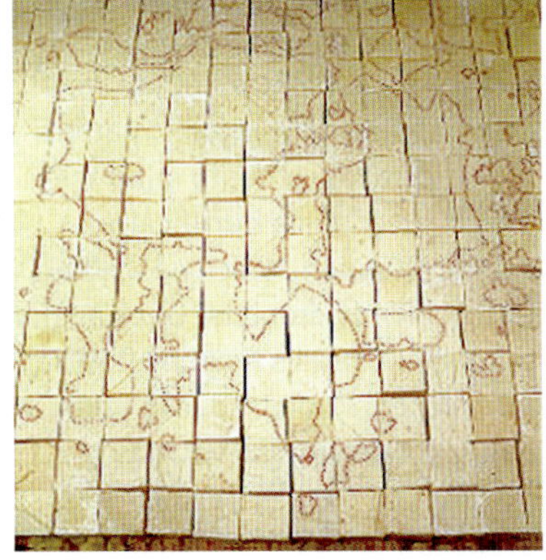

Figure 4
"Present Tense," 1996. Detail. Source: http://www.artfacts.net/ index.php/pageType/exhibitionInfo/ exhibition/7026/lang/1.

cannot go unnoticed. "Present Tense" poignantly alludes to the intimate relationship between the body and land, of how identities are shaped by place, and of how the political has entered and shaped the private sanctity of home.

The idea of home as a disputed territory is also explored with "Mobile Home II" of 2006 (see Figure 5), a large-scale sculptural installation. With this piece Hatoum has created a domestic setting, bringing together a collection of everyday objects: tables and chairs, pots and pans, toys and textiles, which have been arranged and fixed along parallel wires. These wires in turn are fixed to two temporary barriers, between which a process of perpetual motion ensues. A poetic display of order and chaos is played out before us, as these objects are brought together, creating a scene of domestic order, only to be torn asunder moments later. This shuttling process of backwards and forwards is unnervingly captivating, a mobile

trompe-l'oeil perhaps, in which the desired moment of domestic certainty is never quite attained. A form of harmony does prevail however, the immobile barriers, between which this domestic ballet is played, resolutely maintain their function and do not give way. By marrying these utilitarian barriers, which bring disturbing echoes of the temporary boundaries of public demonstrations and police barricades, with the instantly recognizable objects of this homely scene, Hatoum has created an uncanny space. The familiar is turned on its head and contexts are torn apart only to be reassembled in terrifying outcomes. Even the home has become a battleground, a place of continual flux and change, nothing is fixed; all is mobile.

With "Mobile Home" the exile's uncertainty has come full circle. From the universal, arrested motion of "Globe," which sits silently barren, as if fallen from its axis, to the very heart of our private domestic spaces. What is

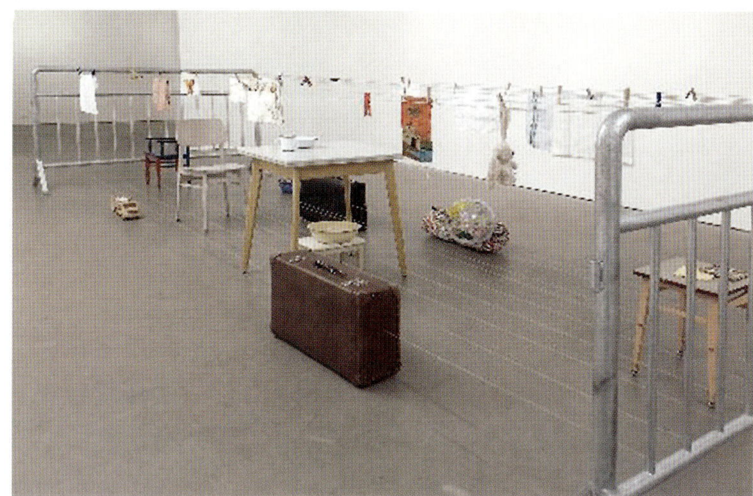

Figure 5
"Mobile Home II," 2006. Furniture, household objects, suitcases, galvanized steel barriers, three electric motors, and pulley system. 46⅞ × 86⅝ × 236¼ in. Source: http://www.yatzer.com/1091_mona_hatoum_at_parasol_unit.

most apparent is a provocative aesthetic language, played out through the acute manipulation of familiar materials and unfamiliar contexts. The potency and power of this is seemingly never ending; a *Present Tense* that echoes beyond the confines of the gallery in its capacity to deliver its message across time, cultures, and place. The critical theoretician, Edward Said, writes on the subject of exile:

> We have become accustomed to thinking of the modern period itself as spiritually orphaned and alienated, the age of anxiety and estrangement ... the age of the refugee, the displaced person, mass migration ... (Said 1984: 159)

With these works Hatoum opens a dialogue with which we can all relate, offering a glimpse of a "perilous territory of not belonging" (Said 1984: 162), especially for those who have not experienced displacement. For it could be argued that the state of exile is very much part of the human condition and hence subjective to all, a *Present Tense*, claustrophobic in its intensity, with no discernable way forward or back. But somehow these works key into this most acute and raw state of being and are able to chart this uncharted terrain.

Note

1. *Present Tense* ran from June 13 to August 8, 2008, at The Parasol Unit, a privately funded charity and not-for-profit gallery space in central London.

References

Hatoum, Mona. 2000. *The Entire World as a Foreign Land*. London: Tate Gallery Publishing.

Rogoff, Irit. 2000. *Terra Infirma: Geography's Visual Culture*. London and New York: Routledge.

Said, Edward. 1984. *Reflections on Exile. Granta 13: After the Revolution*. London: Granta Books.

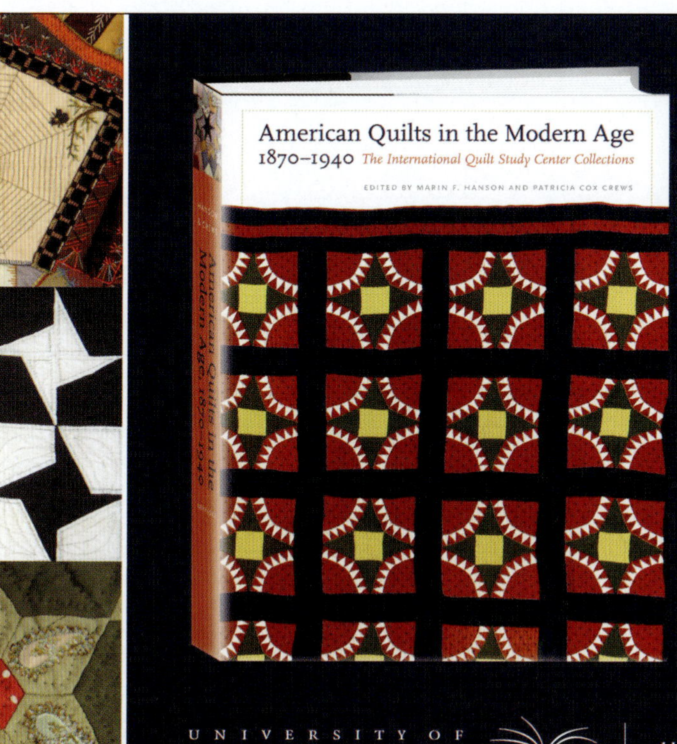

With full-color photographs of over 587 quilts, this book recovers a swath of lost history and shows us some of America's treasured material culture as it was pieced and stitched into place. *American Quilts in the Modern Age, 1870–1940* offers a new visual and tactile understanding of American culture and society, bridging the transition from traditional folk culture to the age of mass production and consumption.

Visit us online for more information!

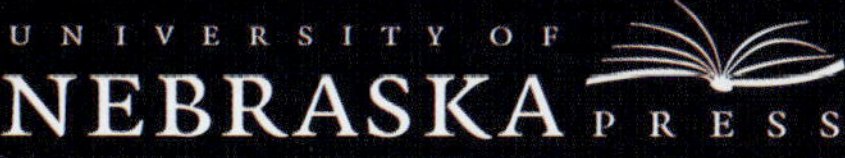

publishers of Bison Books
www.nebraskapress.unl.edu

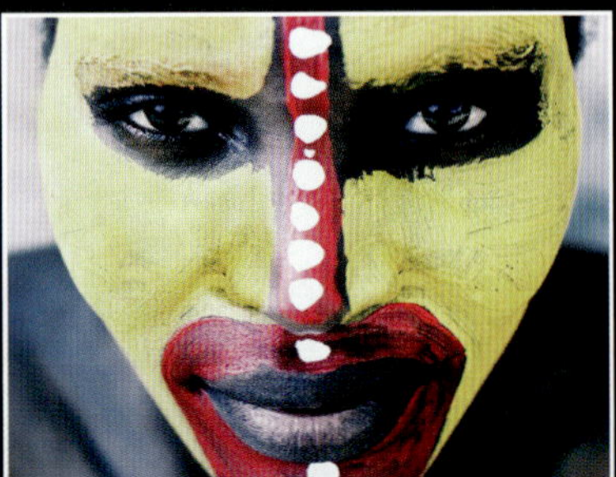
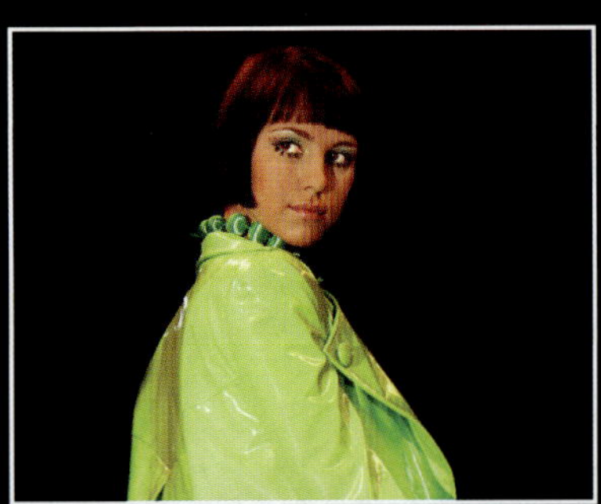
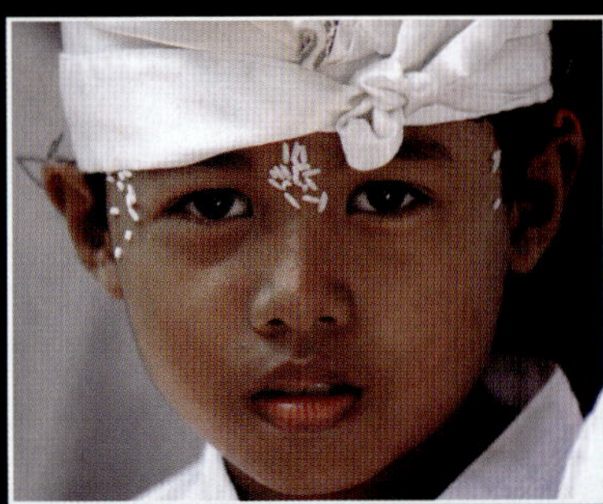
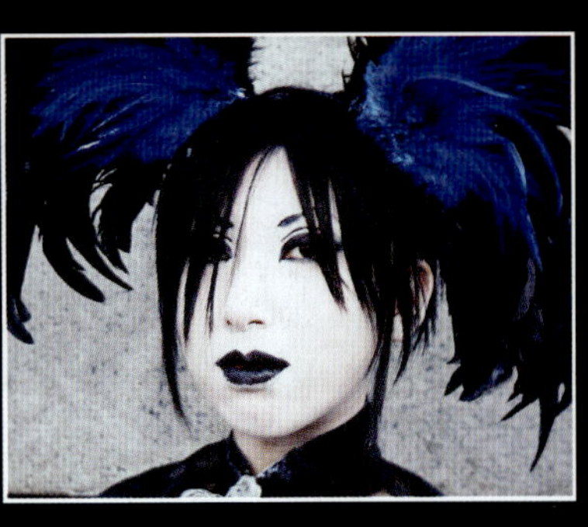

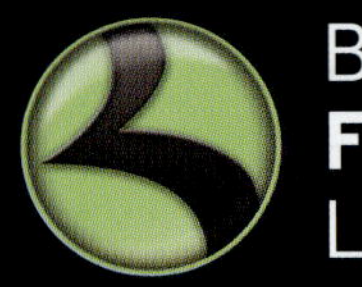

Berg
Fashion
Library.com